THE RO[U]GH [GUIDE TO]

Acce[ssible]
Britain

Fully revised and updated third edition

ROUGH
GUIDES

CONTENTS

FOREWORD

Lara is a writer, actor, model, TV presenter and owner of burlesque fashion label *Kiss My Cherry*. Check out Lara's regular blog at Ⓦwww .accessibleguide.co.uk and her weekly diary for *Marie Claire* magazine at Ⓦwww .marieclaire.co.uk

Welcome to the Rough Guide to Accessible Britain's revved-up third edition. Rough Guides and Motability Operations have teamed up once again, to bring disabled people the information they need to plan **hassle-free and fun outings** the length and breadth of Britain.

Within these pages you will find over 180 ideas for inspirational places to visit. These are the best of Britain's accessible attractions and include some **extraordinary places** you might have presumed would be impossible for people with disabilities to enjoy – such as skiing or dog-sledding in the Cairngorms National Park. With such a wide variety, we hope there will be something to suit everyone.

A team of **discerning disabled reviewers** (including myself!) helped update this revised edition. While out on visits to check each of the sites, access was our key priority, but the complete visitor experience was very important too. Accessible doesn't have to mean boring after all, so even venues with outstanding access facilities were eligible to be included in the guide if they were also highly enjoyable places to visit. Many ideas for the spectacular attractions we have included came from you, our readers – so thanks for the phenomenal feedback we received via our 2009 Reader Review Competition. If you entered, you may even spot your thoughts and recommendations included somewhere in the next eleven chapters.

New to this edition are the **Rough Guide to Accessible Britain Awards 2010** which give special recognition to the attractions that have excelled in making their facilities inclusive for disabled visitors in innovative ways.

This is our best and most comprehensive Rough Guide to Accessible Britain yet and we hope you enjoy it as much as we enjoyed making it – time to get that motor running!

Lara Masters

ABOUT THIS BOOK

Rough Guides are designed to be good to read and easy to use. This Rough Guide is divided into three sections, and you will find **inspiration and practical advice** in each.

This **colour introduction** celebrates the winning and highly commended sites across the five categories of the Rough Guide to Accessible Britain Awards 2010, giving you a feel for the wealth of exciting, accessible days out on offer.

Next, the **eleven regional chapters** contain reviews of a wide range of sites across each region, to suit all interests and abilities. Each review is accompanied with details of where you can eat and drink – if an attraction doesn't have its own café or restaurant on site, we have recommended a venue close by and included its contact details. You will also find **ideas boxes** dotted throughout these chapters. These handy lists should help you with everything from finding an accessible holiday cottage to planning a watersports experience.

Our reviewers have tried to take into consideration all of the **questions and concerns** you may have, but a quick call ahead to check on current conditions at an attraction is always a good idea, especially if you have any specific requirements. Many places can be enjoyed independently, but we have made it clear where someone to offer assistance will help you make the most of the day.

The book concludes with the Rough Guide selection of **useful contacts** that can provide further assistance with planning days out and holidays in Britain, from Blue Badge-enhanced GPS navigation to listings for audio-described theatre performances.

Large print and Braille versions of this Rough Guide are available on request – please call ☎0800 953 7070. An **audio version** can be downloaded from ⓦwww.accessibleguide .co.uk. If you have any thoughts or feedback on this third edition, please share your views with us at ⓔaccessibleguide@motability operations.co.uk.

🏃♿	Assisted wheelchair access
♿	Non-assisted wheelchair access
🚶	Facilities for the mobility impaired
🪑	Rest seats for the mobility impaired
♿wc	Accessible toilets
P♿	Accessible car parking
🛴	Powered scooters available
👂	Hearing loop
🙌	BSL interpreters
👁	Facilities for blind and visually impaired people
🐕	Assistance dogs allowed
☕	Café/refreshments on site
🍴	Restaurant on site

Codes for entry fees

[D] Disabled
[C] Carer
[A] Adult
[Con] Concessions

THE ROUGH GUIDE TO MOTABILITY

This new edition of the **Rough Guide to Accessible Britain** is packed full with more ideas than ever before to inspire you to make the most of your leisure time. The same spirit lies behind the **Motability Scheme**, which has been providing cars, powered wheelchairs and scooters to help disabled people and their families enjoy the freedom of the road since 1978.

Established to enable disabled people to access affordable, worry-free motoring, Motability provides customers with a brand new car as part of an all inclusive lease package that offers insurance, servicing, RAC breakdown assistance and replacement tyres. The Scheme now has over **530,000 customers** and a reputation for outstanding customer service.

For customers, access to a reliable new car enables people to travel confidently to work, medical appointments, visit friends – or indeed to explore the UK and enjoy the best accessible attractions that Britain has to offer.

Motability is available to anyone who receives the Higher Rate Mobility Component of the Disability Living Allowance or War Pensioners' Mobility Supplement – **no other checks or assessments are required**. From April 2011, the higher rate allowance will extend to include those with a severe visual impairment.

This allowance, currently around £50 a week, is transferred to Motability as the monthly lease payment. Those who choose a larger or higher specification model may need to pay an additional advance payment, although over 200 cars carry no further cost. A parent, carer, partner or friend can drive the car if the customer does not drive themselves.

There are over 4,000 cars to choose from, including models from all major manufacturers. There are also Wheelchair Accessible Vehicles and drive-from wheelchair options. If required, a selection of common **adaptations** may be included at no extra cost and there is also a large choice of automatic options available.

- Over 4,000 brand new cars to choose from
- Insurance, annual car tax, servicing and maintenance all included
- Full RAC breakdown assistance included
- Replacement tyres and windscreen included

The Motability Scheme is overseen by the charity, Motability, who may also be able to assist people who require a **financial grant** in order to fund the specific car or adaptations for their needs. The charity also carries out various fundraising activities.

Motability Operations continues its support of the **Rough Guide to Accessible Britain** to inspire disabled people to discover more of the world around them. In turn, Motability hopes to create a better understanding of the Scheme, and reach more people, who could benefit from what Motability offers.

Motability Cars, Powered Wheelchairs and Scooters 0800 923 0000

ACCESSIBLE BRITAIN AWARDS 2010

This Rough Guide is packed with reviews of attractions that provide great services to disabled visitors. And to celebrate and congratulate the cream of the crop, Rough Guides and Motability Operations have launched the **Rough Guide to Accessible Britain Awards 2010**.

Thanks to our team of enthusiastic contributors, the attractions in this third edition were assessed for the awards, on a range of criteria – including information available ahead of a visit, value for money, the attitude and availability of staff on-hand to help and any creativity displayed in meeting the needs of disabled visitors.

From that information, a judging panel of travel and disability experts worked hard to determine the sites that clearly go above and beyond the minimum requirements. Over the next eight pages, we highlight those worthy winners and highly commended attractions across our five award categories – **Best Family Venue, Best Free Venue, Best Heritage Venue and Best Active Venue**. Each of these attractions provide a great experience for every visitor and set benchmarks for the rest of the industry to follow.

The 2009 Reader Review Competition invited readers to submit their ideas for great accessible attractions and days out to the Accessible Britain team. Following the recommendations received, a shortlist of the ten most popular places to visit was hosted at Ⓦ www.accessibleguide.co.uk – visitors to the website were asked to vote for their favourite venue. On p.16 you can see which remarkable attraction received an overwhelming number of votes, to become the winner of the **Readers' Choice** award.

ROUGH GUIDES
ACCESSIBLE BRITAIN AWARDS
2010
Motability

▲ **WINNER Brunel's ss Great Britain** The Southwest • **p.97**
Negotiating your way around an old ship might sound tricky. You'd imagine tight corners and cramped spaces, but nothing could be further from the truth at ss Great Britain, where wonders have been worked to ensure the ship is wheelchair accessible. The ship has been beautifully restored and all visitors are able to become completely immersed in its story. The fantastic visitor centre has audioguides and BSL-interpretation.

▶ HIGHLY COMMENDED **Churchill Museum and Cabinet War Rooms**
London • **p.25** A brilliant insight into those tense war years and one of the most historically important attractions in the UK. To make the museum accessible, organisers have gone above and beyond what should be possible in this space.

◄ HIGHLY COMMENDED **Tate Britain**
London • **p.26** Every aspect of the visitor
experience has been considered at the Tate
Britain and the accessibility of the gallery
cannot be faulted. The guided and personal
tours on offer are a particularly valuable
addition.

▼ HIGHLY COMMENDED **Culloden
Battlefield Visitor Centre** Scotland •
p.163 At this highlight of the Highlands,
the challenging terrain has been overcome
and made accessible. The handheld GPS
audioguides are a great and modern way of
escorting visitors around the many points
of interest.

BEST FREE VENUE

▲ **WINNER Locomotion: National Railway Museum, Shildon** The Northeast and Yorkshire • **p.136** You can't help but marvel at the collection of trains on show here, but impressively it is more than just a big load of machines – it is the social history of Britain. Disabled visitors will be genuinely pleased at the accessibility of the experience and the sheer amount of hands-on interaction possible, especially given the nature of the exhibits.

◀ HIGHLY COMMENDED **Horniman Museum and Gardens** London • **p.35** A constantly surprising place with a wonderfully eclectic range of things to see. The events and exhibitions are always thought-provoking and the museum really has a place at the heart of the local community.

▲ HIGHLY COMMENDED **The National Gallery** London • **p.24** This amazing body of work should be essential viewing for all. And everyone can visit, because great efforts have been made to ensure the treasures on show are accessible. This is a gallery the nation should be proud of.

▼ HIGHLY COMMENDED **National Waterfront Museum** Wales • **p.157** Spacious, airy and everything a modern museum should be – visitors are encouraged to interact and the entire experience is thoroughly engaging. This is the complete history of Wales in one place.

BEST FAMILY VENUE

▲ **WINNER Science Museum** London • **p.28** A classic day out for the whole family where creativity in planning has ensured that the museum is accessible for everyone – including wheelchair users and children. Everything is at just the right height, the exhibits are interactive and everyone can participate in the fun. Visits can be easily planned in advance with the help of the information available on the excellent website. There is ample disabled parking, which is exceptional given the museum's central London location.

◄ **HIGHLY COMMENDED The Alnwick Garden** The Northeast and Yorkshire • **p.130** Given the nature of the attraction, great access is the last thing you'd expect here – visitors should prepare to be surprised. This is a magical day out.

▶ **HIGHLY COMMENDED Eden Project**
The Southwest • **p.112** Very deserving
of its place as one of the country's top
attractions. The Eden Project is fantastic on
every level.

▶ **HIGHLY COMMENDED South Devon
Railway and Totnes Rare Breeds Farm**
The Southwest • **p.110** The owners of
the Totnes Rare Breeds Farm have made
a massive effort to ensure that all visitors
can get fully immersed in farm life. The
partnership with the South Devon Railway
simply adds to the experience – kids love
travelling on these magnificent steam
engines.

▼ **HIGHLY COMMENDED Legoland
Windsor** The Home Counties and
Oxfordshire • **p.62** Visits to Legoland
are effortless. The logistics of how visitors
move from ride to ride have obviously been
considered and it is very easy to plan a day
out there. But what is most admirable is the
way staff are matter of fact when dealing
with disabled visitors – they don't make a
fuss, but just get on with the job.

BEST ACTIVE VENUE

▲ **WINNER Cairngorm Funicular Railway and Ski Centre** Scotland • **p.166** The ultimate marriage of activity and accessibility – the railway carriages are roomy and easy to navigate, allowing an easy journey to the summit, where the scenery is superb and visitors feel on top of the world.

▼ HIGHLY COMMENDED **Manchester Velodrome** The Northwest • **p.123** Tapping into the zeitgeist and making the most of Britain's competitive cycling success at the Olympics and Paralympics, this modern venue has facilities for disabled spectators that are beyond compare. And there is lots of work going on to provide special classes in the future.

▲ HIGHLY COMMENDED **Wicken Fen Nature Reserve** East Anglia and the East Midlands • **p.74** Making the Fens accessible is a near impossible task, but it has been achieved here. The walks, hides and amenities are all first-class, allowing everyone to get face-to-face with nature at its wildest – a pleasure that is sadly denied in many other reserves. The gardening partnership with a local disabled school is a great community initiative.

▶ HIGHLY COMMENDED **Cairngorm Sled-Dog Centre** Scotland • **p.164** At this centre, the owners have a passion that shines through – they love their animals and their sport and want to share that with everyone, going to great lengths to include all visitors in the thrills of dog-sledding.

▶ HIGHLY COMMENDED **Pedalabikeway Cycle Centre** Wales • **p.155** This attraction has been developed with the needs of disabled people in mind. The helpful nature and positivity of the staff is particularly impressive and there is a full range of bikes for hire. This is a lovely way to explore the countryside and a fun day out.

READERS' CHOICE

The **Eden Project** in Cornwall (Southwest • **p.112**) was the clear winner of our Readers' Choice award, and here are just a few of the positive things our readers had to say about this awe-inspiring, feel-good, environmental showcase.

"The staff were extremely helpful and the site almost totally accessible for me and my powered scooter. It seems a lot of thought and consideration for disabled people was involved in designing the layout."

Terence Sutton, Mansfield

"Interesting, unusual and well put together. There are loads of well trained volunteers to help you out."

Ian Cook, Birmingham

"I remember walking into the big biodomes and thinking what a magnificent place this was."

David Parker, Rhyl

"I'm elderly and I really appreciated the many resting places along the way. I was able to finish the walk."

Eileen McBride, Sheffield

"Totally accessible for wheelchair users. The tractor that transports you to and from the biodomes has a trailer with a special section for at least two wheelchairs."

Vicky Stobart, Ipswich

London

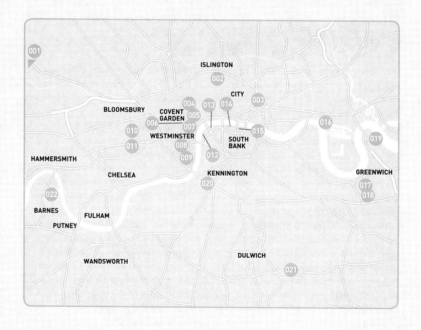

London

Hectic and sprawling, yet full of life, history and culture, London is unmissable. Recent years have seen its institutions reinvented – from Wembley to the British Museum – increasing both their appeal and accessibility. There is a vast amount to do here, whether you're getting lost among priceless antiquities, roaring yourself hoarse at a sporting event, finding tranquillity in surprisingly extensive green spaces or browsing the still-buzzing markets.

001 Wembley Stadium

Address: Wembley HA9 0WS **Website:** www.wembleystadium.com; car parking www
.csparking.com/stadium; accessforall@wembleystadium.com **Telephone:** 0844 980 8001;
disabled bookings 0845 458 1966 **Hours:** check website for events **Dates:** check website
for events **Entry:** varies depending on event and seat; season tickets available

It's the colour of the pitch – such a bright green against the red and grey of the stadium – that hits you, as you wheel out to one of the three-hundred-plus wheelchair spaces around the ground. Visitors never fail to be awestruck and, arguably, wheelchair users can choose from the best seats in the house.

A lot has changed at Wembley and the new stadium is a vastly more accessible place. Lifts and disabled toilets abound; turnstiles, food and merchandise counters are at the right level and the surface is car-showroom smooth. Induction loops are everywhere and the staff are helpful and trained. The match experience is enhanced by a live and highly professional commentary, delivered via headsets available from access points. It's aimed at fans with sensory issues but is available to all disabled spectators. Meanwhile, two useful "dog relieving stations" are available for assistance dogs.

Blue Badge parking is available in the stadium's two car parks but must be booked at least three days in advance, and costs from £12. If you are arriving via public transport, note that Wembley Park Tube does not have level access as claimed; depending on the platform, northbound passengers have a six-inch step up from the train. Thereafter the journey to the stadium is straightforward, if made slightly longer by having to avoid steps. Marshals and police will point you towards a series of slopes leading down to Olympic Way (note that the slopes will be on your right as you leave after the game). You will need to steer your way through the hordes of fans towards the access point. Information on dial-a-ride and shuttle buses are available from the website. Once you've reached the stadium, though, you should be sorted.

Food & drink ▶▶ Wembley food is largely the burger/pie staple diet favoured by football crowds everywhere – and expensive at that. Buy before you arrive!

002 Sadler's Wells Theatre

Address: Rosebery Avenue EC1R 4TN **Website:** www.sadlerswells.com **Telephone:** 0844
412 4300; access officer (two days per week) 020 7863 8096; access information 020 7863
8128/8127 **Hours:** box office Mon–Sat 9am–8.30pm **Dates:** closed 25 Dec and some other
public holidays **Entry:** varies depending on performance and seat, [D]&[C]50% discount

This renowned theatre, specialising in dance, especially modern dance, is inclusive not
only for visitors with disabilities, but also for disabled performers and staff.

The new building, opened in 1998 – the most recent of six theatres to occupy the site
since 1683 – now offers a bewildering array of facilities and a visit here can be an inspirational experience, if only to see what is achievable. From cutting-edge performance to
mainstream contemporary dance, tango to tap and flamenco to family shows, the joy of
movement and the celebration of dance lie at the heart of Sadler's Wells productions and
many have won awards. Most shows only run for a few days; if you think you'll become a
regular patron, the venue can register your seating preferences via their Access Scheme.

There are fifteen disabled spaces in the Sadler's Wells car park that you can book ahead.
The box office has low-level counters and visitors with sensory disabilities can book tickets
via Minicom. Throughout the theatre, textured paths lead to significant areas on every
floor, and as you approach the destination the "feel" changes. Wheelchair users can enjoy the performance from dedicated spaces near the exits (companions' seats are slightly
raised to bring them to the same level) or transfer to theatre seating (the outside armrests
of several aisle-end seats can be raised). Walkers needing extra leg room can specify seats
in the same area, while patrons who can't easily sit up in the auditorium can even ask for
the physio bed. Audio-described performances are a regular feature, and there are BSL-
interpreted pre and post-show talks with regular "Deaf Debating Dance" events. All lifts
have raised and Braille buttons, as well as voice announcements. In short, the theatre is a
model of fantastic access provision.

Food & drink ▸▸ The restaurant offers fine dining most evenings; tables must be booked
by 11am on the day you want to dine (3pm on Friday for a Saturday meal) and orders
made in advance, but your table is reserved throughout the performance. For simpler
food or a drink try the bars or the *Stage Door Café*.

003 Spitalfields Market

Address: Brushfield Street E1 6AA **Website:** www.oldspitalfieldsmarket.com; www
.spitalfields.co.uk **Telephone:** 020 7375 2963 **Hours:** markets Thu & Fri 10am–4pm, Sun
9am–5pm; shops & restaurants open daily, times vary **Dates:** closed 25 Dec **Entry:** free

Long-established Spitalfields Market sits under a glorious vaulted Victorian ceiling in
London's fashionable East End. You can come simply to soak up the atmosphere, but
with so much to taste, try on and check out, you won't be able to resist the temptation
to join in the bustling bargain-hunting for long.

Spitalfields Market

The market buildings were somewhat controversially redesigned in 2003, with many locals and stallholders fearing the loss of the soul of the market. Things have changed, with the arrival of more high-end shops and less space for stalls, but the modernisation certainly hasn't hampered accessibility. Spitalfields still plays host to a changing rota of traders throughout the week: antiques and vintage goods on Thursdays; fashion, arts and crafts on Fridays; and on Sundays a lively mixture of anything and everything, from textiles to gluten-free cakes and freshly harvested oysters. Based around the perimeter of the building, and open every day of the week, are funky art and design shops, some well-known chain restaurants and other independent or family-run cafés selling delicious international foods.

Just over fifty yards from the market entrance on Brushfield Street is a Blue Badge bay with a three-hour limit – but handily, Blue Badge holders can pay and display on single and double yellow lines for an unlimited time throughout the Tower Hamlets borough. The main market area has excellent level access throughout, and the only problems you might face are step-entry to some of the shops and cafés, and busy passages between stalls at peak time – Sundays in particular can get crammed, so arrive as early as you can to avoid the main throng. You'll find the disabled toilets opposite the Doc Martens shop; a RADAR key is required but because the door is monitored by CCTV, staff should bring it along automatically; and if they do not use the contact number displayed. An open seating area by the cafés has benches that are fixed, but at a good height for seating wheelchairs at either end.

Food & drink ▸▸ There are plenty of options to choose from in the market, but as Spitalfields sits parallel to Brick Lane, there's also the option of tucking in to a curry. *Preem Restaurant* (☎020 7377 5252, ⓦwww.preemprithi.co.uk), on the corner of Hanbury Street, is a small, level Indian restaurant with great staff, delicious food and regular deals.

IDEAS ▶▶ ACCESS TO THE ARTS

Access to Art (ⓦwww.access2art.org.uk) operates a service for disabled and elderly visitors to museums and galleries in central London. Members can be accompanied during visits to several major London venues by a volunteer gallery assistant, fully trained on issues relating to disability and equality. They even operate a door-to-door accessible minibus service for those unable to use alternative transport. Membership costs £15 annually.

Artsline (ⓣ020 7388 2227, ⓦwww.artsline.org.uk) is a long-established charity, set up to promote access to arts and entertainment venues. Still going strong almost thirty years later, the charity has a team dedicated to assessing facilities, and an extensive online database of access information for venues from galleries to theatres to cinemas, across London. They also have a handy link-up with the London Open House event, and have assessed over 130 of the fabulous buildings that open their doors to the public for one weekend every September. Although predominantly an online service, queries left on their answer machine will be answered.

Attitude is Everything (ⓣ020 7383 7979, ⓦwww.attitudeiseverything .org.uk; ⓔsuzanne@attitudeiseverything.org.uk) improves deaf and disabled people's access to live music by working with audiences, artists and the wider music industry to implement a Charter of Best Practice. The organisation has worked with many UK festivals and has achieved great improvements for both visitors and artists. Their top accessible UK festival picks are the increasingly recognised Reading and Latitude (ⓦwww.festivalrepublic. com), the long-established Cambridge Folk Festival (ⓦwww.cambridge folkfestival.co.uk) and independently run Guilfest (ⓦwww.guilfest.co.uk), which takes place at Stoke Park. All three events offer a variety of access facilities, ranging from accessible camping areas and viewing platforms to accessible toilets and showers. Organisers also deliver access and transport information online and in different formats well ahead of the event, and where applicable a "2 for 1" ticket deal for disabled customers.

Disability Cultural Projects (ⓦwww.disabilityarts.info) continues some of the work of the National Disability Arts Forum, which sadly ended its seventeen years of campaigning for arts inclusion in 2008, following a lack of funding. DCP's work includes an online database (ⓦwww.arts accessuk.org) of basic access details for arts venues across the UK and a free weekly newsletter, EtCetera. They also have a handy events calendar on the website (searchable by geographical area and artform), as well as a useful directory of links to other organisations involved in disability arts around the UK, from small, local projects to nationwide schemes.

Shape (ⓦwww.shapearts.org.uk) has been campaigning in London for over thirty years with parallel aims to Artsline. Check out the Shape tickets scheme – annual membership costs £25 and provides up-to-date listings of all current productions and events in London including details of assisted performances, a fully accessible online, telephone and postal booking system and regularly reduced ticket prices and waived booking fees. Plus, if you are unable to get to the venue on your own, you can ask for help from a trained team of volunteer access assistants who can assist you to and from the event at no extra charge.

004 British Museum

Address: Great Russell Street WC1B 3DG Website: www.britishmuseum.org Telephone: 020 7323 8000; access information 020 7323 8299 Hours: daily 10am–5.30pm; Thu & Fri till 8.30pm Dates: closed 1 Jan, Good Friday, 24–26 Dec Entry: free, with variations for major exhibitions, [D][C][Con]some discounts apply

The British Museum maintains one of the world's most outstanding and globally representative collections of antiquities, ancient artworks and cultural artefacts: some seven million items, and growing. Founded in the 1750s, the collection was rehoused in its present, Greek Revival-style building in 1852, the most notable recent addition to which has been the stunning, glass-roofed Queen Elizabeth II Great Court, opened in 2000.

This jewel in London's crown provides an amazing and – it's worth emphasising – free day out, and it deserves at least a day's visit. However, if time is at a premium, you could follow one of the one- and three-hour tour cards available from the information desks, which are extremely helpful. The Roman and Greek art collections are perhaps the greatest of all the exhibits here, and unparalleled anywhere in the world. You'll only see more impressive Egyptian exhibits in Egypt itself, while even more niche-interest sections, such as Hittite culture or medieval Southeast Asia, are impressively well served. And visiting children are too, with free art materials and activity backpacks available, themed family trails to suit different age groups ready-mapped, and a family audio tour hosted by Vid the alien.

Parking can be arranged on the main forecourt (call ahead on ☎020 7323 8299). An open lift, to the left of the imposing main staircase, takes you up to the entrance and further lifts are available to all areas. Magnifying glasses can be borrowed at the desks and assistance dogs are welcome; if you drop by the desk in the Great Court they will be given water. Access and what's-on guides and maps are vital accompaniments, not least because once you're through the doors and faced by the awe-inspiring Great Court and Reading Room it's easy to be distracted. The temporary exhibitions are usually accompanied by tactile images and Braille signs. Touch tours and BSL-interpreted gallery talks are regular features, too, as are object-handling sessions and audio-described highlight tours.

Food & drink ▸▸ The *Forum Café* (☎020 7404 1878), on Great Russell Street, opposite the main entrance of the museum, has moveable seating, outdoor tables and a disabled toilet.

005 Donmar Warehouse

Address: 47 Earlham Street, Seven Dials WC2H 9LX Website: www.donmarwarehouse .com Telephone: 0870 060 6624; access information, touch tours & audio performances 020 7845 5813 Hours: Mon–Sat 10am until curtain up Dates: closed Sun & 24 Dec Entry: all performances [D]£12 [C]£12 [A]£15–29 [child]£15–29 [Con]£12 (Thu & Sat matinee)

This former Covent Garden brewery and banana warehouse is one of London's leading theatres – a multi-award-winning space, with a diverse artistic policy that takes in new

LONDON

writing, contemporary versions of European classics, British and American drama and small-scale musical theatre.

Formed in 1961, the Donmar (after the first names of founders Donald Albery and Margot Fonteyn) has only 250 seats and offers a particularly intimate experience for audience and performers alike, demanding an extra dose of chutzpah from actors performing less than two metres from the front row. Under the artistic directorship of stage and film director Sam Mendes, the Donmar became hugely successful in the early 1990s and his successor, Michael Grandage, has built on this reputation. Hit productions have included *Design for Living* (1994), *The Glass Menagerie* (1995), *Uncle Vanya* (2002) and *Frost/Nixon* (2006). *Polar Bears* – the story of a man's struggle to love and live with someone suffering from a psychological condition – is set to be a 2010 highlight. This is the first work for the theatre by Mark Haddon, author of *The Curious Incident of the Dog in the Night-Time*, an awardwinning novel about a teenager with Aspergers' syndrome.

Given the infrastructure of the Donmar, access is pretty good. There's a single, Blue Badge space outside the theatre, only available after 6.30pm. The main entrance from Earlham Street requires a temporary ramp; if for any reason it has not been laid, until 6.30pm you can get to the box office via the Thomas Neal shopping centre, twenty metres to the right. A thirty-inch-wide lift serves both stalls and circle; although the sole wheelchair space is at the rear of the stalls, the accessible toilet and only lowered section of the two bars are at circle level. Walkers will also find fewer, shallower steps in the stalls. An online audio brochure of the theatre and its productions also lists details of signed, captioned and audio-described performances, which need to be booked in advance. The latter are also preceded by free touch tours, on which patrons can explore the set and often meet members of the company – again call ahead to book. Braille and large-print cast sheets, and large-print brochures, are available on request. Assistance dogs are not permitted in the auditorium but can be cared for during performances.

Food & drink ▶▶ In the basement of the Thomas Neal shopping centre – reached by the same lift that you use to access the theatre – the *Progreso* coffee bar (☎020 7379 3608, ⓦwww.progreso.org.uk) sells fairtrade snacks and drinks.

006 The Royal Academy of Arts

Address: Burlington House, Piccadilly W1J 0BD **Website:** www.royalacademy.org.uk
Telephone: 020 7300 8000; access information 020 7300 5732 **Hours:** daily 10am–6pm;
Fri till 10pm **Dates:** closed 24–25 Dec **Entry:** exhibitions [D]£10 [C]free [A]£12 [8–11s]£3
[12–18s]£4 [Con]£10

The Royal Academy of Arts, tucked in a private courtyard just off Piccadilly, was founded by George III and has long been governed by artists – the present board includes David Hockney and Tracey Emin.

Famous for its summer exhibition of some ten thousand works, to which any artist can submit a piece, it is one of Britain's premier galleries. Burlington House, home of the Royal Academy, is an elaborate piece of architecture which has passed through the hands of several patrons of the arts, many of whom have commissioned work on the house over the centuries. The John Madejski Fine Rooms were opened to the public in 2004, having been restored to their eighteenth-century glory. This collection of opulent salons is filled with design influences including Baroque and Neoclassical features, from gold columns to decorative ceilings. Artworks abound, including paintings by Sebastiano Ricci, and Kent's ceiling mural of Jupiter's blessing of the marriage between Cupid and Psyche. The Reynolds Room commemorates the fact that it was here that Darwin presented the draft version of *The Origin of Species*. Works from the main collection are displayed in these rooms, and elsewhere, temporary collections are exhibited, showing the works of renowned artists, of both contemporary and historical significance.

Call ahead to book a disabled parking spot outside. The entrance is ramped and the ticket desk is low. The area of the Academy where the temporary collections are housed is spacious and particularly easy to navigate in a wheelchair, but doesn't have much seating, while the Fine Rooms have heavy doors to open, but stewards who can assist. The library is not accessible for wheelchair users. Available services include wheelchair hire; large print and Braille gallery plans and a tactile gallery map; clear signage and artwork labelling; one-to-one audio-described guided tours; BSL and lip-speaking tours; and audioguides with detailed descriptions of selected works. The gift shop has some low shelves and a supervised lift. For each exhibition that is run, the access department organises a workshop for patrons with learning disabilities.

Food & drink ▶▶ The restaurant and café are well laid out for disabled visitors, but they are pricey – so if you're going to have to splash out anyway, you may as well pop over to Fortnum & Mason's (Ⓦwww.fortnumandmason.com) for a splendid cream tea, served from 3pm.

007 The National Gallery

Address: Trafalgar Square WC2N 5DN **Website:** www.nationalgallery.org.uk **Telephone:** 020 7747 2885 **Hours:** daily 10am–6pm, Fri till 9pm **Dates:** closed 1 Jan & 24–26 Dec **Entry:** free, with variations for major exhibitions

Britain's leading art collection, the National Gallery houses a vast range of paintings of exceptional quality. It's unrealistic to hope to cover everything in a single visit, so it is best to pick up a gallery plan on arrival and head for your favourites.

The steps leading up to the front of this iconic building are imposing and perhaps off-putting but there is level access via the Sainsbury Wing to the west or the Getty Entrance to the east. Once inside, life's a breeze. Most paintings in the permanent collection are on the main floor, linked to other galleries by large lifts with low-level buttons. Highlights of the permanent collection include Italian Renaissance masterpieces, with works by da Vinci, Uccello and Botticelli among many others; Velázquez's provocative *Rokeby Venus*; Dutch and German artists including van Eyck and Holbein; and some wonderful Impressionist art. In 2010 major exhibitions will include "Close Examination: Fakes, Mistakes and Discoveries" and "Venice: Canaletto and his Rivals".

Many of the individual galleries have benches and the Sainsbury Wing theatre and exhibition cinema have wheelchair spaces and induction loops. All levels have toilets, and a wide variety of other access facilities are on offer at the gallery – detailed on the website. You can borrow large print versions of the picture labels from the gallery assistants on duty.

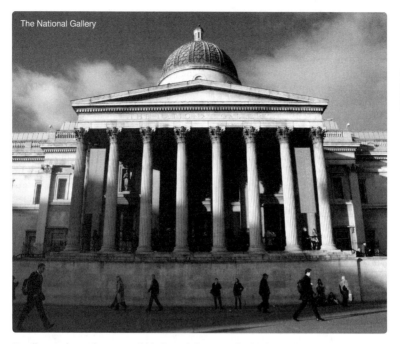
The National Gallery

Excellent audioguides are available free of charge to disabled people, as are guided tours twice daily. There are at least two BSL-interpreted talks and tours each month, while Art through Words sessions for blind and partially sighted visitors are organised on the last Saturday of every month.

Food & drink ▶▶ The stylish *National Café* is a destination in itself. Beautifully presented home-made pies, salads, sandwiches, cakes and tarts are freshly prepared on site.

008 Churchill Museum and Cabinet War Rooms

Address: Clive Steps, King Charles Street SW1A 2AQ **Website:** www.iwm.org.uk/cabinet
Telephone: 020 7930 6961 **Hours:** 9.30am–6pm; last entrance 5pm **Dates:** closed 24–26
Dec **Entry:** [D]£7.75 [C]free [A]£12.95 [under 16s]free [Con]£10.40

Perhaps the biggest surprise is that the Cabinet War Rooms, buried deep under White-hall in a warren of tunnels, are accessible at all. But here they are, and they offer a fascinating insight into how Prime Minister Winston Churchill and his staff managed Britain's day-to-day struggle during World War II.

Opened in 1938, when Nazi bombing raids were being anticipated, the rooms were used for meetings of Churchill's Cabinet for the duration of the war. The rooms remain exactly as they were in 1945, when the intelligence officers and map analysts finally cleared their desks and turned out the lights. As well as cabinet, map and communications rooms, Churchill's domestic quarters are now revealed – including his bed and a rather nice desk – while the Churchill Museum celebrates the great man's life. Running until 30 September 2010, the exhibition "Undercover: Life in Churchill's Bunker" takes a look at the personal stories of the staff who worked with him. Visitors are supplied with a hearing-aid-compatible audioguide to hang round their neck. It's used like a phone, but an earpiece is available to improve the sound quality and leave your hands free. A transcript is also available.

Parking in Westminster is difficult so it's best to look up nearby Blue Badge bay options on Ⓦwww.bluebadge.direct.gov.uk – there is a single one on Queen Anne's Gate. The best access is via Great George Street and the bunkers lie down a twenty-step flight of stairs with a single handrail. However, a lift beyond the ticket office can take you down to the start of the tour (and an accessible toilet). Some of the passageways are quite narrow and the doorway to the Churchill Museum is just over 27 inches wide at its narrowest point – most wheelchair users won't have a problem, but larger powered scooters will struggle. Manual wheelchairs are available to hire. There is limited seating, but you'll find more in the café.

Food & drink ▸▸ *The Switch Room Café* serves British comfort food – sausage and mash, all-day breakfasts, cream teas and home-made cakes.

009 Tate Britain

Address: Millbank SW1P 4RG **Website:** www.tate.org.uk/britain **Telephone:** 020 7887 8888; parking and wheelchair reservations 020 7887 3959; minicom 020 7887 8687 **Hours:** daily 10am–5.50pm (last entrance 5.40pm); 1st Fri of every month till 10pm (last entrance 9pm) **Dates:** closed 24–26 Dec **Entry:** free, with variations for major exhibitions

Tate Britain houses some of the greatest British art from the sixteenth century to the present day, as well as some international modern pieces – touring the rooms gives you a pictorial history lesson.

Works by every influential British artist appear in the collection and a large space is dedicated to some three hundred paintings and thirty thousand sketches by JMW Turner – a riveting body of work covering an astounding range of subjects. The modern exhibits include pieces by Francis Bacon and Damien Hirst and displays are changed annually. But it is Tate Britain's historical story that is the most fascinating: when Henry VIII broke from the Catholic Church, devotional artworks were banned and there was an upsurge in portraiture; as London became prosperous, William Hogarth's painting offered a commentary on the new urban wealth; and, in the eighteenth and nineteenth centuries, John Constable was one of the first painters to popularise naturalistic landscape as a worthy theme.

Allow half a day to complete a tour of the gallery without hurrying. You can call to reserve one of several disabled bays in the gallery's car park and take the back route into the building – but it's much easier to use the Blue Badge bays outside the ramped Manton entrance. Access throughout the site is good: information and ticket desks are low, disabled toilets don't need keys (and have grab rails) and there are several lifts. All gallery areas present the art and accompanying written descriptions at heights low enough to view from a wheelchair, and the gift shops have many low shelves. All the available access facilities are comprehensively listed on the website, but also include large print and Braille exhibition information, portable induction loops, audioguides, guided tours, touch tours and BSL-interpretation.

Food & drink ▶▶ *Tate Britain Café,* has a creative selection of salads, sandwiches, wraps and pastries as well as organic snacks, wines, beers and lots of healthy but tasty options for kids. There are some moveable tables and chairs.

010 Hyde Park and Kensington Gardens

Address: Hyde Park, The Park Office, Rangers Lodge W2 2UH; Kensington Gardens Office, The Magazine Storeyard, Magazine Gate, Kensington Gardens W2 2UH **Website:** www .royalparks.org.uk **Telephone:** Hyde Park 020 7298 2000; Kensington Gardens 020 7298 2000; Liberty Drives 07767 498096 **Hours:** Hyde Park daily 5am–midnight; Kensington Gardens daily 6am–dusk **Dates:** no closures **Entry:** free

Known as the Lungs of London, Hyde Park and its neighbour, Kensington Gardens, are the best places in the city centre to escape the crowds and breathe in some fresh air. Once the private gardens of kings and queens, nowadays everyone can enjoy these green oases, and with such a range of visitor attractions, from modern art exhibitions to adventure playgrounds, there's more to these parks than perfect lawns and duck ponds.

With 760 acres to cover, wheelchair users will appreciate the wide, smooth paths and the half-hourly electric buggy service, run in the summer by Liberty Drives, which takes in the main attractions and is free to anyone with limited mobility. From the hubbub at Speakers' Corner (come on a Sunday to hear the debate), a tree-lined avenue takes you south towards the new 7 July Memorial: a quiet spot in a busy part of London,

Kensington Gardens

and a poignant reminder of those 52 people who lost their lives in the 2005 bombings. Turn west by the Queen Elizabeth Gates and head to the park's watery centrepiece, the Serpentine. In summer the Solar Shuttle can ferry you silently across the water (access is via a ramp, with assistance from the crew) or you can continue along the south bank, past the Hyde Park Lido, famous for its freezing cold Christmas Day swimming race, and café. If you fancy a dip, use one of the accessible toilets and changing rooms; there is a lift to the sun terrace and paddling pool area, and three ramps with handrails leading into the water. Or you can simply dip your feet in the flowing water at the nearby, hugely popular Diana, Princess of Wales Memorial Fountain.

From here, the main footpath continues under Serpentine Bridge and into Kensington Gardens, where children will be pleased to find both Peter Pan's statue and the pirate-themed Diana Memorial Playground. Much of the playground is accessible, including a cleverly designed raised walkway giving access to several slides, so it's a pity that the centrepiece, a huge wooden pirate ship, can only be boarded via tricky rope bridges. Wheelchair access to Diana's former home, Kensington Palace, is very limited, although BSL-interpreted and described tours are on offer – check Ⓦ www.hrp.org.uk or call ahead on ☎ 020 3166 6199 if you're determined to see inside. Heading back east via the Round Pond takes you past the gleaming Albert Memorial and the Albert Hall, and on to the Serpentine Gallery, which is all on one level, dedicated to showing modern and contemporary art and free (it also has has eight medium-sized accessible loos).

Free local parking is available for Blue Badge holders for a maximum of four hours (although the Rangers Lodge at Hyde Park will consider requests for longer stays) and there are five car parks with disabled parking bays within the parks themselves.

Food & drink ▶▶ For something really special, treat yourself to afternoon tea at *The Orangery* in Kensington Palace. Dainty sandwiches and sumptuous cakes are the order of the day, washed down with fine teas and champagne – and much more reasonably priced than at London's top hotels. The restaurant is wheelchair accessible and has limited disabled parking that can be booked in advance via the palace.

011 Science Museum

Address: Exhibition Road, South Kensington SW7 2DD **Website:** www.sciencemuseum.org .uk **Telephone:** 020 7942 4000; minicom 020 7942 4445 **Hours:** daily 10am–6pm **Dates:** closed 24–26 Dec **Entry:** free, with variations for major exhibitions, IMAX cinema and simulators, [D]&[C]some discounts apply

The Science Museum in South Kensington is a buzzing, energetic place, dispelling the myth once and for all that science is boring. With more than two thousand hands-on exhibits, interactive displays and lively demonstrations, exploring everything from space travel to genetics, even the most reluctant visitors would be hard pressed not to find something to engage them. Most people come away enthralled and genuinely enriched by the experience.

A meander through the spacious ground-floor galleries takes you from huge steam-powered machines in the Energy Hall, through the history of rockets in Exploring Space, to Stephenson's Rocket and other iconic objects in Making the Modern World. The Well-

Science Museum

come Wing is home to the IMAX cinema and two very worthwhile exploratory exhibits – Who Am I? and In Future. While the museum is a grown-up institution, there is plenty here to keep children occupied. The three specific children's galleries – The Garden (for 3–6-year-olds), Pattern Pod (5–8s) and the ever-popular Launchpad (8–14s) – are particularly appealing, with a mass of activities easily accessed by most children with limited mobility. Launchpad was relaunched on the third floor in 2007, and now boasts more than fifty interactive exhibits designed to quiz young minds.

If you're arriving by car, you can use one of the four disabled parking spaces outside the museum or the eight more further along Exhibition Road. If you can manage public transport it can be easier: there's a pedestrian subway (but no step-free access) from South Kensington tube station to the museum entrance. General museum access is excellent, with lots of manoeuvring space and low-level exhibits. At the information desk, you should ask for a map, which shows lifts, ramps and accessible toilets. On the first Saturday of every month there is a BSL-interpreter at various free family events. The shop is spacious, with most items within reach of a wheelchair user, and at the time of writing plans were in place to acquire some powered scooters on site. There is one caveat: if you need to use the lifts, you may have a long wait at busy times, as you'll be vying with parents and pushchairs. However, Science Museum Lates are monthly, themed events that allow adults to experience the museum after hours – no kids allowed!

Food & drink ▶▶ All the cafés have moveable seating, but *Deep Blue Café* has waiter service and a selection of well-priced, restaurant-quality, hot dishes, pizzas, salads and great meal-deals for kids – including healthy options.

012–015 The South Bank

Apart from an annoying but doable jink around Blackfriars Bridge, the whole South Bank area is linked by a wheelchair-friendly riverside walkway. It's an attraction in itself on a sunny day, but the area is also littered with a diverse collection of places to visit, all with a high degree of accessibility. We list five great ones here, but there are plenty more to consider. You can find further information at ⓦ www.southbanklondon.com.

012 The London Eye

Address: Jubilee Gardens SE1 7PB **Website:** www.londoneye.com **Telephone:** 0871 222 0188 **Hours:** daily 10am–8pm; later closing during summer months **Dates:** closed 25 Dec **Entry:** [D]£14 [C]free [A]£17.50 [4–15s]£8.75 [Con]£14 (Mon–Fri only, not including Jul & Aug)

Described as "the landmark we never knew we needed", the Eye has become so emblematic of the London skyline that it is hard to remember a time without it.

The graceful thirty-minute "flight" provides an unparallelled view over the city. The pods are fully accessible, and can be slowed or stopped for easier access, but wheelchair users are advised to prebook, as capacity is limited. Disabled visitors should take the side entrance into the County Hall ticket office and use a dedicated ticket desk; those who find queuing a problem can access a fast-track service. A four-minute presentation in 4D (3D plus extra "feel" effects like bubbles) is an exciting and accessible introduction to the Eye experience. An audioguide and Braille guidebook are expected for 2010.

013 National Theatre

Address: South Bank SE1 9PX **Website:** www.nationaltheatre.org.uk (access booking form on disabled access page); access@nationaltheatre.org.uk **Telephone:** 020 7452 3000 **Hours:** Mon–Sat 10am–11pm (some Sun noon–6pm) **Dates:** closed bank holidays **Entry:** building and some exhibitions free; tickets vary depending on performance and seat, [C]free

At the heart of the South Bank complex, the National has produced over six hundred plays, including the highly emotive and controversial *Jerry Springer – The Opera*. Its three auditoriums put on a wide range of drama productions, usually over relatively short runs.

The theatre publishes an access guide online and employs a full-time manager charged with improving access to all the facilities. A visit is now such a seamless experience that the access office is turning its attention to improving life in general for disabled performers and staff. While the National Theatre is well served by public transport, drivers who manage to penetrate London's Congestion Zone are catered for too: if you take your ticket to the underground car park and present it at the box office, with your Blue Badge and theatre ticket, the parking is free.

014 Tate Modern

Address: Bankside SE1 9TG **Website:** www.tate.org.uk/modern; parking and wheelchair reservations ticketing@tate.org.uk **Telephone:** 020 7887 8888; minicom 020 7887 8687 **Hours:** Sun–Thu 10am–6pm (last entrance to exhibitions 5.15pm), Fri–Sat 10am–10pm (last entrance to exhibitions 9.15pm) **Dates:** closed 24–26 Dec **Entry**: free, with variations for major exhibitions

Tate Modern, housed in the cavernous former Bankside Power Station, is filled with post-1900 works of art from around the world. Modern art is awash with isms, and this is where you'll get to grips with the motivations of the protagonists behind Surrealism, Cubism, Minimalism and Vorticism, among other genres. And it's a thrill to enter the vast turbine hall, which often features a stunning temporary exhibit.

Book ahead to reserve one of several disabled bays in the gallery's car park, only a few metres away from a level-access entrance. Access throughout the site is as good as you would expect in a modern gallery, with low-level information and ticket desks, and care is taken to present work so that it is visible to wheelchair users. The permanent collections offer audioguides, guided tours, touch tours and BSL-interpreters at selected times and there are several wheelchairs and two powered scooters available to hire.

015 Vinopolis

Address: No 1 Bankend SE1 9BU **Website:** www.vinopolis.co.uk **Telephone:** 0870 241 4040 **Hours:** Mon, Thu & Fri noon–10pm, Sat 11am–10pm, Sun noon–6pm; closed Tue & Wed **Dates:** closed Tue & Wed; closed 24–31 Dec & 1 Jan **Entry:** wine tours from £19.50

The South Bank doesn't instantly spring to mind as a wine-tasting region. At Vinopolis, however, you're transported to the world's vineyards to swill and spit a multitude of vintages while learning the proper way to evaluate wine, beers and spirits.

There are several Blue Badge bays near the venue and although the local area is cobbled, it's possible to use the pavement to avoid most of the bumps. Vinopolis is largely wheelchair accessible with a ramped entrance to glass doors where assistance is available. The wine-tour ticket desk is low-level and the entire venue is spacious. There are lifts to all floors, plenty of seating and six accessible toilets. Some of the spirit stations are set at high bars, but all are staffed. After the tasting tour, you can continue your downward trend with more wine in *Wine Wharf* (which serves tapas), or various beers in the micro brewery *Brew Wharf*.

Food & drink ▶▶ The South Bank is studded with restaurants, and many are excellent. For a really memorable experience, try the *Oxo Tower Restaurant Bar & Brasserie* (℡020 7803 3888, Ⓦwww.harveynichols.com) or the restaurant on the seventh floor of Tate Modern: both have great menus and startlingly good views. Back out on the riverside, near the Festival Hall, *Giraffe* (℡020 7928 2004, Ⓦwww.giraffe.net) offers global food in a family-friendly setting.

016 Museum of London Docklands

Address: West India Quay E14 4AL **Website:** www.museumindocklands.org.uk **Telephone:** 020 7001 9844 **Hours:** daily 10am–6pm; last entrance 5.30pm **Dates:** closed 24–26 Dec **Entry:** [D]£5 [C]free [A]£5 [under 16s]free [Con]£3

LONDON

This bright and welcoming venue sits in what appears to be the only old building left in London's massively regenerated Docklands district. Happily, though, the rich history of the area is imaginatively described through a range of physical displays and audio-visual media, and the site itself has made great efforts to be as accessible as possible.

The city's story starts on the third floor, in the first century AD, where you're drawn into a well-lit, clearly signed maze of beautifully realised exhibits, telling the story of London's docks from their origins to the present day. You discover that London's reputation as a trading town was established under the Romans and grew to the point where it became the first port of the British Empire. There's a particularly evocative tour through nineteenth-century sailor town, and there are also some much less salubrious tales, such as about the district's complicity in the transatlantic slave trade and – as exemplified by Jack the Ripper – decades of lawlessness.

> "Beautifully situated in a very level location."
>
> **Philip Barron, Croydon**

While the museum is almost adjacent to the West India Quay DLR station, if you're approaching on the tube's Jubilee Line, you may find it more convenient to get off at Canary Wharf and follow the map (available to download from the website). If you come across steps, rest assured there will be a lift nearby. The footbridge immediately in front of the museum is bowed but negotiable. If you're arriving by car, you can drive to the front of the museum, buzz through to security and park free of charge. Access is fine throughout the museum. Apart from one cobbled stretch in the sailor town area, most of the flooring is polished timber. Lifts help you work your way through London's history, back down to ground level.

Food & drink ▶▶ It's worth stopping by the excellent and relaxed museum bar and restaurant, *1802*. There is plenty of seating at different heights, lots of space, and a varied menu from sharing plates to modern British main courses. Kids eat free at lunchtimes!

017–018 National Maritime Museum, Greenwich: the Maritime Galleries and the Royal Observatory

Address: Maritime Galleries, Romney Road, Greenwich SE10 9NF; Royal Observatory, Blackheath Avenue, Greenwich SE10 8XJ **Website:** www.nmm.ac.uk **Telephone:** tickets 020 8312 6608; recorded information 020 8312 6565 **Hours:** daily 10am–5pm **Dates:** closed 24–26 Dec **Entry:** museums free, with variations for major exhibitions; planetarium [D]£6 [C] free [A]£6 [child]£4 [Con]£4, family tickets available

Whether you want to navigate through time, space or the seas, the National Maritime

Museum has it all. Set in the splendid surroundings of London's oldest royal park, the Maritime Galleries celebrate Britain's seafaring history while The Royal Observatory is home to the Meridian Line and state-of-the-art Peter Harrison Planetarium.

The Maritime Galleries, together with the Queen's House, form a magnificent architectural set piece, overlooking the Thames. The collections, ranging from maritime art to model ships and Nelson memorabilia, are imaginatively displayed and include such gems as Captain Cook's sextant, Shackleton's Compass and Captain Scott's furry reindeer-hide sleeping bag. While the child-specific All Hands Gallery could offer more for a child with limited mobility, the museum as a whole has plenty of hands-on features, including the new bridge simulator that lets you experience what it's like to steer a ship at sea. A climb through Greenwich Park brings you to The Royal Observatory, where you can stand astride the Meridian Line: one foot in the eastern hemisphere, one foot in the west. As you'd expect, clocks and telescopes are the mainstay of the galleries housed in Sir Christopher Wren's original Observatory and surrounding buildings. The Astronomy Centre, opened in 2007, is home to three interactive galleries and the award-winning Planetarium, where Royal Observatory astronomers present a programme of lively shows. Recent years have seen much redevelopment of both the Maritime Galleries and the Royal Observatory. All three floors of the Maritime Galleries are completely accessible, as are the royal apartments at the Queen's House, and the new Astronomy Galleries and Planetarium. The Planetarium has dedicated wheelchair seating (prebooking advised). The older parts of the Observatory site have more restricted access, but wheelchair users can experience the Meridian Line and the Time Galleries (via an external lift in the Astronomer's Garden).

The greatest challenge facing those with limited mobility lies in getting between the two sites. There are two pedestrian routes through Greenwich Park, but if gradients are a problem it would be better to drive: the most straightforward route takes five minutes along the eastern side of the park, more or less following Maze Hill (this route is only suitable for vehicles under seven feet wide). Take the Blackheath Gate entrance to the park on Charlton Way for the four disabled bays at the Royal Observatory where Blue Badge holders may park free of charge for up to four hours. Parking at the Maritime Museum is more limited (prebooking advised). The museum has facilities for blind, partially sighted and hard-of-hearing visitors including monthly BSL-interpreted Planetarium shows.

Food & drink ▸▸ As an alternative to the accessible National Maritime Museum cafés, you can try the "Pie of the Day" or rock cakes at *The Pavillion Tea House* located at the top of the park, near the Royal Observatory Blue Badge spaces.

019 The O2

Address: Peninsular Square, Greenwich SE10 0BB **Website:** www.theo2.co.uk **Telephone:** 020 8463 2000; disabled booking 0870 600 6140 **Hours:** daily 9am–late; last entrance 1am **Dates:** no closures **Entry:** building free; tickets vary depending on exhibition, performance and seat

That great white elephant by the Thames, the publicly funded Millennium Dome,

The 02

LONDON

has been reborn as the O2 – a vast and impressive entertainment complex run by the entertainment company, AEG. This hugely successful redevelopment is home to the enormous 23,000-seater O2 Arena, the eleven-screen Vue cinema complex, the 2300-seater IndigO2 venue, the O2 bubble exhibition space and super-club matter.

Acclaimed as the world's top concert venue in 2009, the O2 Arena itself attracts a host of big names. Acts announced for 2010 include Alicia Keys, Rod Stewart, Andrea Bocelli and Peter Kay. But you don't have to be attending a specific event to enjoy the O2. Entertainment Avenue, which circles the main arena, has more than twenty cafés, bars and restaurants. Once you're stuffed, you can indulge in many other experiences, including a chill-out pod and a video "dance-oke" station – both wheelchair accessible.

A state-of-the-art venue like the O2 should rate highly for accessibility and you're unlikely to be disappointed – all the venues at the O2 are wheelchair accessible. Even the small details work: cinema ticket collection machines and car-park pay-points, for example, are at a good height for wheelchair users. The O2 Arena has a number of seating options depending on your level of mobility, including raised wheelchair bays (so you can still see the stage if people in front stand up) on level one, with temporary seating for companions. However, some seats can be some distance from the lifts, so ask when booking if this is an issue. There's plentiful disabled parking but it's expensive on event nights, even with a discount (only for Blue Badge holders: £10; book in advance on ☎0870 600 6140). Car parks 2 and 4 are closest to the entrance at 320 yards and 380 yards away. Visitors are encouraged to use public transport, and North Greenwich tube and bus stations are wheelchair accessible.

Food & drink ▶▶ The places to eat on Entertainment Avenue are all chain outlets – with all the usual suspects present – but there's a great variety, including Thai, tapas and grills. Facilities for disabled visitors are present and correct throughout.

020 The Brit Oval

Address: Surrey County Cricket Club, Kennington SE11 5SS **Website:** www.surreycricket .com **Telephone:** 0871 246 1100 **Hours:** see website for fixtures **Dates:** see website for fixtures **Entry:** varies depending on fixture

This famous old cricket venue, home to Surrey County Cricket Club, has undergone extensive refurbishment over recent years. While the process is not yet complete (floodlights have now been fitted to allow evening fixtures), it already offers a relaxed and accessible environment to disabled fans, wherever you choose to sit.

At pitch level, a visit can be a remarkably intimate experience, as you're sitting just feet from the boundary rope. The playing area is slightly domed towards the centre, offering batsmen excellent opportunities for scoring fours. For a cricket fan, there is surely no better place to watch the game at its highest standard. More than sixty wheelchair-plus-companion seats are available, in four bays spread around the ground. But the higher up you can afford to go, the more spectacular the view.

Parking is available near or, depending on the fixture, in the ground itself (call to check availability). There is level access to the wheelchair bays (toilets here require a RADAR key) and lift access to everywhere else, including the recently built OCS stand and sponsors' boxes. Here, if you can drag yourself away from the hospitality, seats are regularly removed to offer extra wheelchair access to the steep terraces outside. As part of a long-term relationship with Scope, low-level service points are being fitted at catering points and DDA-compliant pads help to open some of the stiffer doors. Induction loops are fitted in seating blocks 7 to 14, which include disabled bays 12 and 13, while assistance dogs are welcome and free audio earpieces (available at the retail outlets) provide a running BBC radio commentary on the match. All staff on site have a basic understanding of BSL. Contact Sharon Eyers on ☎07768 558045 for details of cricket schools for people with disabilities.

Food & drink ▸▸ There are four different vendors on site selling a range of food from burgers to curries, all with low-level service points. Less than five minutes away is a rather nice fully accessible pub, *The Beehive* (☎020 7582 7608).

021 Horniman Museum and Gardens

Address: 100 London Road, Forest Hill SE23 3PQ **Website:** www.horniman.ac.uk **Telephone:** 020 8699 1872 **Hours:** museum daily 10.30am–5.30pm; gardens Mon–Sat 7.30am–sunset, Sun 8am–sunset **Dates:** closed 24–26 Dec **Entry:** free, with variations for major exhibitions

John Horniman, a prosperous Victorian tea merchant, travelled the world for his trade. Fascinated by natural and cultural history he began selecting specimens and treasures to share with the public in his Forest Hill home. Over one hundred years later, his curious discoveries are on display in the accessible Horniman Museum.

The museum and award-winning gardens sit right on top of Forest Hill with glorious views over west London. The original collection – which has been added to over the years – lies at the heart of the museum, but it's the interactive developments and hands-on sessions that really bring the artefacts to life. You can have a go at African drumming, discover the size of a shark's jawbone, conduct a virtual orchestra, or get up close and personal with a busy beehive. From science shows to BSL days, the museum runs a busy and varied programme of touch sessions, family workshops and short courses. Many of these are available for free – so it pays to keep an eye on the website for listings.

The existing museum was constructed in 1901 when the collection outgrew Horniman's home, and a major centenary development has made this Victorian building easy to navigate. A well-situated and good-sized lift allows access to every level, including the new aquarium in the basement – home to a colony of jellyfish. Be aware though that heavy soundproof doors protect some of the galleries, and these can be difficult to open. Outside the paths are good, but care is required on steep ground and steps in some areas. Blue Badge holders should call in advance to book parking in the gardens.

Food & drink ▶▶ The museum café is airy and boasts an outside seating area that is great on sunny days. The choice of dishes reflects the museum's international heritage.

022 WWT London Wetland Centre

Address: Queen Elizabeth Walk, Banstead SW13 9WT **Website:** www.wwt.org.uk/london
Telephone: 020 8409 4400 **Hours:** summer 9.30am–6pm; winter 9.30am–5pm; 24 Dec
9.30am–3pm; last entrance one hour before closing **Dates:** closed 25 Dec **Entry:** [D]£7.40
[C]free [A]£9.95 [4–16s]£5.50 [Con]£7.40

On a 105-acre reserve, by a meander of the Thames in Barnes in southwest London, the Wildfowl and Wetlands Trust's London Wetland Centre is a paragon of ornithological conservation, a mecca for birdwatchers and an internationally recognised Site of Special Scientific Interest.

A maze of paths and boardwalks takes you around the marshes and over the lakes to view birdlife from Britain and migrants from around the world. Apart from the profusion of common mallards and moorhens there are plenty of exotic breeds, such as the orange-headed mandarins and the super-sized Icelandic eider ducks, whose down has the highest thermal rating of any natural substance. Migrants flock here and on-site ornithologists protect rare species and help with global projects such as the reintroduction of the critically endangered Laysan teal back into Hawaii. Hides are scattered across the lakes, enabling you to watch the birds and other wildlife without being obtrusive. From the top of Peacock Tower, you can get out the binoculars and enjoy 360-degree views.

> "Excellent facilities! I'm really glad we live close to the London Wetland Centre."
>
> **Barbara Cocks, Banstead**

There are several disabled parking spots in the car park, adjacent to the main visitor centre. This centre has some heavy doors but staff can assist. The paths are mostly asphalt, with boardwalks and some compacted shingle, though in the World Wetlands area there are lots of wildlife gates to be opened and closed. There are several accessible toilets, and all but two of the hides are single storey with level entry, as is the Sand Martin Nest Bank. The nearby Peacock Tower hide has a lift allowing everyone access to the dramatic views across the lakes.

Food & drink ▶▶ As well as neatly tended picnic areas, the centre has the *Water Edge's Restaurant* too – eat on the terrace and observe the wandering moorhens. The menu is clearly displayed on a chalkboard.

The Southeast

The Southeast

As the region where Londoners weekend, the southeast can be prone to high visitor numbers, both from the capital and from nearby Europe. But steer clear of the obvious tourist traps, and you'll find many places offering respite from the crowds, with elegant tended gardens and broad tracts of unspoilt field and woodland proving this verdant region the deserved bearer of the title "the garden of England".

023 Bolderwood Deer Sanctuary, New Forest National Park, Hampshire

Address: 3 miles west of Lyndhurst at the northern end of the New Forest Bolderwood Ornamental Drive (nearest postcode SO43 7GQ) **Website:** www.new-forest-national-park .com **Telephone:** Lyndhurst visitor centre 023 8028 2269 **Hours:** no closures **Dates:** no closures **Entry:** free

Hampshire's ancient New Forest has almost one hundred miles of cycle tracks, many of which are suitable for wheelchairs. Approached via Lyndhurst through a drive of ornamental trees, Bolderwood Deer Sanctuary ticks all the boxes for anyone looking for a day of fresh air and exercise in this newly created National Park.

The grassy picnic area by the car park is lovely, but you'll be keen to explore the trails that head off into the beautiful woodland. The three accessible trails – Deer Watch, Jubilee Grove and Radnor – are finished with compacted gravel and start from the car park. They're of varying length (the longest is two miles), rated moderate, and feature some 1:15 to 1:20 gradients, as well as some short stretches of 1:5 gradients, which larger, more robust scooters can manage with care. Although still recovering from the ravages of the 1987 storm, some of the tallest trees in the forest – Douglas fir and Redwoods – can be found in this area among the native beech and oak. Although deer are prevalent in the New Forest, they can be surprisingly elusive, so if you visit in the summer months, make sure you're there between 1.30pm and 2.30pm when the local herd of fallow deer are fed by rangers. You'll find an accessible viewing platform that overlooks the feeding meadow, around 160 yards down the Deer Watch trail. As well as the deer, New Forest ponies roam freely in the area and a huge variety of wildlife depends on the delicate environment being sustained.

> "My relations took me to visit the deer sanctuary. The weather was perfect and I had no problems using my wheelchair."
>
> **Jean Ruff, London**

Bolderwood car park has plenty of disabled parking and an accessible toilet. The information centre, situated in the picnic area, is staffed during summer weekends and school holidays. If you're tempted by the eight-mile-long Bolderwood cycle trail, which also starts from the car park, be aware that it includes several cattle grids.

Food & drink ▶▶ Every day in summer, and most of the rest of the year, you can buy award-winning New Forest Ice Cream from a mobile vendor in the car park. For something more filling, Lyndhurst has a range of tearooms, pubs and restaurants: *La Pergola* (☎023 8028 4184, ⓦwww.la-pergola.co.uk) is an Italian restaurant on Southampton Road that has brand-new and fully accessible facilities.

024 British Disabled Flying Association, Hampshire

Address: Lasham Airfield, Alton GU34 5SS **Website:** www.bdfa.net **Telephone:** 01256 346424 **Hours:** daily 9am–6pm **Dates:** no closures but weather-dependent **Entry:** flight experience in plane or glider £50 (approx one hour)

Flying a plane is something you might dream about, but never expect to do. One visit to the British Disabled Flying Association at Lasham will have you questioning your preconceptions, and realising just how easily the barriers can be broken down.

The BDFA charity enables people with disabilities to experience flying light aircraft and

Preparing for a trial flight at the BDFA Lasham Airfield

IDEAS ▶▶ FLYING

The British Disabled Flying Association is not the only association that can help you take to the skies:

The APT Charitable Trust (☎01722 410744, ⓦwww.disabledflying.org.uk, ⓔadmin@disabledflying.org) has microlight aircraft with modified controls. Based at the Old Sarum airfield in Wiltshire, staff have over fifteen years of experience giving physically disabled people an opportunity to fly.

Flyability (ⓦwww.flyability.org.uk, ⓔcontact@flyability.org.uk) is the disability initiative of the British Hang-Gliding and Paragliding Association. Tandem flights are available with Flyability, but the charity also encourages people with disabilities to train as pilots alongside able-bodied students.

Walking on Air, in Scotland, provides specially adapted gliders. See p.173 for more information and contact details.

gliders. If you want, you can go on to gain flying hours and eventually get your pilot's licence. The charity has use of three light planes and a glider. The flights are heavily subsidised, offered at around half the going rate, but have to be booked in advance. The planes have either two or four seats with easy access to the cockpit and full dual controls in the front seats. Once airborne, you're encouraged to take the controls to get a feel for how the plane handles: the qualified pilots, some of them disabled themselves, are always in full control. It's a thrilling, potentially life-changing experience, and even on your first flight, with the reassurance and simple explanations of your instructor about the dials and gauges, you'll get enough of an insight to want to go up again.

When you first call or email to book your flight, your instructor will let you know how to get through the entrance barrier and where to go. Disabled parking is adjacent to the clubhouse, which has an accessible toilet. A wheelchair accessible golf buggy can take you to the aircraft. There are two types of planes, giving options for cockpit entry for those with reduced mobility. The aircraft wings are strong, and low enough to step or transfer onto easily, followed by a few steps or a shuffle into the cockpit. For those with less movement, an electric hoist can aid transfer. If you have sight, hearing, cognitive or learning disabilities you can also participate: BDFA say they've never turned anyone away.

Food & drink ▶▶ The *Lasham Gliding Society Restaurant* sells drinks and snacks – a great place for a flight de-brief.

025 Frensham Pond Sailability, Surrey

Address: Pond Lane, Churt, Farnham GU10 2QA Website: www.frenshampondsailability .org.uk Telephone: 01252 850089; call to book a "try sail" Hours: times vary, contact the club Dates: sailing days Apr–Oct Thu & Sat Entry: [D]£5 per session; annual fee £35

This vibrant sailing club – voted Royal Yachting Association Club of the Year 2009 – has been offering accessible and highly affordable sailing facilities for more than 25 years. Set in beautiful Surrey countryside, Frensham Ponds Sailability caters for disabled people – both groups and individuals (aged 10 and over) – with its fleet of Access and Wayfarer dinghies, a Challenger trimaran and several 2.4-metre mini-keelboats.

No previous experience is required. Although it caters for all levels of ability and ambition, the club has built a reputation for breeding top-class racers: current members include British and French National Access champions. If you fancy competing with Team GB in the 2012 London Paralympics, this is a good place to start (though you'll need to put in a lot of practice). However, there is no pressure and gentle cruises around the eighty-acre pond are a weekly feature. While organised sailing such as this is restricted to the summer months, Sailability members race or cruise with the main Frensham Pond Sailing Club all year round.

Access is first class. On-site parking is flat and level. Sailors have access to the main clubhouse where an induction loop is available and the disabled-friendly shower rooms and toilets are excellent. The new pavilion allows cover for wheelchairs while their users are out on the water. Hoists are available to transfer the less mobile in and out of the boats. The Access, Challenger and mini-keelboats are designed to be sailed solo, and some of them are fitted with joystick controls. All three classes are also designed not to capsize, although in a stiff breeze, you might be forgiven for thinking that's what's about to happen – thrilling stuff. For another UK Sailability experience, see p.69.

Food & drink ▶▶ After an hour on the water, you'll need some sustenance: the café in the clubhouse is open at weekends and on special occasions, offering tasty home-made snacks. Regular barbecues are hosted in the summer months, and there is a licensed bar on site.

026 RHS Garden Wisley, Surrey

Address: Woking GU23 6QB **Website:** www.rhs.org.uk/wisley **Telephone:** 0845 260 9000
Hours: Mar–Oct Mon–Fri 10am–6pm, Sat, Sun & bank holidays 9am–6pm; Nov–Feb
10.30am–4.30pm; last entrance one hour before closing **Dates:** closed 25 Dec **Entry:**
[D]£9.50 [C]free [A]£9.50 [6–16s]£3 [Con]members free

RHS Garden Wisley

As the flagship garden of the Royal Horticultural Society (RHS), you would expect Wisley to be pretty special, and you would be right. This is a dream-garden destination, with plenty for everyone, experts and novices alike.

What sets Wisley apart from other public gardens are attractions like the Fruit Mount, a spiral-shaped viewpoint, which looks out over Fruit Fields to the Surrey countryside beyond. There are world-class examples of all gardening styles, from formal to wild and inspirational model gardens to stimulate the senses. The newest and most spectacular jewel in Wisley's crown is the Glasshouse, a state-of-the-art climate-controlled greenhouse. Inside, in various climatic zones, amazing plants of all sizes in realistic settings show how horticulture can be theatre as well. The result is breathtaking, as well as educational. You can take a wheelchair below the surface to see how roots grow underground, and even go behind a waterfall. The Wisley events calendar is becoming increasingly busy, so keep an eye on the website for news of seasonal and special events, many of which are free and educational.

There are sixty disabled spaces in the car park, and loan wheelchairs available, including electric buggies by arrangement. All Wisley's shops and restaurants have level entry, including the excellent tea shops. This is a hilly site spread over almost 250 acres, so inevitably you will come across steps, and some rough paths. There is, however, an extensive wheelchair route which is easy to follow and takes you to all the best attractions. Even this route can be steep in places, and you might prefer to wait for the mobility vehicle, which runs every twenty minutes. There are five disabled toilets scattered around the site, of various sizes – the newly refurbished one in the car park is the best. The guided tours are free, and some are BSL-interpreted; they can be booked in advance for groups and cost £1 per person.

Food & drink ▸▸ The seasonal food at the *Conservatory Café and Restaurant* is great – lookout for unusual sausages, novel English cheeses and the locally brewed Gardeners Tipple ale.

027 Brighton Pier, East Sussex

Address: Madeira Drive, Brighton BN2 1TW Website: www.brightonpier.co.uk Telephone: 01273 609361 Hours: pier daily 10am–11pm weather-dependent; attractions vary Dates: pier closed 25 Dec; some attractions close Sep–Mar Entry: free access to pier; charges vary for individual attractions

It's brash and tacky, the rides are overpriced and the food is the stuff of heart attacks, but for a few hours of unadulterated fun-seeking at its finest, it's hard to beat. Welcome to Brighton Pier, the archetypal British seaside experience.

There are theme-park rides – both traditional and terrifying – huge arcades of slot machines, penny-pushers and video games, side stalls, tin-can alleys, beer gardens, karaoke bars, candyfloss, fish and chips, doughnuts and, of course, Brighton rock. Despite the free entrance onto the privately owned pier, money is all too easily frittered away. If you can resist all the temptations, perhaps the pier's gentlest pleasure is just to sit and admire the view back over the beach and city. Most visitors don't know that Britain's most commercially successful pleasure pier is also an architecturally notable

Victorian iron structure, not to mention Grade II listed.

Parking can be tricky in the busy high season, but there are disabled spaces for roughly fifteen cars just to the left of the pier. Otherwise, Blue Badge holders can park without time limit at pay and display or voucher bays (indicated by a green tick). For wheelchair users, navigating the pier is easy: a special strip of walkway minimises judder, entrance to all the buildings is step-free, and many of the arcade games and side stalls have low-level slots. There's plenty of seating and deckchairs are free. There are two wheelchair accessible toilets, both requiring a RADAR key. The first is situated right in the middle of the Palace of Fun near the pier entrance – be aware that you may have to navigate a congested and noisy route to access it. The second disabled toilet is near the far end of the pier, in the fun area for kids. The only really problematic area of the pier is the funfair – access to the rides may be tricky, if not impossible for some disabled visitors.

Food & drink ▶▶ The *Palm Court Restaurant* on the pier is pretty special: the tasty portions of fish and chips can be served with not just a side order of mushy peas, but a glass of bubbly too!

028–029 The Royal Pavilion and Brighton Museum & Art Gallery, East Sussex

Address: The Royal Pavilion, 4–5 Pavilion Buildings, Brighton BN1 1EE; Museum and Art Gallery, Royal Pavilion Gardens, Brighton BN1 1UE **Website:** both attractions www .royalpavilion.org.uk **Telephone:** both attractions 0300 029 0900 **Hours:** pavilion Apr–Sep daily 9.30am–5.45pm, Oct–Mar daily 10am–5.15pm; museum Tue–Sun 11am–5pm **Dates:** pavilion closed 25–26 Dec; museum closed Mon except bank holidays, 1 Jan & 25–26 Dec **Entry:** pavilion [D]£7.50 [C]free [A]£9.50 [5–15s]£5.40 [Con]£7.50; museum free

Built to impress by a bored Prince Regent, George IV, the Royal Pavilion in Brighton is a unique combination of eccentric architecture and sumptuous interior design. From outside, with its palladian symmetry and meringue-like topping of onion shaped domes, the Pavilion looks like a cross between Buckingham Palace and the Taj Mahal.

Inside the Chinese styling is as extravagant as George IV's lifestyle was scandalous. And while it may not be to your taste, you can't fail to be impressed by the opulence of the decoration – known as chinoiserie – the quality of the craftsmanship and the ambition of the design. Probably the most impressive example is the Banqueting Room. Here, suspended from the domed ceiling, a red-tongued silver dragon clutches a thirty-foot chandelier, weighing more than a tonne, from which extend six more fire-breathing dragons. Equally ostentatious in its own way is the Great Kitchen, where multi-course banquets were prepared. Even this domestic room is spectacular, with high ceiling lights and iron columns in the shape of palm trees. The grandeur persists as you move through the ground floor rooms, and culminates when you arrive at the Music Room with its breathtaking domed ceiling, lined with 26,000 individually made hand-gilded scallop shells.

There aren't many places to sit and rest on the way round, but manual wheelchairs are

The Pavilion Gardens

available to borrow, and the staff are very helpful and happy to lend a hand. Unfortunately, the first floor is only accessible by a flight of thirty shallow stairs with a handrail. If you can manage these, you can visit the bedrooms used by George IV's brothers and Queen Victoria's bedroom. But if you can't, rest-assured the highlights are downstairs. At the reception desk you can pick up a free audio tour that has a T-switch for hearing aids. Specialist tours for groups of visitors with sensory disabilities – including signed and tactile – can be booked in advance.

Just across the beautiful Pavilion Gardens – about one hundred yards away – you'll find the Brighton Museum and Art Gallery. The museum is free to enter, and small enough to be a perfect addition to your visit. Inside you will find collections of world art, fashion and style, local Willett's pottery, and a fascinating collection of photographs of old Brighton. The most eye-catching exhibits are in the museum's diverse twentieth-century collection, home to pieces from the early Art Deco period to contemporary works. There is a pair of giant lips that are actually a sofa, ceramic art by the Turner Prize winner Grayson Perry, and beautiful domestic objects that your granny might have owned. The museum has level access, some seating, an accessible toilet, and a lift between floors. You won't find any parking next to the museum or Pavilion, but in Brighton street parking is free for Blue Badge holders in the pay and display and voucher bays. Disabled visitors can advance book 'drop-offs' and 'pick-ups' closer to the entrance.

Food & drink ▶▶ *The Royal Pavilion Tearoom* is on the first floor of the building, and so out of reach for some visitors. But all is not lost – at the museum, tasty tea and scones are served in the accessible tearoom overlooking the main exhibition area.

030 Bedgebury National Pinetum and Forest, Kent

Address: Park Lane, Goudhurst, Cranbrook TN17 2SL **Website:** www.bedgeburypinetum.org .uk **Telephone:** 01580 879820; bike hire shop 01580 879694 **Hours:** daily Jan & Dec 8am–4pm; Feb & Nov 8am–5pm; Mar & Oct 8am–6pm; Apr & Sep 8am–7pm; May–Aug 8am–8pm **Dates:** closed 25 Dec **Entry:** free; parking £7.50 per car, £30 for a minibus; concessions by advance arrangement; Go Ape [A]£30 [10–17s]£20

Bedgebury National Pinetum and Forest isn't just a beautiful collection of trees: the Forestry Commission has worked hard to develop it into an "activewood", and one of the largest and most popular family-orientated outdoor destinations in southeast England.

With fifteen miles of trails, adventure play areas, a unique collection of pine trees from around the world, and the tallest tree in Kent, there is plenty to keep even the most active family busy. Much of the site is accessible. The visitor centre can provide you with maps and directions to the various activities. The trails are mostly well surfaced and fun to explore – the tranquil Pinetum Trail is mostly level with plenty of rest stops; the Forest Trail has fairly easy access but rougher paths; and the Family Cycle Trail is the most adventurous route, but it's still reasonably accessible, if somewhat hilly. Kids are well served with a Play Trail and a pirate-themed play area where efforts have been made to make some of the equipment accessible to children of all abilities.

Also on offer is archery, for all abilities, and Go Ape, a high-wire forest trail, which takes you on a three-hour treetop adventure, via Tarzan swings and ziplines. It's not for the fainthearted, although participants are securely wired the whole time. Call ahead to book and discuss any requirements you have – the Go Ape guideline for accessibility is: "if you can climb a rope ladder you should be fine", so if this is you, then give it a go. On arrival, you'll find the disabled parking bays on asphalt near the visitor centre, which is home to a RADAR-key-accessible toilet and level-entry shower. There is a bike shop here too, which hires out adapted bicycles, tricycles and a powered off-road scooter.

Food & drink ▶▶ Bedgebury is an amazing place to picnic, and there's enough space to ensure that everyone can find a scenic spot. If you'd prefer not to bring your own food, then try the *Pineatery*, for fresh, local ingredients and lovely cakes.

031 The Historic Dockyard Chatham, Kent

Address: Chatham ME4 4TZ (use ME4 4TY for satnav) **Website:** www.chdt.org.uk **Telephone:** 01634 823800 **Hours:** daily 13 Feb–27 Mar 10am–4pm; 28 Mar–23 Oct 10am–6pm; times vary throughout Jan, Oct, Nov & Dec **Dates:** closures vary throughout Jan, Oct, Nov & Dec **Entry:** [D]£12.50 [C]free [A]£15 [5–15s]£10.50 [Con]£12.50

The Historic Dockyard Chatham celebrates more than four hundred years of Royal Navy shipbuilding. And while a day out on an old, sprawling eighty-acre riverbank site might not sound ideal for disabled visitors, the museum is remarkably accessible.

The museum's emphasis on the people who built these magnificent vessels, as much as the ships themselves, helps visitors to appreciate the dockyard's story on a human scale. In the Wooden Walls gallery, adjacent to the entrance, a tour led by a guide in costume explains how these wooden warships were built, as described by the 1758 diary entries of a young apprentice boy. There is a vast amount of history to take in at Chatham – HMS *Victory* was built here, as were some of the ships that defeated the Spanish Armada. An exhibition traces the dockyard's involvement in slavery, and at the quarter-mile-long Ropery, another guide in period dress explains how rope has been made here for four centuries. Tickets are valid for re-entry for a year, which is a good thing, because there is much more here than you can see in one day.

There is a substantial mobility vehicle to take you around and manual wheelchairs are available to borrow, but if you are on foot, watch out for tramlines, cobbles and other trip hazards. The Big Store and particularly the adjacent National Lifeboat Collection are both easy to access, and both the Wooden Walls gallery and the Ropery have lifts. Unfortunately, getting around the warships is really only for those who can climb ladders – if you can you're free to explore a World War II destroyer, and a Cold War nuclear submarine. Wheelchair users can get onto the deck of HMS *Gannet* – a Victorian warship – via a ramp. There are currently four reasonably large accessible toilets, and at the time of writing, a brand-new exhibition space, No.1 Smithery, was in construction and planned to be launched in summer 2010.

Food & drink ▶▶ Visit the aromatic *Nelson Brewery* at the dockyards for a tour and a taste of their award-winning traditional Kentish ales – Trafalgar Bitter, Loose Cannon and Pieces of Eight. You can take some home too.

032 Leeds Castle, Kent

Address: Maidstone ME17 1PL **Website:** www.leeds-castle.com **Telephone:** 01622 765400 **Hours:** daily Apr–Sep 10am–6pm; Oct–Mar 10am–5pm (last entry earlier, times vary) **Dates:** closed 7–8 Nov & 25 Dec **Entry:** [D]£13.50 [C]free [A]£16.50 [4–15s]£9.50 [Con]£13.50

Built for beauty rather than defence, the majestic, if confusingly named, Leeds Castle has the grandest of designs and is a perennially popular place to visit. The castle puts on displays and activities throughout the year, so it's good to know that your ticket gives you unlimited free re-entry for twelve months.

This magnificently sited castle, part of it set on an island in a lake, and the whole thing surrounded by five hundred acres of parkland, has been built up, added to and improved on over a thousand-year period. The castle's interior is just as impressive as its dramatic external appearance: the main building was sumptuously furnished in the early twentieth century by the last owners. A stone bridge (with stairlift) takes you over the lake to the island, and the second part of the castle. This beautiful building – known as the Gloriette – has been refurbished to give an idea of its appearance in medieval times, complete with the banqueting hall and the bedroom used by Queen Elizabeth I. Other accessible attractions include an oasis of aromatic plants and herbs known as the Culpeper Garden, the world-renowned aviary, and the delightfully eccentric museum of dog collars. Plus there are interactive daily falconry displays, an accessible children's play area and the Knights Realm adventure playground to enjoy too.

Leeds Castle

There is plenty of disabled parking near the entrance, where you can also pick up an excellent map and mini-guide to the facilities. This site is large, but the paths are good with lots of rest points, and everything is clearly marked out in the guide. The woodland garden and the duckery walk (which is less than a mile long) are both accessible and have seating. If you do need a bit of extra help getting about the grounds, take the Land Train which makes various stops around the estate – it's accessible to manual wheelchair users.

Food & drink ▶▶ There are several places to eat at Leeds Castle, but the *Fairfax Hall Restaurant* is highly recommended – it has a great menu, an accessible dining terrace and stunning views across the moat to the castle.

033 Dungeness National Nature Reserve, Kent

Address: RSPB visitor centre, Boulderwall Farm, Dungeness Road, Lydd TN29 9PN; RHD railway (check website for details of stations and stops) **Website:** www.dungeness-nnr .co.uk; RSPB www.rspb.org.uk/reserves; RHD railway www.rhdr.org.uk **Telephone:** RSPB 01797 320588; RHD railway 01797 362353 **Hours:** RSPB reserve daily 9am–9pm (or sunset if earlier); RSPB visitor centre daily 10am–5pm; RHD railway timetable varies, check website **Dates:** RSPB closed 25–26 Dec; RHD railway timetable varies check website **Entry:** RSPB reserve [D]£2 [C]free [A]£3 [5–16s]£1 [Con]£2; RHD railway ticket prices vary check website

Dungeness National Nature Reserve

Set on the largest shingle bank in Europe, Dungeness is a unique place. Being here feels like being perched at the edge of the world, the land as flat as a pancake in every direction as far as the eye can see.

In the marshes behind this remarkable landscape lies an RSPB nature reserve, home to more than six hundred species of plants and many unusual insects, and its gravel banks and small lakes are a haven for migratory birds. There's a nature trail of packed shingle that is almost two miles long – disabled visitors on foot will be fine with this surface, but should take a little extra care, while manual wheelchair users can usually manage, but will probably need an assistant to push. Six bird hides are on or near the trail, all of which are wheelchair accessible. The area is famous among birdwatchers for frequent sightings of bittern and bearded tit, and for the marsh harriers spotted in 2007. If you park at the RSPB visitor centre, you'll find disabled toilets nearby and the closest birdwatching hide just metres away.

Surprisingly, the fenced-off Dungeness nuclear power station fits into this desolate scenery rather well. Somehow, the local collection of windswept fishermen's cottages and artists' studios are reassuringly defiant in its presence. Most famous of these is Prospect Cottage, the former home of the artist Derek Jarman. You'll find this delightful house – with its inspirational shingle garden, made from hardy plants and beachcombed materials – less than a mile along the road up the coast, towards Lydd. You can make another enjoyable journey in the area using the picturesque Romney, Hythe and Dymchurch Railway, a narrow-gauge steam railway beloved of generations of children. Wheelchair accessible carriages are available, but there's a height restriction and they must be booked in advance, so call ahead to enquire. The station is over three miles by road from the RSPB visitor centre.

Food & drink ▶▶ Fishing boats still launch from the shore at Dungeness, and the aromatic (or plain smelly, depending on your taste!) *Dungeness Fish Shop* (☏01797 320789, ⓦwww.dungenessfish.co.uk) specialises in locally caught and smoked varieties that you can take home to cook. Many local places to eat are famed for their gigantic portions of fish and chips: fill your boots at either the *Pilot Inn* (☏01797 320314, ⓦwww .thepilot.uk.com) or the *Light Railway Café* at Dungeness Station.

034 Samphire Hoe, Kent

Address: signposted south off the A20, 2km west of Dover CT17 9FL **Website:** www .samphirehoe.com **Telephone:** 01304 225649 **Hours:** daily 7am–dusk **Dates:** no closures **Entry:** free; pay and display car park [30 mins]50p [1 hour]£1 [2 hours+]£2 Blue Badge holders free

The 6.4 million cubic yards of rock that came out of the Channel Tunnel had to go somewhere: it was piled in the sea below the cliffs at Dover and the result is a unique, isolated stretch of chalk meadowland – now a nature reserve – called Samphire Hoe. It's a haven for wildlife and human visitors alike.

This brand-new piece of Kent is a magical and ever-changing place: tucked in under the cliffs, it can be a peaceful sun trap and picnic spot on a hot day, but in rough weather the waves can come crashing in. The Hoe is landscaped with small lakes and sown with local wild flowers – look out for granny's toenails (also known as bird's-foot trefoil) – and is home to the rare early spider orchid, which you can see in April and May. Many species of insects and birds have rapidly colonised the area, and if you're quiet, and very lucky, you might see an adder. If you like sea-fishing, then try your luck along the sea wall – you could even win the fish-of-the-month competition. And be sure to check out the sound sculptures, which evoke the history and beauty of the nature reserve. These installations have been created by local artists, who have combined pictures, sculpture and sound recordings to tell the stories of the people who used to live here under the cliffs, and to evoke the haunting natural sounds and beauty of the Hoe.

Next to the car park – which has four designated disabled bays – there is a tea kiosk with a RADAR-key-accessible toilet. The kiosk has free maps of the Hoe which show all the paths, the many benches, and the wheelchair accessible route. The full circuit is just over a mile of asphalt and gravel path, changing to concrete back along the sea wall, with an aver-

Samphire Hoe

age gradient of 1:15, but sometimes steeper. The other paths are quite challenging: if you're an adventurous family you might enjoy the Treasure Trail (maps available from the kiosk), but you'll have to be prepared for some rugged paths. The small shingle beach is accessed by steps, and on rough days the sea wall may be closed, indicated by red flags flying.

Food & drink ▶▶ Samphire Hoe is a great place to picnic, but there is a kiosk in the car park which has a range of reasonably priced hot and cold drinks, traditional snacks, sandwiches and cakes.

The Home Counties and Oxfordshire

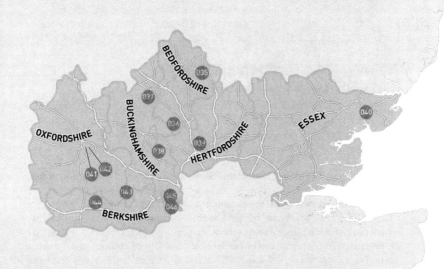

The Home Counties and Oxfordshire

Arching around the peripheries of London, the "Home Counties" of England form London's commuter belt. Beyond the suburban sprawl, however, there is plenty to entice. The countryside is at its most appealing amid the picturesque Chiltern Hills, and the region is dotted with pleasant little villages and market towns, although the lively university city of Oxford remains the main attraction.

035 The Shuttleworth Collection, Bedfordshire

Address: Shuttleworth Aerodrome, Old Warden, Nr Biggleswade SG18 9EP **Website:** www .shuttleworth.org **Telephone:** 01767 627927 **Hours:** Apr–Oct 9.30am–5pm; Nov–Mar 9.30am–4pm; last entrance one hour before closing **Dates:** closed 1–2 Jan & 24–31 Dec **Entry:** [D]£9 [C]free except on event days [A]£10 [under 16s]free [Con]£9; prices vary for events

The Shuttleworth Collection is a world-famous presentation of aircraft, flying machines and flight-related exhibits, showcasing the first hundred years of human flight. It includes a huge range of civilian and military aircraft, as well as cars and carriages.

More than forty planes in flying condition are housed in eight floodlit hangars. You can trace the history of the aeroplane, from the one used by Louis Blériot – the first aviator to cross the Channel in a plane rather than a lighter-than-air balloon – through to the Spitfire of Battle of Britain fame. Air shows are held on event days between May and October, when you can witness the magnificent sight of the Edwardian flying machines taking to the skies. For keen aerophiles, one of the highlights of a visit is the chance to see aircraft restoration in progress in the workshop. Also on the Shuttleworth site are the Regency-style ornamental Swiss Garden, the Bird of Prey Centre and the expansive Jubilee Play Centre, which will delight children of all ages and abilities (different entry charges and opening hours apply to each attraction).

The brown tourist signposts for Shuttleworth are somewhat misleading: the entrance is actually in Hill Lane about a mile east of the village of Old Warden. The parking area near the entrance is level. Access to the shop, where you'll find the ticket desk, is easy. Further on, however, there are varying surfaces, including some trip hazards (gullies and hangar door rails), and some awkward doors. Trickiest are the steep ramps between hangars, which may prove too much for manual wheelchair users visiting without an assistant, and may be difficult if you're a walker with impaired mobility.

Food & drink ▶▶ The spacious, level and reasonably priced café and restaurant serves hot favourites like sausage and chips, as well as cold snacks.

036 ZSL Whipsnade Zoo, Bedfordshire

Address: Dunstable LU6 2LF **Website:** www.zsl.org/zsl-whipsnade-zoo **Telephone:** 01582 872171 **Hours:** times vary seasonally, check website **Dates:** closed 25 Dec **Entry:** ticket prices vary seasonally; car entry, allowing you to drive through the park £16 (free to Blue Badge holders); car park £4; disabled visitors entitled to either car park OR carer free

The Zoological Society of London's Whipsnade Zoo is one of Europe's largest wildlife conservation parks, home to more than 2500, mostly endangered, animals. Occupying six hundred acres of countryside on the edge of the Chiltern Downs, this is very different from the traditional city zoo and provides a really enjoyable and worthwhile day out.

Whipsnade has big open paddocks that allow a relatively natural habitat for many large species, including camels, bison and rhino, though the big cats are securely penned. The Children's Farm allows close contact and the whole family can join the charming lemurs in their enclosure. Wallabies, mara (long-legged relatives of the guinea pig), muntjac deer and peacocks wander freely through the park. The "Passage through Asia" route – allowing you to drive through a section where all the animals are unenclosed – is a particular highlight, though watch out for yak and camel jams ahead.

Taking your car in is the best option as you can get to much of the park and see many of the larger mammals from your car – and there's parking throughout. If you don't want to drive through, you may want to avoid the steep slopes from the car park by being dropped off at the gates. A wheelchair accessible bus and train are also available. If you decide to explore on foot or using a wheelchair, you'll find access is step-free almost everywhere, but some paths are steep and even rutted, and the Woodland Bird Walk has a bark-litter floor. To see absolutely everything on foot does require covering long distances and gradients, so either a powered wheelchair or a fit pusher are probably essential. There are good disabled toilets around the park, but those nearest the entrance are surprisingly difficult to access. Kennels are available for assistance dogs.

> "We saw a baby elephant and wallabies jumping around! There are lots of park staff, and they are all caring and well informed."
>
> **Maureen Kirchin, Luton**

Food & drink ▸▸ Whipsnade's café is on a hillside overlooking the beautiful Dunstable Downs. The larger restaurant has great views of the lake, and has daily barbecues during the summer, but beware that the indoor tables and chairs are bolted to the ground.

037 Bletchley Park, Buckinghamshire

Address: The Mansion, Bletchley Park, Sherwood Drive, Bletchley, Milton Keynes MK3 6EB **Website:** www.bletchleypark.org.uk **Telephone:** 01908 640404 **Hours:** Apr–Oct Mon–Fri 9.30am–5pm, Sat & Sun 10.30am–5pm; Nov–Mar daily 10.30am–4pm **Dates:** closed 1 Jan & 24–26 Dec **Entry:** [D]£10 [C]free [A]£10 [12–16s]£6 [Con]£8; car park £3

By 1939 the looming threat of war had become a reality. British intelligence was looking for a safe base well away from central London, and chose Bletchley Park with its solid road, rail and teleprinter links. Posing as a shooting party, British code breakers took over the estate, and Bletchley became the nation's best-kept secret.

This government intervention rescued Bletchley from demolition – plans for developing the land into a housing estate were abandoned, so the elegant mansion and parklands survived, and have been open to the public since 1994. The grounds are a great place for families to relax, but it's the exhibits at these wartime headquarters that really fascinate. The Block-B centre and the famous Enigma and Lorenz cipher machines help to illuminate the complexities of code breaking, and the vital role of this decryption work in the war effort – it's well worth planning ahead to join one of the revealing guided tours, which make sense of it all. There are many collections to see and some have varying opening times, so a quick check before visiting is recommended.

There are two parking areas but you should choose the one to the left of the main entrance, which has eight Blue Badge bays. This is a dedicated disabled car park and close to the main entrance, but the surface is incompletely concreted with compacted gravel in some areas. There is an accessible lift to the left of the six steps that lead up to the reception. Powered scooters are permitted outdoors, and manual wheelchairs are available for free to use inside the building. The majority of the preserved buildings and exhibits are accessible by wheelchair, with only a few exceptions. Wheelchair users may need assistance with the door to Hut 8 (one of the wartime constructions), and the privately owned collection of Churchill memorabilia has some high cabinets, which may prove difficult to view. There are three accessible toilets dotted around the park.

Food & drink ▶▶ Fifty custom-made Fabergé eggs were recently sold to raise funds to transform a former code-breaking hut into *The Galley Bar and Restaurant*, which is large and has reasonable prices. Try to avoid the lunchtime rush.

038 Roald Dahl Museum and Story Centre, Buckinghamshire

Address: 81–83 High Street, Great Missenden HP16 0AL Website: www.roalddahlmuseum
.org Telephone: 01494 892192 Hours: Tue–Fri 10am–5pm, Sat & Sun 11am–5pm Dates:
closed Mon except bank holidays and some school holidays; check ahead for Christmas &
New Year opening Entry: [D]£4 [C]free [A]£6 [5–18s]£4 [Con]£4

Roald Dahl was determined that all his papers, manuscripts and photographs should remain together in Britain. The result is a charming, family-friendly museum set up by his widow, Felicity, which immerses you in Dahl's mischievously subversive world.

Most of the exhibits are aimed at children aged around 6 to 12 with a creative bent, though there is enough to keep little ones – and grown-ups for that matter – interested too. Budding writers and Dahl enthusiasts will get the most out of the museum. Two galleries, Boy and Solo, tell the story of the author's life, while the Story Centre inspires young minds to get inventive with plot, character and language. All of this is based around a large, accessible courtyard with the shop and galleries on one side, the Story Centre across the end, and "Miss Honey's Classroom" and the worryingly named "Children Eating Room" opposite. The courtyard itself provides an overspill eating area for *Café Twit* and hosts refreshingly amateurish storytelling sessions on sunny days.

The museum is in the centre of Great Missenden, and while there's a Blue Badge bay about one hundred yards down the High Street, the nearest convenient parking is the pay and display car park 270 yards away, with a pavement approach to the museum entrance. Getting into the disabled toilets can prove tricky if the courtyard gate is open.

Food & drink ▸▸ The whole museum is step-free, except for a single step into the *Café Twit*. A ramp is available, but the inside is so small that wheelchair users are probably best off with the courtyard seating if stopping for a delumptious home-made treat.

039 Verulamium Museum, Hertfordshire

Address: St Michael's Street, St Albans AL3 4SW **Website:** www.stalbansmuseums.org
.uk **Telephone:** 01727 751810; group bookings 01727 751820 **Hours:** Mon–Sat 10am–
5.30pm, Sun 2–5.30pm; last entrance 5pm **Dates:** check ahead for Christmas & New Year
closures **Entry:** [D]£2 [C]free [A]£3.50 [5–18s]£2 [Con]£2

Verulamium, founded by the Romans, was the site of Britain's first Christian martyrdom, when a Roman soldier called Alban was executed for sheltering a Christian priest in 209 AD. The extraordinary story of the city of St Albans and its Roman origins is brilliantly told in this museum.

Home to some of the finest Roman mosaics and frescoes in northern Europe, and set in an enormous area of parkland, the museum displays everyday life in Roman Britain in a highly accessible manner. The exhibits include re-created Roman rooms, hands-on discovery areas, video presentations and touch-screen databases. Look into the kitchen of a Roman housewife and learn about the food she prepared; see the lead coffin of a wealthy citizen and hear an actor tell his story; visit the reconstructed carpenter's workshop and absorb the sounds of the workshop and the bustling street. The attractive shop sells a well-judged selection of high-quality souvenirs and books. For only 10p, you can pick up a fun learning pack for children, while an in-depth museum guide is available for £4. Out in Verulamium Park, a neighbouring building (free entry) showcases a typically magnificent town house, with a display of Britain's earliest central heating system – the underfloor, hot-air hypocaust, clad in a mosaic floor. In the other direction, across the road, you'll find the impressive Roman theatre (£2 entry).

There is a bit of a slope up from the disabled parking spaces to the step-free museum entrance. There are good, even surfaces throughout the museum and ample space to get around. Most displays are at a good level for wheelchair users, but some of the older cabinets are a little high. Accessible toilets are downstairs (there's an excellent lift hidden behind the reception desk), and a manual wheelchair is available from the shop if required. Groups of visitors with visual disabilities can call Brian Marpole on ☎01727 751820 to book a handling session, and an audioguide covering the outdoor sites is available for a £20 deposit. If you want to visit the hypocaust, you might come across some tricky and steep areas outside, but the shop can also provide a powered scooter.

Food & drink ▸▸ *Inn on the Park* (☎01727 838246, ⊛www.inn-on-the-park.com) is an accessible place to grab lunch, less than five minutes away from the museum. Outdoor seating overlooks the park, and in the summer mini golf is played nearby.

040 The Beth Chatto Gardens, Essex

Address: Elmstead Market, Colchester CO7 7DB **Website:** www.bethchatto.co.uk
Telephone: 01206 822007 **Hours:** Mar–Oct Mon–Sat 9am–5pm, Sun 10am–5pm; Nov–Feb Mon–Sat 9am–4pm, Sun 10am–4pm **Dates:** check ahead for Christmas & New Year closures **Entry:** [D]£5 [C]free [A]£5 [under 14s]free

Almost fifty years ago Beth Chatto began nurturing an overgrown wasteland into beautiful gardens, despite the poor soil, gravel and bog conditions she faced. Now in her late 80s, and winner of ten Chelsea Flower Show gold medals, Beth still lives in a small house overlooking the site and regularly tends the gardens.

This is not only a lovely spot to spend a gentle afternoon, but a showcase to inspire the public to contend with their own difficult soil types. The site is broken up into three independent and informal gardens: the gravel garden is home to drought-loving plants from around the world; the water garden with its four large ponds is planted with lush foliage that thrives even in moist silt and sticky clay; and the dark woodland garden, is especially pretty in spring when blanketed with daffodils. If you feel encouraged to make a start on your own patch, visit the concrete-floored nursery, which sells gardening books written by Beth, as well as plants, shrubs and bulbs. Unfortunately the nursery has some tight passages but staff are ready to assist and will pass on their knowledge

The Beth Chatto Gardens

to help you pick the right plants for your plot.

With such a helpful team available on hand, a chat at reception is a useful way to start a visit, especially if you'd like advice on the best route to take around the gardens. Ian Palmer, a nursery gardener, runs guided tours for a fee of £2, and these can be tailored to focus on scent and touch – do call ahead to check he will be in. If you're in a manual wheelchair, and unless you're super fit, you'll need to bring a companion along to help, as some of the pathways are undulating and have rough surfaces. But these are gardens to explore slowly and you won't want to make your way around too briskly – on the shady route through the water garden there's a bench every twenty yards or so. Parking is flat and close to the entrance, but on grass. Assistance dogs are welcome, but otherwise dogs are not allowed.

Food & drink ▸▸ A fantastic tearoom overlooks the nursery, serving home-made soup and other hot meals. The ice cream is local and award-winning – a real treat.

041 Christ Church College, University of Oxford, Oxfordshire

Address: Oxford OX1 1DP **Website:** www.chch.ox.ac.uk **Telephone:** visitor enquiries 01865 276492 **Hours:** Mon–Sat 9am–5pm, Sun 2–5pm; last entrance 30 minutes before closing **Dates:** closed 25 Dec **Entry:** [D]free [C]free [A]£6 [5–17s]£4.50 [Con]£4.50; family tickets available

Christ Church is Oxford University's most magnificent college; it was founded in 1525 and incorporates England's smallest cathedral, which is also the college chapel.

Christ Church is a working college and provides a highlight of any visit to Oxford. It encompasses the stunning Cathedral Church; the huge Tom Quad and its enclosing buildings; the cloisters; Sir Christopher Wren's gatehouse and bell tower, which houses the bell known as Great Tom; the Great Hall (which played Hogwarts Hall in the Harry Potter films); and the square tower with its beautiful vaulting. A door at the rear of the cathedral leads you to the cloisters, which survive from the seventh-century St Frideswide's monastery. Here you can watch a video charting the history of the cathedral and college. Next door, the chapterhouse includes a shop and a collection of cathedral plate. The college has a gallery with a collection of old masters and drawings (entry fee applies). South of the college are the Great Walk and Christ Church Meadow – a tranquil pasture, bordering the rivers Cherwell and Isis, and open to all for walks and picnics.

Oxford may be a flat city, but it is an old place, and general access is less than perfect. On the streets, you'll have to navigate past masses of other visitors, and over uneven flagstone pavements – but in such a historically and architecturally fascinating place, your efforts will quickly be rewarded. Arrive early to secure one of the popular Blue Badge spaces next to Tom Quad. Disabled visitors should enter Christ Church via the main gate by Tom Tower. There's a ramp up to the south side of Tom Quad and another into the cathedral by the West Door. Sadly some parts of the college are still inaccessible to wheelchair users, and visitors on foot need to be careful of cobblestones and uneven stone stairways without handrails. Efforts towards improvements are being made (for example, a lift is being built to provide access to the Dining Room), but development of such an architecturally significant site is obviously problematic. Staff are keen to assist where they can, and will welcome advance notice of your needs. A manual wheelchair can be borrowed, and assistance is sometimes available to help disabled visitors view the Great Hall. Braille and large print guides are available. You can reach Christ Church Meadow on foot from the college, but wheelchair users need to leave by the Tom Gate and travel one hundred yards to the War Memorial Garden for ramped access.

Food & drink ▸▸ Unsurprisingly there are many quaint but inaccessible places to eat in Oxford. *The Mitre* (℡01865 244563, Ⓦwww.beefeater.co.uk) – a Beefeater restaurant on the High Street – has a traditional pub feel, moveable chairs, a disabled toilet and an induction loop. Take care with the slightly undulating floors.

042 Botanical Gardens, University of Oxford, Oxfordshire

Address: Rose Lane, Oxford OX1 4AZ **Website:** www.botanic-garden.ox.ac.uk **Telephone:** 01865 286690 **Hours:** daily Apr–Nov 10am–5pm; Dec–Mar 10am–4.30 **Dates:** closed weekends; closed 1–3 Jan & 22–31 Dec **Entry:** [D]free [C]free [A]£3 [under 16s]free [Con]£2.50

Oxford's botanical garden is a compact oasis in the heart of the city, where plants are grown for conservation research. It's a national reference collection with seven thousand different varieties of plant and in fine weather makes a lovely spot for a picnic.

The walled garden is laid out formally, with lawns, borders, trees and a centrepiece fountain. Plants here are grouped in a number of different ways: by country of origin, botanic family or economic use. The area outside the walled garden contains classic features – a water garden, lily pond, rock garden, orchard, vegetable beds and autumn and spring walks. It's a beautiful place, particularly in summer, and at one side of the grounds, visitors can watch as day-trippers punt down the river. The glasshouses, which can be accessed from the walled garden or by a gravelled riverside walk, hold a range of strange and beautiful tropical flora – highly recommended if a little tricky to access. The duckboard walkways are flat but narrow and overhung with plants, while the doors between the various sections are heavy, manual and have ramped thresholds.

There's a car park off St Clement's Street just over half a mile away, or you can park, using your Blue Badge, in the disabled bays or on Rose Lane, from where there is level access. Other than that, you have to take your chances on the High Street. Look out for cobbles and flagstones at the entrance to the ticket office, which has wide glass doors. The garden's hard-gravelled paths are mostly level, and at the time of writing they were set to be further improved for spring 2010. There's a RADAR-key-accessible toilet at the rear of the conservatory but access for a wheelchair is tight. You can also use your ticket to visit the Harcourt Arboretum in Nuneham Courtenay, just outside Oxford.

Food & drink ▸▸ *Queen's Lane Coffee House* (℡01865 240082) on the High Street is a pleasant spot for afternoon tea. It has moveable tables and a flat entrance, but can get busy.

043 River and Rowing Museum, Oxfordshire

Address: Mill Meadows, Henley-on-Thames RG9 1BF **Website:** www.rrm.co.uk **Telephone:** 01491 415600 **Hours:** daily May–Aug 10am–5.30pm; Sep–Apr 10am–5pm **Dates:** closed 1 Jan & 24–25 Dec, 31 Dec **Entry:** [D]£5 [C]free [A]£7 [4–16s]£5 [Con]£5

Set in a picturesque water meadow beside the Thames at Henley, the River and Rowing Museum gives visitors a glimpse into the historic relationships between the town of Henley, the River Thames, and the sport of rowing for which it is renowned. Designed by the award-winning British architect David Chipperfield, this bright, modern, airy museum is a very welcoming place for disabled visitors.

The permanent displays introduce the Thames, from source to estuary and review the sport of rowing through the ages. There is a look at adaptive rowing and a celebration of the GB paralympic arms-only-rowing gold medallists. Visitors can take a virtual tour around the town and then travel through its history, through artefacts, models, boats, video displays and interactive exhibits. The museum hosts a varied programme of special exhibitions and a busy schedule of talks and workshops for children as well as adults. It also houses The Wind in the Willows Gallery – a permanent exhibition of delightful dioramas with an audioguide (headphones or loop antenna), which brings Kenneth Grahame's classic story to life. Visiting this part of the museum should be a great experience for visitors with sensory disabilities – there are many sounds and smells to take in, and even an atmospheric chill in the wild wood.

The museum is a flat and easy ten-minute walk from Henley station and has a free car park at the rear. An enjoyable alternative means of getting here is on the combined river and museum trip from Reading to the museum's jetty – there's a new, wheelchair accessible boat now operating on this service. At the museum itself, ramps run up front and rear to the main foyer, the shop and pleasant café, and a broad sun deck with benches and

Henley-on-Thames

tables. There's also a disabled toilet on this lower level. There is plenty of room for wheel-chairs through most of the site, and staff are happy to assist. The exhibits are on two floors, with a drive-through lift which takes a chair and a couple of helpers, and most displays are at low level with easy to reach buttons. The gallery doors are wide but manual and one-way, though quite easy to open. Much work has been done with disability groups in the area, and touch tours for local groups can be organised in advance.

Food & drink ▸▸ The terrace café has seating indoors and outside the picnic benches have seating at the end suitable for wheelchair users. You can grab cold snacks and a small selection of great quality hot meals.

044 The Living Rainforest, Berkshire

Address: Hampstead Norreys RG18 0TN **Website:** www.livingrainforest.org **Telephone:** 01635 202444 **Hours:** daily 10am–5pm **Dates:** closed 24–26 Dec **Entry:** [D]£7.75 [C]free [A]£8.75 [3–4s]£5.75 [5–14s]£6.75 [Con]£7.75

As you pass through the Living Rainforest's screens you're transported into a hot, damp jungle and the presence of luxuriant flora and beautiful birds and insects. Your ticket is valid for a year so you can go back to see the ever-changing forest – whenever you visit, it's guaranteed to be warm inside, so remember to leave your coat in the car!

The Living Rainforest is housed in two giant glasshouses. As you follow the path, foliage brushes your face, and you quickly adjust to the sights, sounds and aromas of an equatorial forest. There's a wide range of creatures to discover, most spectacularly the free-flying and brilliantly coloured butterflies and birds from Amazonia and southeast Asia. Meanwhile, snakes, playful Goeldi's monkeys and the rare West African dwarf crocodile are kept safely behind barriers to protect them from human visitors – and the visitors from them. Look out for insect-eating plants and bird-eating spiders; watch graceful stingrays and the miniature miracle of a butterfly emerging from its chrysalis. Presentations and workshops led by the expert staff give you a genuine understanding of their conservation work and educational motives. The routes are well signposted, and large-print notices describe the exhibits. The building itself is interesting too – it is constructed from sustainable timber and recycled brick, insulated with newspaper and heated with a woodchip-fired biomass boiler.

The accessible car park is laid with compacted gravel, but a little uneven, and there's a one-hundred-yard-long tarmac path to the entrance. There are wheelchairs available to borrow, and scooters are permitted. The patio is accessible and the play area is on level grass. The toilets are reached through the café. The paths inside the glasshouses have been made of scored concrete – they are damp, and with appropriately muddy patches in places, but generally not slippery. Most of the site is level, with the exception of two shallow troughs from which to view eye-level exhibits. There are steps at one end of these, so wheelchair users may need to reverse out.

Food & drink ▸▸ The popular on-site café is open at the weekends serving all the usual suspects – baguettes, pasties, chips etc – but the locally produced, home-made cakes are especially tasty.

THE HOME COUNTIES AND OXFORDSHIRE

045 Thames Valley Adventure Playground, Berkshire

Address: Bath Road, Taplow, Maidenhead SL6 0PR (use SL6 0EP for satnav) **Website:** www
.tvap.co.uk **Telephone:** 01628 628599 **Hours:** Tue–Thu & Sat 10am–3.30pm, Fri 10am–5pm
(over 16s only) **Dates:** closed Sun & Mon; usually closed 24–26 Dec but call ahead to check
Entry: [D]£6 per child, based on voluntary contribution [C]free; advance booking essential

It's not flash nor fancy and the paint is peeling off a little, but this place doesn't feel run-down, just well loved. And it's really not hard to see why the children and their families who come to the Thames Valley Adventure Playground (TVAP) love it. This is a playground where children of all abilities can play together: whatever your child's disability, even if they are a wheelchair user, they could have a go on pretty much everything.

Roundabouts? No problem – just wheel right on board and make sure the gate shuts behind your son or daughter so their chair doesn't fly off. Swing? They've got one that will take a wheelchair, or a swinging bed if you prefer. Surely not the zipwire…? Yes, there is even a zipwire with a secure bucket seat and a wooden fort with wheelchair access up to the top. Indoors, you'll find a soft-play room, sensory room and music room, all adjacent to a lovely bright airy space filled with toys and craft tables. The new extension over the lake even has a glass floor feature through which you can watch the water and fish beneath.

For most of the week TVAP is open exclusively for children with special needs and their families (Fridays are exclusively reserved for special-needs adults). As you would expect, everything is completely accessible. There is lots of parking outside, though none designated as disabled (it doesn't need to be). The toilets are equipped with hoists, a large changing bed, grab rails and various seats. All staff are trained to deal with all kinds of disabilities and they're a very friendly bunch too.

Food & drink ▸▸ There isn't any catering on site, but there is plenty of space, indoors and out, to picnic. Handily, there is even use of a kitchen to help you prepare.

IDEAS ▶▶ FUN FOR KIDS

Eureka! (℡01422 330069, Ⓦwww.eureka.org.uk), the National Children's Museum in Halifax, exists to educate children through play. Bursting with multi-sensory and hands-on exhibits for children aged under 11, Eureka! has level access, lifts between floors and an induction loop.

BeWilderwood (℡01603 783900, Ⓦwww.bewilderwood.co.uk) is a "curious treehouse adventure" in Norfolk, and has charming delights galore – boat rides, giant slides, aerial walkways and zip wires are all set in beautiful eco-friendly wood- and marshland. While some of the woodland floor can be hard-going if you're pushing a wheelchair or pushchair, there is some disabled play equipment on site. The Slippery Slope slide is suitable for more than one person to go down at the same time.

ZSL London Zoo (℡020 7722 3333, Ⓦwww.zsl.org/zsl-london-zoo) is the world's oldest scientific zoo, and an exciting place for families to visit. Kids will particularly enjoy the recently opened Gorilla Kingdom and the Clore Rainforest Lookout, where South American monkeys roam free.

046 Legoland Windsor, Berkshire

Address: Winkfield Road, Windsor SL4 4AY **Website:** www.legoland.co.uk **Telephone:** 0871 222 2001 **Hours:** daily 10am–5pm, Sat & Sun 10am–6pm, summer school holidays 10am–7pm **Dates:** closed Nov–mid Mar; closed some weekdays in Apr, May, Sep & Oct **Entry:** [D]£37.80 [C]free [A]£37.80 [3–15s]£28.61; discounts online; annual passes available

Legoland Windsor

Ask any family with a child with special needs where to go on a day out and the answer is almost unanimously Legoland. It's not just that the park is 95 percent accessible to wheelchair users: Legoland has a positive attitude to disability that's reflected not only in the services they offer but also in the can-do attitude of the staff.

Set in 72 acres of attractively landscaped grounds, the park is divided into zones, roughly by age, from Duploland to Adventure Land. Very much a family park, there aren't any of the white-knuckle rides that attract thrill-seeking teenagers. LegoCity is good for kids who can't leave their wheelchairs, with its Orient Expedition safari train ride, with wheelchair accessible compartments. Aero Nomad is a ferris wheel which has a gondola that can accommodate a wheelchair. Every visitor can also enjoy Miniland, the showcase model village built with 35 million Lego bricks, re-creating some of the world's most famous landmarks.

> "We didn't have a single moan from the kids all day."
>
> **Jackie Trollope, Devon**

Parking is free and very well controlled, with plenty of marshals, and disabled bays closest to the entrance. Once inside, there are no steps, but some paths are quite steep and will require a strong pusher behind a manual wheelchair. For children who have social difficulties with queuing, the theme park operates an exit pass scheme, allowing the guest-plus-three to enter the ride via the exit. You'll need to show an official diagnosis or statement of your child's condition, however, and, on busy days, you may need to queue at Guest Services to get the pass in the first place. There is no shortage of accessible toilets.

Food & drink ▸▸ All the refreshment areas at Legoland are accessible, but City Walk in LegoCity is particularly spacious, with seating areas inside and out.

East Anglia and the East Midlands

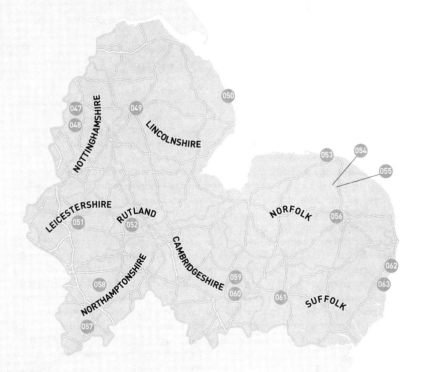

East Anglia and the East Midlands

Renowned for its wide skies and flat landscapes, East Anglia's scenery – from the once inhospitable fenlands to bucolic river valleys and unspoilt stretches of coast – is undoubtedly its main draw. The East Midlands, by comparison, can initially seem a little short of star sights, but don't be fooled. There is plenty to explore, with the area's industrial history playing a key role in many of its attractions.

047 Clumber Park, Nottinghamshire

Address: Worksop S80 3AZ **Website:** www.nationaltrust.org.uk/clumberpark **Telephone:** 01909 544917 **Hours:** park open during daylight hours; cycle hire centre times vary seasonally, check ahead **Dates:** park closed 25 Dec; cycle hire centre dates vary seasonally, check ahead **Entry:** free; car park approx £5

These four thousand acres of park and woodland south of Worksop in northern Nottinghamshire are owned and operated by the National Trust. Although large, Clumber is a disabled-friendly park and one of the most popular tourist targets in the region.

The park is famed for its handsome woodland walks, stunning views, unique variety of deciduous trees and fine Gothic revival chapel. It was once the country seat of the dukes of Newcastle, and it was here in the 1770s that they constructed a grand mansion overlooking their own personal lake. The house was dismantled in 1938, when the duke sold the estate, but many of the outbuildings – including stables and barns – have survived. And many of these structures have been adapted to provide high quality and accessible visitor facilities. The shop, conservation centre and tearoom have ramped access with spacious, light interiors suitable for wheelchair users. Even the chapel has a ramped entrance, but you'll have to be prepared for limited space and low lighting. In another part of the park is the Walled Kitchen Garden, which has a wheelchair accessible glasshouse – you'll come across a turning point at the far end. The disabled parking bays are around 170 yards from the main facilities, and the accessible toilets are near the main visitor area. There is also a RADAR-key-accessible toilet behind the conservation centre, with its "feeling chamber" full of natural items like deer antlers and animal fur.

Clumber has over twenty miles of safe cycle routes; a useful access leaflet, which you can pick up from the visitor centre, details the distance and path surfaces of three accessible routes. The longest route stretches four miles, and the shortest has resting seats and smooth, flat paths. There is a bike hire centre, close to the car park. While cycle hire is charged (£6.50 for two hours or £13 per day), all adapted cycles and powered scooters are free – although donations towards their maintenance are welcomed. You can borrow manual wheelchairs, tandems, trikes, buggies for kids and a trandem – an adapted wheelchair/hand-cycle combination that needs to be powered by a reasonably fit companion. Try and book in advance, and remember to bring identification. Other activities in the park include horse riding, fishing and orienteering – you can find details and prices on the website. The park also hosts many events, and these are listed in a National Trust leaflet. You can request a large print version on ☎01909 486411.

Food & drink ▸▸ The refurbished, fully accessible restaurant in the main visitor centre offers lunches and afternoon teas – some of the produce is even home grown. There is a newly established BBQ area too.

048 Sherwood Forest National Nature Reserve, Nottinghamshire

Address: Swinecote Road, Edwinstowe, Mansfield NG21 9HN **Website:** www .nottinghamshire.gov.uk/countryparks **Telephone:** 01623 823202 **Hours:** mid Feb–end Oct 10am–5pm; end Oct–mid Feb 10am–4pm **Dates:** closed 25 Dec **Entry:** free; car park £3 (seasonal) but free for Blue Badge holders

Sherwood Forest was once a vast royal woodland of oak, birch and bracken covering all of northern Nottinghamshire. Most of it was cleared in the eighteenth century, and nowadays it's difficult to imagine the protection it provided for generations of outlaws, most famously Robin Hood.

These days, a little less than 450 acres of surviving woodland make up Sherwood Forest National Nature Reserve. It's a transformed landscape, but still a great family attraction. The Major Oak – the creaky tree where Maid Marion and Robin are supposed to have "plighted their troth" – still stands proud. Children aged between 5 and 12 will particularly enjoy the various medieval-style Robin Hood-related entertainment: accessible activities include archery, jousting and a fairground which functions between March and October. Of the three colour-coded walks through the forest, the mile-long blue walk that passes the Major Oak is fully accessible for wheelchair users. The path, which has gentle slopes, is surfaced with picnic tables and benches en route. The red and green routes are longer, not fully surfaced, have some steep slopes and tend to get muddy in places during wet weather.

Parking is easy and all the buildings at the visitor centre have flat or ramped access, though some buildings are small, with only standard-width doorways. A seasonal programme, downloadable from the website, outlines a range of activities and events coming up, and these are coded to indicate their suitability for visitors with disabilities. There are disabled toilets on site. Two manual wheelchairs and two powered scooters can be borrowed from the centre, but advance booking is recommended and identification will be requested on collection. The nearby craft centre has access (if sometimes rather tight) to all workshops.

Food & drink ▸▸ *Forest Table Restaurant* is amazingly good value: the Sunday roast carvery is only £4.99 for adults, and £1.99 for children. You'll find the restaurant, with its wheelchair accessible tables, in the visitor centre.

049 Lincoln Cathedral, Lincolnshire

Address: Minster Yard, Lincoln LN2 1PX **Website:** www.lincolncathedral.com **Telephone:** 01522 561600 **Hours:** 29 Jun–28 Aug Mon–Fri 7.15am–8pm, Sat & Sun 7.15am–6pm; 29 Aug–28 Jun Mon–Sat 7.15am–6pm, Sun 7.15am–5pm **Dates:** check ahead for closures due to special services and bank holidays **Entry:** [D]£5 [C]free [A]£5 [5–16s]£1 [Con]£3.75

This beautiful church, right in the heart of the historic city centre, dominates Lincoln's skyline. While the cathedral's architecture and interior are imposing, it is also a place of peace and spirituality and a must-see if you're in the area.

The entrance is through the west door into the nave with its vast vaulted ceilings and massive pillars. Down the left side, a series of beautiful and tactile wooden sculptures depict the stations of the Crucifixion. Beyond them, the north–south transept is illuminated by a unique pair of rose windows – the Bishop's Eye and the Dean's Eye. You then come to the oldest part of the building and the heart of the cathedral, St Hugh's Choir, with its beautiful oak carvings. Behind the high altar is the aptly named Angel Choir, the well-camouflaged home of the celebrated and much-searched-for Lincoln Imp. Through the northeast transept is the cloister, a tranquil setting for quiet reflection, which provides access to the nine-sided chapterhouse and a fine library designed by Sir Christopher Wren. There are interesting and informative free guided tours at intervals throughout the day.

Lincoln Cathedral

Parking is the only major access problem at Lincoln Cathedral. The streets in the surrounding area are narrow and cobbled, with limited access for vehicles. Although disabled parking is permitted for up to three hours in the restricted areas, it gets busy, so you'll have to arrive early to secure a spot. The ground floor of the cathedral is wheelchair accessible, with the exception of the three side chapels dedicated to the armed forces. Just inside the entrance there is a touch model of the building, including a site layout, with a foot-operated audioguide. And in the northeast transept there is a touch exhibition with Braille descriptions. The recently constructed toilet block has two disabled toilets.

Food & drink ▶▶ The *Cloister Refectory*, although quite small, provides snacks and lunches. But for something more cosmopolitan, pop out to *Café Zoot* (☎01522 536663, Ⓦwww.cafezoot.co.uk), close to the cathedral in the bustling Bailgate area. It ticks all the basic boxes for accessibility, with ground-floor eating and toilets available, and regularly offers deals as reasonable as two meals for £9.99.

050 Black Cat Equestrian Centre, Lincolnshire

Address: Huttoft Road, Sutton-on-Sea LN12 2QY **Website:** www.blackcatequestriancentre .co.uk **Telephone:** 01507 442631 **Hours:** riding lesson times vary, check ahead **Dates:** closed Thu; check ahead for Christmas & New Year closures **Entry:** riding lessons £12 per half-hour; £14 per hour (groups of more than four)

This riding centre has a wide range of facilities: one indoor and two outdoor paddocks, a show-jumping course, a cross-country course, harness driving and two mounting blocks. It also has the advantage of being in Sutton-on-Sea, one of Lincolnshire's prettier coastal resorts, just south along the coast from Mablethorpe. A visit can easily be combined with a trip to the seaside.

A family-run business, the Black Cat Equestrian Centre is carefully designed to suit people of all ages and abilities at every level of experience – from the nervous and apprehensive to the confident and self-assured. They usually have around twenty horses at the centre, so if you book ahead, you'll find a mount to suit your abilities and style. And because of the centre's connection with Lincoln College's Reach-Out course for people with learning difficulties, Black Cat staff are experienced at providing literally hands-on equine encounters for people of every ability.

The staff are helpful, experienced and happily allow extra time for assisting visitors with disabilities. But contacting them prior to visiting is a good idea, as the exact nature of your disability will determine whether you are able to ride or learn carriage-driving. People with learning disabilities, sensory impairments and mobility difficulties are regular visitors, though wheelchair users can find it difficult to move their chairs over the gravel surface. The car park and path surfaces are mostly uneven, so extra care is needed, and there's a shallow step into both the otherwise accessible toilet and reception area.

Food & drink ▶▶ You'll find only a hot drinks machine on site, so remember to take a packed lunch along if you think the exercise will make you peckish.

051 National Space Centre, Leicestershire

Address: Exploration Drive, Leicester LE4 5NS **Website:** www.spacecentre.co.uk
Telephone: 0845 605 2001; access enquiries 0116 261 0261 **Hours:** term time Tue–Fri
10am–4pm, Sat & Sun 10am–5pm; school holidays daily 10am–5pm **Dates:** closed Mon in
term time; closed 24–26 Dec & 1 Jan **Entry:** [D]£11 [C]free [A]£13 [5–16s]£11 [Con]£11

The UK's largest planetarium and exhibition of space exploration is a highly stimulating
and visually arresting place – visitors realise that on arrival, when they first take in the
centre's famous rocket tower building.

Whether or not you consider yourself a fan of space matters, you could easily spend
the day here. But if you are an enthusiast, you'll be enthralled by Tranquility Base where
you can test your suitability for a career as an astronaut. Elsewhere around the site, six
spacious galleries tell stories of the origins of the universe; of unmanned space probes; and
of space travel – all illustrated by genuine space artefacts, including rockets, food packs
and even a space station toilet. Many hands-on activities provide fun for visitors of all ages.
In Project Apollo, a joystick-controlled simulator gives you a chance to have a go at a
moon landing. The futuristic cinema experience in the Space Theatre is a highlight of any
visit. Stunning thirty-minute-long films are projected onto the huge, domed ceiling. The
theatre has step-free access and six wheelchair spaces where companions can sit alongside.

There are plenty of disabled parking spaces, though there's a long exposed transfer down
a significant slope to the entrance itself. Automatic doors open onto the spacious main
lobby. A lift takes you to the upper level and a larger lift is available on request – from there
the rocket tower lifts take you to the rest of the levels. Displays are easily accessible and spacious, though a few of the interactive features are out of reach to wheelchair users and the
flight deck simulator is up a short flight of steps. Touch tours can be arranged in advance,
large print guides are available, and most audio exhibits are subtitled. There are disabled
toilets off the main lobby and at the back of the ground-floor galleries.

Food & drink ▸▸ Beneath the gigantic rockets is *Boosters*, serving a small range of drinks,
sandwiches and snacks. Chairs can be moved and the tables are well spread out.

National Space Centre

052 Rutland Sailability, Rutland

Address: Rutland Sailing Club, Gibbet Lane, Edith Weston, Oakham LE15 8HJ **Website:** www.rutland-sailability.org **Telephone:** contact Alan Naylor for further information & booking 01162 719170 **Hours:** weather permitting Apr–Oct Thu 9.30am–3.15pm, Sat 9am–noon **Dates:** closed Mon–Weds, Fri & Sun; closed Nov–Mar **Entry:** first visit free, second visit £5, third visit £45 annual membership required

Sailing is freedom: there's nothing that quite compares with the splashes on the hull and the breeze on your face as you skim across the surface of the water.

Sailability exists to help disabled people gain the confidence to fulfil their sailing potential – this charity proves that this exhilarating sport can be enjoyed regardless of any disability. At Rutland Sailing Club, they have 23 boats, ranging from small, single-sail craft through two-person twin-sail boats to multi-hulled craft for six people. And recently acquired are two new Windrider trimaran boats – fast but very stable. Rutland Sailability claim never to have had to turn anyone away on account of their disability, and indeed their professionalism and expertise are impressive, enabling most

> "Rutland Water is perfect for a weekend break."
>
> **Michael Skinner, Harlow**

people to be sailing with an instructor after only minutes of being on the water. The lake is a good size and invariably has a breeze, even on a seemingly still day. Rutland Water is actually one of the most important wildfowl sanctuaries in the country – during the summer you may even see osprey fishing over the water.

Parking is no problem and an electric cart can transfer you from car to jetty if required. The volunteers are friendly, experienced sailors, knowledgeable about the sailing adaptations available. The jetty has four hoists and there's plenty of specialist sailing kit to allow anyone, even if they have very little mobility, to sail completely independently. The accessible changing rooms, with multiple wet rooms, shower chairs and ceiling hoists, put many other disabled changing rooms to shame. They also have on-site adapted residential accommodation.

Food & drink ▸▸ The sociable and spacious clubhouse serves hot and cold food, and has a licensed bar. The large outdoor deck has splendid views over the lake.

IDEAS ▸▸ WATERSPORTS

Sailability has clubs all over the UK – for another experience, see p.40.

The British Disabled Water Ski Association (☏01784 483664, ⓦwww .bdwsa.org; ✉info@bdwsa.org) has seven centres across the UK, including in Yorkshire and Scotland, and aims to introduce newcomers to the sport, regardless of any disability they may have.

Jubilee Sailing Trust (☏023 8044 9108, ⓦwww.jst.org.uk) owns the only two tall ships in the world designed to be sailed by people of all physical abilities. Day Sails are available, as are voyages of several weeks.

SabreScuba (☏07803 044755, ⓦwww.sabrescuba.co.uk/about.php) are Wiltshire-based Scuba Diving trainers, offering diving experiences to disabled people. Train for a PADI certificate that you can use in warmer climes.

053 Sheringham Park, Norfolk

Address: Wood Farm, Upper Sheringham NR26 8TL **Website:** www.nationaltrust.org.uk /main/w-sheringhampark **Telephone:** 01263 820550 **Hours:** dawn–dusk **Dates:** closed 25 Dec **Entry:** free; car park £4

If you fancy a leisurely stroll and some bracing country air, then Sheringham Park, with its beautiful sea views and extensive woodland, is ideal place to visit. Considered an outstanding example of the work of the eighteenth-century landscape designer Humphry Repton, the park was purchased by the National Trust in 1986.

There are various paths which you can take on foot but only one, laid with concrete, that is wheelchair accessible. This route takes you through woodland, past Sheringham Hall – a private residence – and onto some marvellous coastal views. It's not a circular walk, so you'll have to turn round and retrace your route back the way you came, but this isn't really a problem: you'll be bowled over by the displays of specimen trees and, in May and June, azaleas and rhododendrons in bloom. At a moderate pace, the walk takes about one and a half hours.

National Trust members can park in the Blue Badge bays free of charge, though non-members need to pay. The visitor centre is fifty yards away, and overall its disabled facilities are excellent. If you want to borrow a powered scooter, you may be asked to take a short driving test and have to agree to stick to the concreted route through the park. Braille and large print information sheets are available. The disabled toilet is RADAR-key-accessible.

Food & drink ▶▶ The refreshment kiosk in the open courtyard has only outdoor seating, but sells steaming hot drinks to keep visitors warm on cold days, as well as ice creams for when the sun shines.

054 Blickling Hall Gardens and Park, Norfolk

Address: Blickling, Norwich NR11 6NF **Website:** www.nationaltrust.org.uk/blickling **Telephone:** 01263 738030 **Hours:** check ahead for seasonal variations **Dates:** closed Tue; house closed Nov, Dec & Jan; gardens closed 24–26 Dec with other seasonal variations **Entry:** [D]£9.75 [C]free [A]£9.75 [under 16s]£4.85

Set in beautiful gardens and surrounded by historic parkland, this splendid Jacobean house, dating from the 1620s, is one of the finest in Britain.

Blickling Hall commands your attention straight away. On arrival, your eyes are drawn down the main drive, tunnelled between two-hundred-yard-long, four-yard-wide yew hedges, towards the elegant Jacobean facade. Inside, the rooms have all the fine furnishings and fabulous views of the surrounding lake and gardens that you could hope for. Elaborate plasterwork is a major feature, especially in the immense Long Gallery which houses the library – a significant private collection of more than twelve thousand books. The splendour of the house is matched in the extensive gardens and parkland. The floral borders are seasonally graced by daffodils and rhododendrons, and many other vibrantly coloured flowers and plants. There are woods and lakeside walks to enjoy – three powered scooters are available and there's a circular route suitable for wheelchairs, just less than two miles long.

There are nine Blue Badge spaces for disabled visitors, but they aren't clearly marked, and parking can be casual. In this courtyard there is an accessible toilet (others are in the more distant main car park and at the visitor centre), and the entrance to the secondhand bookshop (wheelchair accessible, if tight). The 110-yard route to the house has a steep, paved ramp, but as you enter the building, the restaurant and shop are both fully accessible. Beyond the shop is the visitor centre, which has a hearing loop. A lift allows most of the house to be accessible and wheelchairs are available for use inside. Braille and large print guides are available, and there is a tactile collection too.

Food & drink ▶▶ You can eat alfresco in the *Courtyard Café*, or in the restaurant which dishes-up estate produce, including apples and cakes. Don't miss the local Norfolk crab cakes.

055 Bure Valley Railway, Norfolk

Address: Aylsham Station, Norwich Road, Aylsham NR11 6BW **Website:** www.bvrw.co.uk **Telephone:** 01263 733858 **Hours:** check website for railway timetable **Dates:** check website for seasonal variations **Entry:** return ticket [D]£11 [C]£11 [A]£11 [5–16s]£6

This narrow-gauge, fifteen-inch railway runs for around eight miles through the picturesque Norfolk countryside, between the market town of Aylsham and the Broads capital of Wroxham – with three intermediate halts at Brampton, Buxton and Coltishall.

Bure Valley Railway was constructed in 1990. The line is mainly operated by steam locomotives, so if you thrill at the smell of soot and the rhythm of the rails, then this is the outing for you. The scenery on the 45-minute journey is varied – the line crosses farmland and water meadows, skirts woodland and passes water mills. The track's narrow gauge does make for a slightly bumpy ride though, and passengers require a flexible spine and the ability to duck their head on entering. Once you're seated, the purpose-built carriages are very comfortable. A special boat train combines the nostalgic locomotion trip with a cruise on the Broads (March to October; £17 adult return); a fifteen-minute walk or push from Wroxham station is required to link passengers with the fully accessible boat. Staff are happy to arrange a taxi link but you'll need to book that in advance.

If you start your journey at Aylsham, you enter the station via a paved ramp from the large car park, which has three adjacent Blue Badge bays. Manoeuvrability in the booking office and shop does require a little skill, but all the facilities at both Aylsham and Wroxham are level. The staff are very helpful and it can be fruitful to call ahead to make reservations – they are happy to answer questions. The train's specially designed wheelchair coaches can accommodate four manual chairs (though fewer powered scooters) plus seating for companions. Access is via double doors with detachable ramps. When a full service is in operation each train has two of these coaches.

Food & drink ▶▶ *Whistlestop Café* at Aylsham station has sufficient space and modern fittings, with good value snacks and meals from easily readable menus.

056 Sainsbury Centre for Visual Arts, Norfolk

Address: University of East Anglia, Norwich NR4 7TJ **Website:** www.scva.ac.uk **Telephone:** 01603 593199 **Hours:** Tue–Sun 10am–5pm, Wed 10am–8pm **Dates:** closed Mon including bank holidays; closed 1–3 Jan & 24–31 Dec **Entry:** Sainsbury Centre collections free; special exhibitions [A]£4 [Con]£2

The Sainsbury Centre for Visual Arts houses an impressive collection of international work – including pieces by Francis Bacon and Henry Moore – and mounts special exhibitions which change every few months. The centre, which opened in 1978 to house the Robert and Lisa Sainsbury Collection, forms part of the University of East Anglia.

At the heart of the Sainsbury Collection is the Living Area, housing the permanent display, which mixes works from across the world, and across the millennia. As well as Bacon and Moore, the exhibits cover five thousand years of output, with pieces from other modern Europeans such as Alberto Giacometti, Jacob Epstein and Pablo Picasso. And there is ancient art – a ceramic hippo from Egypt's twelfth dynasty is among the 1300 early pieces on show. The building itself, designed by Norman Foster, is a vision of high-tech, and was once described by Sir Robert Sainsbury as "the best thing in the collection". It was extended underground in 1991 to allow space to house the Lisa Sainsbury collection of modern pottery, and expanded again in 2006. It looks set to acquire more new levels and wings in the future.

Access is via the main entrance to the university, from where visitors can follow signs into the centre. There are four Blue Badge spaces immediately outside the main entrance and level access into the building. The galleries are fully accessible for wheelchair users, and a manual wheelchair is available on request. A hearing loop is installed in parts of the building, and there are handsets to assist during the regular talks and lectures. A lift links the main gallery to the shop and the lower Crescent Wing, where temporary exhibitions are displayed.

Food & drink ▸▸ You can get snacks and meals at the *Gallery Café* and the *Garden Restaurant,* which are ideal for coffee and cake.

057 Silverstone, Northamptonshire

Address: Towcester NN12 8TN **Website:** www.silverstone.co.uk **Telephone:** 0844 372 8200 **Hours:** 8am–6pm; check ahead for events **Dates:** closed 1 Jan & 25 Dec **Entry:** race days from [D]£15 [C]free [A]£15 [under 15s]free; driving experience from £69

You can drive a car or watch from the trackside at the home of British motor-racing. Either way, the throaty roar of straining engines, the scent of fuel mixed with scorched rubber, and the exhilaration of speed – felt in your gut or vicariously – all make the hairs on the back of your neck stand up.

Silverstone's place in the history of motor-racing is assured: since 1948, the driving legends and manufacturers who have done battle around this three-mile circuit are essentially

EAST ANGLIA AND THE EAST MIDLANDS

Ferraris at Silverstone

motor-racing's roll of honour. Numerous race days take place at Silverstone throughout the year, with the biggest being the British Formula 1 Grand Prix – now securely at home on the Silverstone track for the next seventeen years. Approach roads can get very congested on race days, so set off as early as you can. If you have a Blue Badge it should be clearly on display when you arrive – though it's wise to double check with the marshals in attendance that they are directing you to the disabled parking correctly. This parking area has a concrete surface, but there is a distinct lack of drop kerbs. Avoid the turnstile at the visitor entrance, by heading in through the main gate (you'll have to wait for someone to open this). Ramped viewing platforms and disabled RADAR-key-accessible toilets (keys available to buy on site) are situated all around the course. With the exception of race days, it's also possible to transfer between the platforms during your visit. Entry is free for two assistants attending with a disabled visitor in receipt of the Middle or Higher Rate Mobility Component of the Disability Living Allowance.

If you want to try the driving experience, you will be able to choose from several cars. If you require hand controls, the exclusive option is the Ferrari 360 F1 Modena – although few budding racers will be unhappy about that. Alternatively, you can elect to be driven around the circuit by a professional instructor or arrange to take your own car onto the track. The Silverstone staff are trained to deal with the needs of disabled visitors, though calling in advance is highly recommended. The organisation has taken on suggestions from previous disabled users and all visitors are treated individually and sensitively. For some people, getting into the vehicle is tricky, but with prior notice Silverstone staff will do their best to allow you to experience the track as a passenger or driver, whatever your disability, and even, with an instructor, if you're blind.

Food & drink ▶▶ There is a Costa Coffee outlet at the track. If you need to unwind from the thrill and speed of Silverstone, try the *Boat Inn* (℡01604 862428, Ⓦwww.boatinn .co.uk) in Stoke Bruerne. This friendly pub by the Grand Union Canal is around fifteen minutes' drive away.

058 Brixworth Country Park, Northamptonshire

Address: Northampton Road, Brixworth NN6 9DG **Website:** www.northamptonshire.gov.uk **Telephone:** 01604 883920 **Hours:** car park & toilets daily 9am–5pm; visitor centre Apr–Oct 10am–4.30pm; Oct–Mar 10am–4pm **Dates:** closed 1 Jan & 25 Dec **Entry:** free; powered scooters £2 first hour & £1 per extra hour

Set in the heart of beautiful rural Northamptonshire, Brixworth Country Park is a national showpiece for an accessible countryside. This small yet perfectly formed park offers great possibilities if you want to picnic, walk, push or cycle in woodland, meadow and reservoir surroundings.

There are three short circular routes round the park, all signed and colour-coded – they each do a great job of immersing you fully in the outdoors while remaining accessible. The paths are hard surfaced, with some undulations but no steep gradients, so regular wheelchair users should be able to manage independently or with a little assistance. The shortest route is 550 yards, and the longest just over a mile. You can stroll quietly through the woods and meadows, or pause to watch from the accessible viewing hide, where you may catch a glimpse of wildlife, including foxes, squirrels, waterfowl and woodland birds. For more of a challenge, and a half-day adventure, the walking routes also give access to a seven-mile circuit around the reservoir. Although there are no hand-bikes stocked in the bike hire shop, they do have two types of passive seating that can be attached to bikes, as well as two trampers (very sturdy powered scooters) and manual wheelchairs.

Disabled parking is free of charge and situated just in front of the visitor centre and small shop – selling nature books, umbrellas and walking sticks etc – at the start of the walking trails. Wide doorways equipped with push buttons are fitted throughout the visitor centre and there is a well-kept disabled toilet next to the shop. There is a sensory garden, too, and the children's play area is wheelchair accessible.

Food & drink ▶▶ *The Willow Tree* serves meals at lunchtimes, and snacks and drinks until the park closes. Indoors it has widely spaced tables, plus an outdoor patio with a gentle view of the park. A new paved area links the visitor centre to the picnic tables and BBQ stands.

059 Wicken Fen Nature Reserve, Cambridgeshire

Address: Lode Lane, Wicken, Ely CB7 5XP **Website:** www.wicken.org.uk **Telephone:** 01353 720274 **Hours:** daily Feb–Oct 10am–5pm; Nov–Jan 10am–4.30pm **Dates:** closed 25 Dec **Entry:** [D]£5.75 [C]free [A]£5.75 [5–17s]£2.95

Wicken Fen is one of Britain's oldest nature reserves and one of the most important wetlands in Europe. It's home to more than seven thousand species of wildlife in-cluding otters and rare butterflies. The reserve has a raised boardwalk which makes it an ideal place for disabled visitors to explore the fens.

A remnant of the once extensive Cambridgeshire fenlands, this area has been managed for centuries by sedge-cutting and peat-digging, resulting in this unique habitat. It is now one of England's most diverse wetland sites and a nationally important habitat for molluscs, with 88 species of slugs, snails and bivalve shellfish recorded here. It's a great birdwatching area (bitterns and marsh harriers being frequent visitors), and if you're quiet and visit the more out of the way areas, you may see frogs, toads, newts and even a grass snake. Konik ponies (originally from Poland) and Highland cattle can be seen grazing in the reserve too. You can take the leisurely half-mile walk along the boardwalk or a more challenging two-mile route along either the nature trail or the adventurers' trail. All three routes have hides along the way. Borrow a pair of binoculars on arrival to ensure you have a good chance of seeing some of the more timid wildlife, as well as the birdlife.

Wicken Fen has two disabled parking spaces and two manual wheelchairs to borrow. The boardwalk is completely flat and very easy to walk on, but it can get a little slippery in wet weather. The hides are also fully accessible, with moveable benches, so it is possible to get up really close to the windows. Braille and large print information is available.

Food & drink ▶▶ The café serves a variety of warming home-made dishes including stews and pasties. The fresh vegetables are grown locally in a school for disabled children.

060 Anglesey Abbey Gardens, Cambridgeshire

Address: Quy Road, Lode, Cambridge CB25 9EJ **Website:** www.angleseyabbey.org **Telephone:** 01223 810080; powered scooter booking 01223 810086 **Hours:** gardens daily Jan–Feb & Nov–Dec 10.30am–4.30pm; Mar–Oct 10.30–5.30pm; times vary for other areas of estate **Dates:** closed 24–26 Dec **Entry:** [D]£9.75 [C]free [A]£9.75 [5–15s]£4.90; reduced rate in winter

The gardens of Anglesey Abbey – a Jacobean mansion on the site of the original, thirteenth-century priory – make for a fine day out. They are a perfect setting for a summer family picnic, and full of hidden surprises.

The 114-acre grounds are well laid out, with meandering paths leading you through formal gardens, numerous themed areas and past hidden treasures, including more than a hundred sculptures and a working watermill – the Lode Mill – dating from the eighteenth century. And if you want to go off the beaten track there are also wide expanses of lawn and meadows of wild flowers to explore. The January and February snowdrop display is famous; in the spring the garden flaunts an impressive array of more than four thousand hyacinths; and in late summer the dahlia feast is something to behold. Unfortunately, the house itself remains barely accessible – if you are a wheelchair user or you struggle with stairs, your tour will be limited to two rooms on the ground floor, and the on-screen virtual tour is scant compensation.

> "The staff are kind, and the gardens are excellent in every way. My wife's mother was once in service at the house, so we understand how difficult it would be to overcome the limitations of such an old building."
>
> **Ron Mann, Rickmansworth**

Anglesey Abbey has fourteen disabled parking bays, all on tarmac and the furthest no more than sixty yards from the house. A new visitor centre has recently opened and the shop and garden centre are all fully accessible. There are nine powered scooters and one five-seater vehicle with driver available. The main drive to the abbey is tarmac-surfaced and the other paths, although loose gravelled, are still easy to push a wheelchair over. Blind and visually impaired visitors can call ahead to organise tours around the garden, many areas of which have been planted for scent.

Food & drink ▸▸ The fully accessible restaurant is worth a visit, not least for the Lord Woolton vegetarian bake – named after the World War II Minister of Food who urged people to be creative with their rations. Adapted tables and cutlery are available for those who would prefer to picnic.

061 Theatre Royal, Bury St Edmunds, Suffolk

Address: 6 Westgate Street, Bury St Edmunds IP33 1QR **Website:** www.theatreroyal.org **Telephone:** 01284 769505 **Hours:** check website for performance dates and times; box office Mon–Sat 10am–6pm; open door (dependent on performances) Tue & Thu 2–4pm (guided tour 2pm), Sat & Sun 10.30am–1pm (guided tour 11am) **Dates:** closed 25 Dec; check ahead for occasional closures **Entry:** tickets vary depending on performance and seat [D]£2 reduction at some performances [C]free; open door £1.50; guided tours £6

The Theatre Royal is the only surviving example of a Regency playhouse in the country. Opened in 1819, it has recently been restored and is thoroughly worth a visit. In fact, if you're going to a show, it's worth arriving half an hour early to explore the building as far as you can, or even popping in to look around during an "open door" session.

In the care of the National Trust, the Theatre Royal is one of only eight Grade I-listed theatres in the country. The refurbishment has restored the entrances to the pit, the Georgian fore-stage and the dress circle boxes – the latter approached on level access from the foyer, and containing the only four wheelchair accessible seats in the house. Entering your box, you're instantly absorbed by the original, Neoclassical design and the elegant curve of the two rows of boxes. The colour scheme, from the dark earth-hued floor to the stone tones of the dress circle and up to the painted sky on the ceiling – together with the kind of perspective scenery which would have been used two centuries ago – all serve to create a perfect, all-round illusion that is on a human scale, while constantly impressive.

Theatre Royal box office staff and stewards are all knowledgeable and fully aware of the issues facing disabled patrons. There is access from two kerbside Blue Badge spaces, with two more, available for evening performances, at the Greene King Brewery Museum, opposite. Dropping off at the front then parking in the Greene King staff car park (220 yards from the back of the theatre) is the best option (note there's no wheelchair access from this car park). Inside the theatre, the pit, reserved in Georgian times for the hoi polloi, is not wheelchair accessible, and only accessible to those on foot via 25 broad, shallow steps with a handrail on both sides. The upper circle and gallery are inaccessible. Three or four specific performances per season are captioned, signed or BSL-interpreted.

Food & drink ▸▸ The accessible *Greene Room* is the new foyer bar-restaurant which serves tasty meals, including vegetarian options, from two hours before the performance.

062 Southwold Pier, Suffolk

Address: North Parade, Southwold IP18 6BN **Website:** www.southwoldpier.co.uk
Telephone: 01502 722105 **Hours:** daily May–Sep 9am–late (times vary); Oct–Apr 10am–
4pm **Dates:** closed 25 Dec **Entry:** free

As you'd expect, Britain's only twenty-first-century pier is a thoroughly accessible place to visit. Southwold Pier was actually built at the beginning of the twentieth century, but storms, drifting sea mines and World War II each played a hand in its destruction and subsequent reconstructions. The latest, and hopefully final rebuild was completed in 2001.

Southwold is as charmingly English a seaside town as you could hope for, and the award-winning pier is the perfect introduction to it, commanding views of the picture-postcard colourful beach huts, golden sands and bustling harbour. Traditional fun is the name of the game in the amusement arcade on the pier – there isn't a fruit machine in sight. Not quite so tasteful is the wacky Under the Pier Show, which is packed with a selection of obscure, hand-built games ideal for fun-loving visitors of all ages. Some of the machines require a fair degree of physical participation, so aren't suitable for everyone, but there are a lot to choose from. To take on the challenge of the cheeky but entertaining Mobility Masterclass, you'll need to be able to manage one step up and to stand while manoeuvring an unsteady platform. The three accessible shops are crammed with hard-to-resist paintings, photographs and ceramics produced by local artists.

A car park with four disabled bays is just a few hundred yards north of the pier, up a gentle incline on a tarmac surface. A RADAR-key-accessible toilet is nearby, and there are also disabled toilets in *The Boardwalk* and the shop Seaweed & Salt on the pier. With level decking outside and in all the facilities, it's a smooth experience for visitors in wheelchairs and powered scooters. It gets breezy, though, so those on foot will ap-

Southwold Pier

preciate the wind-protected seats where you can simply sit and soak up the sights and sounds of the seaside.

Food & drink ▶▶ There are three places to choose from on the pier: the fully licensed *The Clockhouse*; *The Promenade* which offers snacks and takeaways; and finally *The Boardwalk*, which serves award-winning fish and chips.

063 Dunwich Heath Coastal Centre and Beach, Suffolk

Address: Dunwich, Saxmundham IP17 3DJ Website: www.nationaltrust.org.uk/main /w-dunwichheathandminsmerebeach Telephone: 01728 648501 Hours: dawn–dusk; visitor centre hours vary, call ahead Dates: no site closures; dates vary for information kiosk and café Entry: free; car park £4.20

Dunwich Heath is an area of outstanding natural beauty with tracts of heather and gorse, woods, sandy cliffs, unspoilt beaches and lots of local wildlife. While certainly appealing to natural history enthusiasts, this lowland heath has a wonderfully remote feeling, enabling you to blow away the cobwebs, and many visitors find they want to come back often.

There are three designated paths to take you over the heath – the 2.5-mile gorse walk, the 1.2-mile heather walk and the 1.1-mile birch walk. All three routes provide magnificent displays of gorse and heather in the spring and summer, but, as suggested by their names, they take you over different parts of the heath. It is best to decide which walk you want to explore depending on what you most fancy seeing. If you walk down the path to Minsmere Beach, you may glimpse a sand martin returning to its nest in the cliffs. There is also a sea-watch hut with lookout points where you may, if you're lucky, spot seals and harbour porpoises, as well as many sea birds. Ashore, the wildlife-viewing is less uncertain, with the area home to many different species, from glow-worms to red deer.

The car park has eight Blue Badge bays, two within twenty yards of the visitor centre and six with views across the beach and just more than fifty yards away. There's a single powered scooter and one three-seater buggy with driver available for disabled or elderly visitors – staff at the visitor centre can give you the details of where these vehicles are permitted to go. The heath's paths are laid with the sort of gravel you can push a wheelchair over, although the path down to the sea has seven shallow steps, while the beach itself is shingle. Assistance dogs are welcome on the heath, but limited to certain parts of the beach.

Food & drink ▶▶ Just by the old Coastguard Cottages, you'll find a tearoom that serves hot drinks and cakes, as well as substantial lunches – including the excellent sausage plait.

The West Midlands and Derbyshire

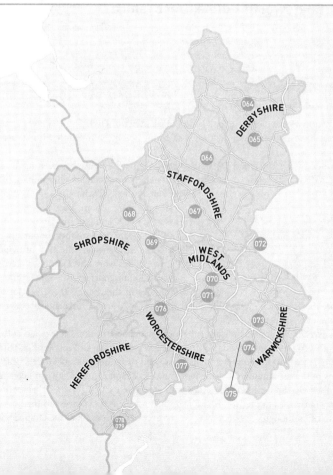

The West Midlands and Derbyshire

Birthplace of the Bard, Cadbury's chocolate and the industrial revolution, the West Midlands offers a range of attractions to suit all visitors. Although parts of the region are undeniably bustling and built up, this is a mostly quiet area, characterised by rolling countryside, stately homes and castles and Britain's first national park, the awe-inspiring Peak District, which offers every outdoor activity imaginable, from the sedate to the strenuous.

064 Chatsworth House, Derbyshire

Address: Bakewell DE45 1PP **Website:** www.chatsworth.org **Telephone:** 01246 565300; access information 01246 565314 **Hours:** house daily 11am–5.30pm; garden 10.30am–6pm; last entrance one hour before closing **Dates:** closed 24 Dec–mid Mar **Entry:** [D]£12.65 [C]free [A]£12.65 [3–16s]£6.90 [Con]£10.45; car park £2 [D]free

Chatsworth House, on the edge of the Peak District in Derbyshire, is a vast, extraordinarily handsome mansion, dating back to the seventeenth century. It is deservedly popular.

Owned by the Duke and Duchess of Devonshire, the house has been updated and expanded over the centuries, but the current incarnation remains a harmonious whole.

> "At Chatsworth, we were given all the assistance we needed to see the house, and the afternoon tea was delicious."
>
> **Keith Raithby, Alfreton**

The four-poster bed where George II died and the Great Dining Room – set as it was for the visit of George V and Queen Mary in 1933 – are showpiece exhibits. Another enduring highlight is the magnificent collection of paintings. Chatsworth has works by Tintoretto, Van Dyck and even Rembrandt, whose *Portrait of an Old Man* hangs in the chapel. There is a lot to see outside the house too, in the glorious grounds, from a grotto and artificial waterfall to a nursery and assorted greenhouses.

An excellent clear map indicating the location of benches, accessible toilets and varying path surfaces is downloadable from the accessibility page of the website. Disabled parking is close to the entrance to the house and there are accessible toilets nearby, as well as in the restaurant and at the farmyard. An adapted golf buggy can take visitors from the lodge up the hill to the shops and refreshments, while a wheelchair accessible trailer offers rides to the woods and lakes behind the house. Access to the house is a little trickier, though the north wing can be accessed by a ramp at the Orangery shop.

Chatsworth House

Building work due to be completed in 2010 will include the installation of a new lift and improved access through the visitor route. It is possible to organise a full access visit in advance, but only if you are planning to visit during a quiet period (recommended if you want some breathing space out in the grounds). All the refreshment venues and shops have flat access and, with the exception of the garden shop, plenty of space. The main children's attraction, the farmyard and adventure playground, has a lift and ramp access. Book powered scooters before you visit.

Food & drink ▸▸ Treat yourself to a luxurious brunch, or even a champagne tea, at the award-winning *Cavendish Rooms*.

065 Cromford Canal, Derbyshire

Address: Cromford Wharf, Matlock DE4 4LS **Website:** www.derbyshire-peakdistrict.co.uk /cromfordcanal.htm; pumphouse www.middleton-leawood.org.uk **Telephone:** countryside services 01629 823204 **Hours:** no closures **Dates:** no closures **Entry:** free

The Cromford Canal flows through the Derbyshire countryside – a gentle stroll along the towpath is a picturesque and low-key outdoor trip.

Linking into the Erewash canal – which in turn runs into the River Trent – the canal ultimately provided Cromford with a transport link to Derby, Nottingham, Manchester and Liverpool, when it was built in 1794. The towpath is walkable for around 5.5 miles from Cromford to Ambergate. The first 1.8 miles of this stretch – as far as High Peak Junction – are suitable for wheelchair users. Wildlife enthusiasts will enjoy the diversity in the area, renowned for its butterflies and dragonflies; the southern, less accessible stretch, between Whatstandwell and Ambergate, runs through a Site of Special Scientific Interest managed by Derbyshire Wildlife Trust. Back at the terminus in Cromford, the canal is close to the Cromford Mill – the world's first hydro-powered spinning mill. Leawood Pumphouse is nearby too, with its fine old beam engine that once maintained the water level in the canal. The engine has been restored and is usually fired up on holiday weekends and during other busy periods, to the delight of enthusiasts. Specific dates and times are available from the pumphouse website; visitors are usually welcomed between noon and 5pm on open days.

If you are a wheelchair user, or struggle to manage stairs, you may be restricted to the ground floor of the pumphouse. The canal itself is cared for by a dedicated band of waterway enthusiasts, the Friends of Cromford Canal. Sufficient disabled parking can be found at Cromford Wharf, which also has a RADAR-key-accessible toilet. The well-compacted towpath can be navigated reasonably well, whether you're on foot or in a wheelchair. Care should be taken on some stretches of the path, but most of it is very easy-going and there are benches at intervals if you need to take a breather.

Food & drink ▶▶ Take along a picnic to enjoy when you reach High Peak Junction before you turn around and head back to Cromford. Or if you can wait until your return, have coffee, sandwiches and cake at the café by Cromford Wharf.

066 Alton Towers, Staffordshire

Address: Alton ST10 4DB Website: www.altontowers.com Telephone: 0871 282 5176
Hours: daily 10am–5pm (later openings during holidays) Dates: mid-Mar–Oct Entry:
[D]£18.50 [C]£18.50 [A]£37 [4–11s]£28 [Con]£18.50; discounts available online

Thrills and speed: Alton Towers rapidly dispenses these fixes from white-knuckle rides contrived to excite even the most hardened adrenaline junkie. It's an exhilarating place, but if high-speed rollercoasters are not your thing, the five hundred acres also have gardens, a water park and a resort spa, which might appeal more.

Disabled visitors can obtain enviable priority passes: pick one up to ensure you can enter the rides via the exits, therefore avoiding the (sometimes very) long queues, and making the most of your time. The passes can also permit up to two carers to accompany you on the rides, and to help you with taking your seat, because while staff can allow extra boarding time for disabled visitors, they are unable to physically assist. Unsurprisingly, access to some rides is challenging and the level of enjoyment you'll get from Alton Towers depends to some extent on your own abilities. A very helpful leaflet – available online, or from the park – has detail on boarding and safety requirements for every ride, and it's perhaps worth having a look at it before you book tickets. Wheelchair transfer onto the infamous "big four" stomach-churners – Air, Nemesis, Oblivion and Rita Queen of Speed – is possible, but visitors have to be prepared for seat height variations, and difficulties getting chairs close to the rides. The Flume and Congo River

Rapids are trickier and might need more consideration.

Disabled parking is available for Blue Badge holders in the express parking area, close to the main entrance, and all the park's toilets are wheelchair accessible. Guest services are located just inside the park entrance: staff can provide all the access information you could need and are always happy to answer queries. A £20 refundable deposit is required if you would like to borrow a manual wheelchair.

Food & drink ▸▸ Alton Towers has even more fast-food outlets than you would find on a typical high street. *Rita's Chicken and Ribs* in Fountain Square is modern and relaxed, with healthy options and a licensed bar.

067 Shugborough Estate, Staffordshire

Address: Shugborough, Milford, Stafford ST17 0XB **Website:** www.shugborough.org.uk **Telephone:** 01889 881388 **Hours:** times vary seasonally, check ahead **Dates:** closed mid-Oct–mid-Mar **Entry:** [D]£9.50 [C]free [A]£12 [5–16s]£7 [Con]£9.50

Shugborough Estate is a historic farm in Staffordshire. From the costumed workers to the food in the tearoom, everything on the estate has been restored – as far as visitor comfort will allow – to eighteenth-century conditions.

Shugborough could easily be cheesy in tone: the guides are in character as real-life people who were once estate workers, but their evident enthusiasm keeps it all fresh. A day at Shugborough is structured around various scheduled events, each one offering you the chance to participate: visitors can have a go at cheese-making, see how the flour mill operates, watch the ironmonger at work in the forge and get a sense of what life was like as a servant. Outside, the farm animals will keep children entertained, and afterwards you can treat them (and yourself) to a gobstopper or a stick of licorice from Mrs Fagan's Sweet Shop.

Disabled parking is located by the reception. The estate is big, so a handy accessible shuttle and land train service transfers visitors to the house. Although the walk is flat, relatively smooth, and takes in some lovely countryside, the paths become more uneven near the servants quarters and coach house. Many of the estate buildings are listed, which inevitably means that some are difficult for wheelchair users to get around. Some provision has been made to overcome these problems. A stair-climber is available at the manor house (unaided transfer required), but you'll still need to be able to manage stairs to get to the first floor. The helpful staff indicate alternative routes where access is difficult. The mill block can be accessed via a side path (ask at the farm shop), but you'll need to be able to manage two internal steps to see the actual equipment. A video tour of all areas, including those that are inaccessible, is available at a couple of spots on the estate. There are two disabled toilets, though at opposite ends of the estate.

Food & drink ▸▸ *Lady Walk Tearoom* has a hot and cold menu, inspired by Mrs Steins – who was head cook in the estate kitchen in 1876. Food is locally sourced where possible; some of it is grown in the walled garden and the excellent Shugborough ale (added to the steak casserole) is brewed on site.

068 Hoo Farm, Shropshire

Address: Preston-on-the-Weald Moors, Telford TF6 6DJ Website: www.hoofarm.com
Telephone: 01952 677917 Hours: 21 Mar–6 Sep daily 10am–6pm; 8 Sep–2 Nov & 28
Nov–23 Dec daily 10am–5pm; 24 Dec 10am–3pm; last entrance one hour before closing;
variations over Halloween Dates: closed Mon; closed 3–27 Nov, Jan & Feb Entry: [D]£6.50
[C]£6.50 [A]£6.50 [2–14s]£5.95 [Con]£6.25

Hoo Farm is one of an enterprising band of farms up and down the country that have
turned land over to the creation of farm-themed family attractions. The formula is simple but effective – play areas and lots of animals to keep young children happy.

A family can easily be entertained for a whole day on Hoo Farm. As well as the standard pigs, sheep, goats, cows and ducks to visit, and the obligatory rabbits and guinea
pigs to pet, it is home to a surprising variety of wildlife, including foxes, owls and deer
– plus unexpected exotic creatures, like meerkats, raccoons and wallabies. If you want
to see all the animals, you may need to drag your kids away from the go karts, sandpits,
bunny beauty parlour and bouncy farm. There is a timetable of events throughout the
day – including animal-feeding and pony rides (extra fees). The comedy highlight has
to be the sheep steeplechase, where visitors bet on their favourite woolly wonder, then
cheer as they jump helter-skelter over fences, topped by woollen "riders" bobbing entertainingly on their backs.

There is disabled parking with three bays right next to the entrance, and a disabled
toilet just as you enter. Access around the site is level, though the gravel paths have
relatively big stones, and the wooded areas can get muddy in wet weather, so wheelchair
users may need assistance. Powered scooter hire requires a £5 deposit. Hand-washing
facilities are at an appropriate height.

Food & drink ▸▸ *The Hungry Shepherd Coffee Shop* is open at weekends and during
school holidays. It is accessible, but cramped and basic, so you might prefer to take a
picnic.

069 RAF Museum Cosford, Shropshire

Address: Shifnal TF11 8UP Website: www.rafmuseum.org.uk Telephone: 01902 376200
Hours: visitor centre 10am–5pm; test flight 10am–5.30pm; war planes 10am–5.30pm; Cold
War 10am–6pm; Hangar One 10am–6pm; Fun 'n' Flight Interactive Mon–Fri 10am–4pm, Sat
& Sun 11am–4pm; last entrance at 5pm Dates: closed 24–26 Dec and early Jan Entry: free

Even non-aviation buffs will get something out of a visit to the RAF Museum at Cosford
– the whole family will benefit from the fun, yet educational exhibits, and should leave
with a valuable sense of what life is like in active service.

This is the sister site to the RAF Museum in Hendon, north London. Over seventy
aircraft are housed here, in four hangars: there are many fascinating things to see, including experimental aircraft, engines, missiles and World War II planes. Captured

enemy aircraft provide an interesting comparison with the British models on show, while the Cold War exhibition extensively covers the subject. The displays are interactive throughout, but the Learning Zone in the test-flight hangar is particularly brilliant, and well engineered for kids.

Access to the visitor centre from the conveniently located disabled parking spaces is along a downhill tarmac path. Pedestrian entry is through a rotating door but there's a separate entrance for wheelchair users. RAF Cosford is pretty well set up for wheelchair users, although a fair amount of transferring between buildings is required. Maps are on hand to help with navigation from hangar to hangar (keep an eye out for Hangar One, as it isn't as well signposted as the others). The four museum buildings each have an accessible toilet, and are level and spacious, although in one of them the pedestrian walkways could be better indicated for visitors with visual disabilities. The one split-level building housing the Cold War exhibition has an induction loop and a lift giving access to a very effective viewing gallery. The overall site has a slight gradient and some visitors may find the return trip to the car park quite steep. Four powered scooters, and some manual wheelchairs are available for free. Braille and large print guides can be supplied.

Food & drink ▸▸ The glass-fronted café *Refuel* is very light, modern and spacious. Chairs and tables are moveable, and the children will love the menu: plenty of pizzas, burgers and chips.

070 Thinktank, Birmingham

Address: Millennium Point, Curzon Street B4 7XG Website: www.thinktank.ac Telephone: 0121 202 2222 Hours: daily 10am–5pm Dates: closed 24–26 Dec Entry: [D]£7.25 [C]free [A]£9.25 [3–15s]£7.25 [Con]£7.25

Bursting at the seams with hands-on exhibits, Thinktank is a fun museum, covering the sweep of past, present and future science and technology.

Although often awash with young children, there is plenty to engage big kids and adults too, and a family will need at least half a day to enjoy it all. This diverse learning experience is spread over four galleries on four floors. Down on Level 0, the journey starts in The Past, where there's a full-size spitfire, and a look at the steam machinery of the Industrial Revolution that was so instrumental in Birmingham's expansion. From there, as you work your way up the building, and through the three further areas, The City, The Present and The Future, all the exhibits are colourful, tactile and utterly compelling. You can play with a drum-playing robot, solve a crime, create a dance workout and control the arm of a JCB digger. The diverse programme of events and activities for adults changes regularly – if you're interested in subjects like the future of human evolution, or the links between art and science, check the website for dates of evening lectures, and for BSL-interpreted events. If that's not enough to keep you entertained, there is a Planetarium too and an IMAX cinema out in the wider Millenium Point complex where Thinktank is based.

Launched in 2001, Thinktank was created in partnership with the visual impairment specialists at Queen Alexandra College. Subsequently, it is a beacon of great design,

Thinktank

with every element of the space crafted to ensure accessibility for all. The displays are unusually low-level, there's plenty of free space around the exhibits and captions on the walls are generally large. Large print and Braille guides are available, as well as magnifying glasses. There is plenty of Blue Badge parking near the entrance, and the accessible toilets are spacious and clean.

Food & drink ▶▶ At the time of writing, renovation was planned for the catering facilities at Thinktank. Once opened, this new lounge-style café should serve child-friendly food, and lots of vegetarian options.

071 Cadbury World, Birmingham

Address: Linden Rd, Bournville B30 2LU **Website:** www.cadburyworld.co.uk **Telephone:** 0845 450 3599 **Hours:** variations throughout the year, check website for details **Dates:** daily Mar–Oct; variable closures Nov–Feb **Entry:** [D]£13.90 [C]free [A]£13.90 [4–15s]£10.10 [Con]£10.50; group and family tickets available

Visiting Cadbury's chocolate factory in the heart of Bournville, where they boast the biggest chocolate shop in the world, is the stuff of childhood dreams. It's the closest any of us will probably ever get to visiting Willy Wonka's chocolate factory.

For a commercial operation, largely conceived to encourage you to consume more of the sweet stuff, the tour combines amusements, heritage and education in a surprisingly appetising way. Divided into fourteen zones, from the Aztec Forest, via The Cadbury Story, and through to the state-of-the-art Purple Planet, you'll learn a lot about chocolate here. There are detailed insights into how chocolate is made, how Cadbury came to be and the Quaker beliefs that made Bournville what it is today, though not, apparently, much about cacao plantations or the cocoa trade. The last fifty years of Cadbury's advertising are celebrated in the new advertising and media area – providing a chance for a trip down memory lane, and to gawp at the famous animatronic gorilla who passionately pounds away on the drums to a Phil Collins track. In Essence, where sweets and other treats are available to help you create your very own cup of flavoured liquid chocolate, even the healthiest eaters will struggle to remain disciplined.

Facilities are largely inclusive and the whole place is accessible for all, with just two exceptions: the staircase to the factory packaging facility and the exclusively fixed seating in the picnic area outside. Without fuss, a wheelchair accessible Beanmobile can be cleverly slotted into the Cadabra ride. Assistance dogs are not permitted in production areas, but a dog-sitter can be provided, while visitors make their way through those parts of the site. Queues can sometimes be a problem, but wheelchair users and others requiring assistance are usually given priority.

Food & drink ▶▶ After all that free chocolate, you'll be stuffed. But if you are in need of something savoury, visit the *Cadbury Café* which has a menu that has been designed with kids in mind.

072 Twycross Zoo, Warwickshire

Address: Burton Road, Atherstone CV9 3PX **Website:** www.twycrosszoo.com **Telephone:** 01827 880250 **Hours:** 5 Mar–29 Mar 10am–5pm; 30 Mar–24 Oct 10am–5.30pm; 25 Oct–4 Mar 10am–4pm **Dates:** closed 25 Dec **Entry:** [D]£6 [C]free [A]£11 [3–16s]£7 [disabled 3–16s]£5 [Con]£9; family tickets are available

Who knew that the largest protected collection of monkey and ape species in the world has its home just off the M42 in Leicestershire? Since its modest opening in 1963, Twycross Zoo has grown to become not only one of Britain's major zoos, but to win international status as the World Primate Centre.

As well as monkeys, the zoo is home to all sorts of other species – lions, elephants and giraffes, for starters – but it's the size and diversity of the primate collection, and the dedication to research and conservation, that set Twycross apart. It's reassuring to see so much space and stimulation provided in the animals' enclosures; spider monkeys and gibbons, for example, have plenty of room to swing effortlessly through the branches in their areas. Vantage points for visitors are great and well considered too – although when you're sitting three inches away from an enormous silverback gorilla, mimicking your every movement, you may feel like you're the one being observed. The zoo and its staff have a commendable grasp of the needs of visitors with disabilities, and seem keen to improve accessibility further. At the time of writing, a brand new Himalaya visitor centre was set to open in early 2010.

> "Disabled access at Twycross Zoo is second to none."
>
> **Richard Bramall, Rotherham**

Twycross is wonderfully flat with very few slopes, and certainly no steep ones. All path surfaces are hard gravel or tarmac, including in the car park, which is close to the entrance with plenty of disabled parking available. Powered scooters can be rented for £8, and manual wheelchairs for just £1. All the cafés, shops and toilets are easily accessible, as are all the animal houses, except for inside the lemurs' abode. Unfortunately assistance dogs can't go near the enclosures for apes, elephants or some of the large carnivores, as their presence can cause distress. Some large print guides are available and induction loops can be picked up at reception. Sign language interpretation has to be arranged in advance and is not available at weekends – but the zoo seems keen to promote its use, as diagrams of how to sign different animals' names appear in some areas.

Food & drink ▶▶ New in 2010, the state-of-the-art Himalaya centre is planned to have a large restaurant selling fairtrade and organic food with views over the snow leopard enclosure.

073 Warwick Castle, Warwickshire

Address: Warwick CV34 4QU **Website:** www.warwick-castle.co.uk **Telephone:** 0870 442 2000 **Hours:** 4 Apr–Sep 10am–6pm; Oct–3 Apr 10am–5pm **Dates:** closed 25 Dec **Entry:** prices vary seasonally [D]£9.14 [C]£9.14 [A]20.43 [4–16s]£15.33 [disabled 4–16s]£5.11 [Con]£17.32–18.34; car park £3; discounts available online; family tickets available

The great mass of Warwick Castle still keeps an eye on the town of Warwick as it did hundreds of years ago. Built in 1068 by William the Conqueror, fortified in the fourteenth century and restored in the nineteenth century to the magnificent sandstone hulk you see today, the castle is a perennially popular attraction.

Owned by the same entertainment operators who manage Alton Towers and Madame Tussaud's, Warwick Castle tries to be more than a historical site – indeed some visitors think it's anything but. With its period-costumed character guides hamming it up and lashings of additional entertainment, it may not be David Starkey or Simon Schama, but it's still a lot of fun, and the voices of minstrels and jesters and the clash of battling knights all add to a slightly frenetic and robustly commercial theme-park atmosphere that kids in particular love. Whenever you visit, there'll be a lot going on, both inside the castle itself and beyond the walls, in the relatively peaceful grounds where lawns and woods sweep down to the river. If you go to River Island, though, the jousting and merriment is likely to be in full swing: you may even get to watch the firing of the trebuchet – the world's largest siege machine.

> "Entertaining for all, even teenagers. The parking is good, there is plenty of seating and the staff are friendly. Take your own food though!"
>
> **Georgina Collins, Trowbridge**

There's accessible parking on site and Blue Badge bays in Warwick town centre. Outdoor paths are hard and most gradients aren't steep, but unless you are a fit wheelchair user, you may require assistance anyway. To avoid the cobbled main entrance into the castle, follow the path that leads you between Bear and Clarence Towers. Inside the medieval castle, access can be tricky. Steps and narrow corridors prevent access to some areas, but there's plenty of seating and good handrails on some of the difficult steps. Although some areas – including the Great Hall and State Rooms – are out of bounds to disabled visitors, there is plenty that can be seen. Pick up the useful "suggestions for wheelchair users" leaflet at the entrance for helpful advice. Touch tours can be arranged in advance.

Warwick Castle

Food & drink ▶▶ *The Coach House Restaurant,* in the Stables Courtyard area, serves a basic selection of food, including breakfast, cream teas and healthy options.

074 Charlecote Park, Warwickshire

Address: Warwick CV35 9ER **Website:** www.nationaltrust.org.uk/main/w-charlecotepark
Telephone: 01789 470277 **Hours:** house 28 Feb–1 Nov Fri–Tue noon–5pm, 7 Nov–20
Dec Sat & Sun noon–4pm; park & garden Feb & 2 Nov–31 Jan 10.30pm–4pm, Mar–1 Nov
10.30am–6pm **Dates:** house closed 21 Dec–27 Feb; park & garden closed 24–25 Dec and
some restricted access on Wed & Thu **Entry:** [D]£9 [C]free [A]£9 [5–15s]£4.50 [Con]£9;
reduced rates for park and gardens admission only

Charlecote Park is a remarkable, seven-hundred-year-old estate with a superbly maintained Tudor mansion and exquisite gardens, surrounded by a landscaped deer park. A few miles east of Stratford, Shakespeare is said to have been caught poaching here.

Inside the house, the décor is preserved in all the heavy, Elizabethan-style Victorian refurbishment of the mid-nineteenth century. Charlecote has been owned by the Lucy family since the fourteenth century: they have a vast collection of portrait paintings and antiques on display in their home. On days when the house is open, the main tours start at 11am and last for an hour, when it opens to non-guided visitors. Sadly, if you can't manage stairs, the upper floor is inaccessible, but photographs of the furnishings are available. Visitors can participate in traditional Tudor games on Capability Brown's formal lawns, or enjoy the sensory garden, and there are acres to explore on a country walk. Throughout the year, tours of the outbuildings, costume talks and family trails keep visitors busy and entertained. In October, during the rutting season, a tractor pulling a passenger carriage provides a safari around the deer park. The carriage has ramped access and adapted seating, but spaces must be booked in advance.

Great care has been taken to make as much of the property as accessible as possible. On arrival, disabled visitors can ask for the gate code that allows entry to the disabled parking area. The car park is around two hundred yards from the house, but a powered scooter is available to help disabled visitors make their way down the driveway. The paths in the grounds are wide, but mostly loose gravel, and not all easy for unassisted manual wheelchair users to navigate. In the house, doorways are wide enough even for powered scooters, and there is ramped access everywhere except the second floor. There are three disabled toilets. Large print and Braille guides are available.

Food & drink ▶▶ The *Orangery Restaurant* has a ramped side entrance, and a pleasant outdoor terrace. Local artists exhibit paintings of Charlecote Park along the walls.

075 Royal Shakespeare Company, Warwickshire

Address: The Courtyard Theatre, Southern Lane, Stratford-upon-Avon CV37 6BB **Website:** www.rsc.org.uk **Telephone:** 0844 800 1114; access information 01789 403436 **Hours:** check website for performance dates and times **Dates:** check website for performance dates and times **Entry:** varies depending on performance and seat

The Royal Shakespeare Company is one of the most prominent publicly funded companies in the UK that aims to keep Shakespeare's work at the forefront of British theatre.

The Courtyard Theatre is a one-thousand-seater temporary structure making way for the new Royal Shakespeare Theatre across the road – set to be complete late in 2010. Until then the Courtyard is an impressive and beautifully designed stand-in, blending industrial-style theatre space with traditional notes: it doesn't feel temporary at all. The atmosphere of the theatre is one of energy and informality, reflected in all the productions with the envelopment of the audience in the action on stage. As well as Shakespeare, the RSC puts on a variety of plays by contemporary writers – a total of some eight to ten productions each year, with recent appearances by the likes of David Tennant and Sir Ian McKellen.

RSC productions are extremely popular and you should book disabled seats as far ahead as possible. The theatre has disabled parking, with further Blue Badge bays directly outside, but arriving late can be a problem, with the road cluttered up with cars and coaches. Once you're inside, every aspect of your RSC experience will be straightforward and enjoyable, from the low-level reception desk to the wide corridors throughout the building. Visitors with sensory disabilities are well catered for. Signage is clear; audio and captioned performances and touch tours take place regularly; large print and Braille cast lists are available; assistance dogs are permitted in the auditorium or can be looked after by front-of-house staff; and audio notes on the plays can be downloaded from the website or provided on CD. Visitors who can transfer from their wheelchair into the auditorium seating can arrange for their chair to be safely taken away, and returned at the interval and end of the performance. Transfer is not necessary though – there are sixteen wheelchair spaces with excellent visibility, while theatre seating can be removed to create space for powered scooters. There are clean, spacious disabled toilets on every level.

Food & drink ›› The theatre bars are low-level and close to the disabled seating. For a filling pre-performance meal deal, try *Café Pasta* (☎01789 262 910, Ⓦwww.cafe-pasta .co.uk) on Sheep Street, a few hundred yards towards town. Enter via the single-step double-door front entrance, or the flat but single-door side entrance.

076 West Midland Safari and Leisure Park, Worcestershire

Address: Spring Grove, Bewdley DY12 1LF **Website:** www.wmsp.co.uk **Telephone:** 01299 402114 **Hours:** mid-Feb–early Apr 10am–4pm; early Apr–early Nov 10am–5pm; early Nov–mid-Feb 10am–3pm; closing times vary further, a detailed schedule is available on the website **Dates:** generally closed weekdays in Jan, early Feb & Nov but dates vary **Entry:** prices vary seasonally [D]£11.50 [C]free [A]£12.95 [child]£12.50 [Con]£11.50; prices vary for pedestrian visitors; family tickets are available; extra charges apply for the leisure park

With elephants, rhinos, giraffes, zebras, tigers, hunting dogs, cheetahs, antelopes and the only pride of rare white lions in the UK, West Midland Safari and Leisure Park gives you a taste of Africa from the comfort of your own car.

You can easily spend a couple of hours driving around the park's one hundred acres, observing the wildlife and stopping to take photographs along the way. Some of the less dangerous species can be fed from car windows, so it's well worth buying a bag of the special feed (£2.50) at the entrance. Feeding is fun and a great way to see the animals up close, but remember to have some tissues with you, as you may be left with slobber to

West Midland Safari and Leisure Park

wipe off your hands! On weekends, public holidays and normal days between 11am and 2pm, the route can be a little congested and slow-moving, which gives you the chance to observe some of the animals for a good while – but if you don't want to be restricted to your car for too long, try and avoid those times. You are welcome to drive round as many times as you wish, should you want to see any of the animals again. Guided mini-bus tours are available, but you need to be able to board the vehicle on foot.

After the safari experience, there is even more to enjoy in the rest of the leisure park: animal enclosures, reptile houses, tanks of creepy crawlies and even white-knuckle rides. As the park is a pedestrian area you'll need to leave your car in the disabled parking area near the entrance. There are some considerable distances to cover, and a few slopes to negotiate, but rest stops are provided along the way. Manual wheelchairs can be borrowed too – but do call ahead to book and note that your car keys or driving licence will need to be left as a deposit. Access to most animal houses, including the ramped high walkway over the hippo enclosure, is reasonable, although disabled visitors should be prepared for some steep and uneven surfaces. The park boasts thirty rides and unsurprisingly not all of them are accessible, but if you can transfer from your wheelchair, the intense Venom Tower Drop and the delightful Jumbo Parade family ride, among others, are manageable. A very brief, but useful, overview of each ride is available on the "fun" section of the website, along with lots of other information.

Food & drink ▶▶ The *Explorers Café* is midway through the park and has plenty of healthy options, a children's menu, disabled toilet and lots of outdoor seating with movable chairs.

077 Croome Park, Worcestershire

Address: near High Green WR8 9DW **Website:** www.nationaltrust.org.uk/main /w-croomepark **Telephone:** 01905 371006 **Hours:** check ahead for seasonal variations **Dates:** check ahead for seasonal variations **Entry:** [D]£6 [C]free [A]£6 [5–15s]£3 [Con]£6

Croome Park is significant as Capability Brown's first design triumph. He started work here in 1751, before his career took off and he transformed many other country estates. Brown designed both the grounds and the house, Croome Court.

While perhaps previously not receiving the recognition it deserves, extensive restoration work is currently under way at Croome, and it is finally being seen for the superb example of Brown's landscaping that it is. The fine Worcestershire countryside all around only adds to the appeal. In its entirety, the property spreads over around 670 acres, but the pleasure ground area has a manageable two-hour walk that takes in all the main sights. It's a lovely route, littered with architectural, sculptural and natural delights, including the Church of St Mary Magdalene (a Brown design), the Temple Greenhouse (Robert Adam) and the stunning lake at the bottom of the property (Brown again).The gravel path is hard packed in most places, but has some steep hills, and tricky bridges over the lake that have little ground clearance – wheelchair users will need some assistance.

Croome Court's doors were reopened to the public in 2009 – visitors can admire the restored furnishings in six rooms on the lower floor. A powered scooter is available to help disabled visitors navigate the steep slopes between the visitor centre and the house. Access into the building is via a large front staircase: a mechanical stair climber allows wheelchair users access to the top. As you wheel in and your chair is tipped backwards, the device can initially feel a little unnerving, but is very sturdy and safe. The visitor centre, canteen and toilets all have wide entrances, while the staff are extremely friendly and knowledgeable.

Food & drink ▶▶ Recent restoration work has seen a 1940s theme emerge, with the visitor centre now housed in the old RAF buildings. Hearty, homely food is on the menu in the World War II-style English canteen, where the cakes are fantastic.

078–079 Symonds Yat Rock and Symonds Yat East, Herefordshire

Address: Ross-on-Wye HR9 **Website:** www.visitherefordshire.co.uk **Telephone:** tourist board 01432 260621 **Hours:** no closures **Dates:** no closures **Entry:** free

Straddling the river Wye, where England meets Wales, is the quaint village of Symonds Yat East. Symonds Yat Rock is a nearby limestone outcrop that rises some five hundred feet from the banks of the Wye – views from the top are breathtaking.

Much has been done to make the Yat Rock viewpoint accessible for all: a Heritage Lottery Fund grant of almost £3 million was spent building a new all-ability trail to the top, unveiled in April 2009. Visitors should start their journey at the well-signposted disabled car park and follow the path that leads to a clearing with picnic tables, snack shop and disabled toilets – from there a solid wooden footbridge starts the path up the hill. The total distance from the car park to the summit is around 550 yards. The inclines along the way are not too extreme but if you are using a manual wheelchair, assistance may be required in some places. At the viewpoint, low walls allow wheelchair

View from Symonds Yat Rock

IDEAS ▶▶ SPECTACULAR VIEWPOINTS

The Giant's Causeway (☎028 2073 1855, ⓦwww.giantscausewaycentre. com) This sixty-million-year-old World Heritage site is absolutely amazing; geology at its most magical and a truly unique landscape. A shuttle bus leaves the information centre for the causeway every fifteen minutes – call ahead to check timings for the accessible bus with chairlift.

Rhossili (visitor centre ☎01792 390707, ⓦwww.nationaltrust.org.uk) Right on the tip of the Gower Peninsula, Rhossili has one of the most spectacular coastal panoramas in Britain. The massive sweep of golden sands extend to the distance, backed by sand dunes, grassy downs and the high peak of Rhossili Down, while off to the west the rocky promontory of Worm's Head rises above the waves to be cut off by the incoming tide twice a day. Although access is limited, the views repay the long, twisty drive down Gower's narrow country lanes. There's also a lovely, accessible clifftop path out towards Worm's Head, which offers great views of the surfers riding the waves in the bay below.

Spinnaker Tower (☎023 9285 7520, ⓦwww.spinnakertower.co.uk) This 558-feet-high tower in Portsmouth has become one of the south's most impressive tourist attractions, thanks to the stunning views that take in Portsmouth harbour, the Solent and the Isle of Wight. The tower's smooth high-speed lift whisks you up to a series of viewing platforms, and the tummy-flip-inducing glass floor.

Stonehenge (customer services ☎01980 623108, ⓦwww.english-heritage. org.uk) Although always a glorious – not to mention mind-boggling – sight, Stonehenge is undoubtedly at its most beautiful at sunset. Disabled parking is close to the entrance, and the paths around the outer circle are tarmac and grass. The audio tour has an induction loop.

users to enjoy the glorious views and the first-rate birdwatching possibilities. RSPB members are often on hand with twitching tips and telescopes powerful enough to see right inside bird nests. If you visit between April and August, you might even spot the rare breeding pair of peregrine falcons that nest in the area.

Cosy Symonds Yat East is only a two-mile drive away, and is the perfect place to rest after making your way down from the viewpoint. The tiny village is no more than five hundred yards long, so it's not far from the car park to wherever you choose to stop and relax. There are a few undulations along the way, but most of the cafés and restaurants have ramped access. Once you've picked your riverside spot, there is little more to do than tuck into a cream tea while watching the unusual hand-pulled ferry travel back and forth across the Wye – unfortunately this boat is only accessible to visitors on foot.

Food & drink ▶▶ A pleasant place to eat in Symonds Yat East is *The Saracens Head* (☎01600 890435, ⓦwww.saracensheadinn.co.uk). It has outdoor seating overlooking the river, and a ramped side entrance and disabled toilet.

The Southwest

The Southwest

The past is perhaps at its most tangible in England's southwest, where ancient Neolithic sites and charming historic houses pepper the predominantly rural landscape. This handsome region is not one for instantly striking visitors with dramatic scenery and imposing vistas – it settles instead on beguiling them with its genteel towns, bucolic landscapes and crumbling coastline, gently but effectively coaxing them to return time and time again.

080 The National Arboretum at Westonbirt, Gloucestershire

Address: Near Tetbury GL8 8QS **Website:** www.forestry.gov.uk/westonbirt **Telephone:** 01666 881218 **Hours:** Apr–Nov Mon–Fri 9am–8pm, Sat & Sun 8am–8pm; Dec–Mar Mon–Fri 9am–5pm, Sat & Sun 8am–5pm; closing always dusk if earlier **Dates:** closed 1–2 Jan & 24–31 Dec **Entry:** 2 Jan–28 Feb [D]£4 [C]free [A]£5 [5–15s]£2 [Con]£4; Mar–Sep [D]£6 [C] free [A]£7 [5–15s]£2 [Con]£6; Oct–Nov [D]£7 [C]free [A]£8 [5–15s]£2 [Con]£7 Dec £5 car parking payable only 9am–4pm

Magnificent displays of rhododendrons and azaleas herald the spring at Westonbirt Arboretum; leafy glades and wild flowers follow in the summer and the trees sparkle magically on frosty winter days – but it's the glorious colours of the Japanese maples in autumn that are most spectacular of all.

Westonbirt's collection of trees, plants and shrubs is vast. There are over fifteen thousand individual specimens on site, including Westonbirt's "champion" trees, the largest of their kind in the UK, which you can have fun tracking down. With such variety, it's well worth visiting for some fresh air and a stroll in any season. Two different areas make up the six hundred acres of Westonbirt: the "old" arboretum is fairly level and has plenty of activities for kids, while the larger Silk Wood has some steeper slopes (especially near the entrance) but benches to rest on. There are seventeen miles of hard paths through the arboretum, but bark trails off the beaten track may prove difficult for wheelchair users to navigate, particularly after rainfall. Powered scooters allow disabled visitors to freely explore the whole of Westonbirt, and using one is recommended – the visitor centre has seven available for free, but you must call ahead to book one. You can get advice on the best trail to choose from helpful volunteers working in the accessible Great Oak Hall – pop in there before you set off on a route. There is also a handy map available on arrival. Keep an eye on the website for events that take place throughout the year – from photography workshops to woodland management courses.

The arboretum can get busy, particularly during autumn so if you're visiting on a weekend or a sunny day and want to secure the most accessible parking, arrive as early

The National Arboretum at Westonbirt

as possible. There are eight disabled spaces on a tarmac surface close to the visitor centre, and a couple more on gravel by the plant centre. If these are already full when you arrive, use the additional disabled parking on grass. The disabled toilets, visitor centre, restaurant, café, play area and shop are all located in the centre of the park, but if you fancy shopping in the plant centre, it's best to drive down to it and park by the entrance. Some of the trees' identification labels are high in the branches but most signs are low-level.

Food & drink ▶▶ There is plenty to choose from: *Maples Restaurant* with indoor and outdoor seating, the open-air *Courtyard Café* in the centre of the arboretum and mobile caterers on site – but on a sunny day it's a lovely place for a picnic.

081 Brunel's ss Great Britain, Bristol

Address: Great Western Dockyard BS1 6TY **Website:** www.ssgreatbritain.org **Telephone:** 0117 926 0680 **Hours:** Jan & Nov–Dec 10am–4pm; Feb & Mar 10am–4.30pm; Apr–23 Oct 10am–5.30pm **Dates:** closed 11 Jan & 24–25 Dec **Entry:** [D]£10.95 [C]free [A]£10.95 [5–16s]£5.95 [Con]£8.50

When you step aboard Brunel's ss *Great Britain*, you enter the era of Victorian ingenuity and self-confidence. The visit is a slickly presented, behind-the-scenes immersion in the story of the first ocean liner, and the biggest passenger ship of the era.

The *Great Britain,* for decades a rusting hulk in the Falklands, has been lovingly restored to some of her former glory in the Bristol dry dock where she was built. Visitors journey through the interactive dockside museum and then board the ship. With a choice of free audio and BSL guides you can find out what life was like for passengers and crew, from the elegance of the first-class cabins to the cramped and noisy steerage accommodation. Then, if you descend under the rather beautiful glass "sea", you can view the magnificent hull, which is now protected by a state-of-the-art system to control moisture that would corrode the metal.

There are disabled parking spaces about 160 yards from the entrance. This is a Victorian ship and dockyard, so inevitably there are sloped areas, uneven paths and tight corners – but the level of effort that has gone into making the site wheelchair accessible is commendable. There are many ramps and wide doorways. There are lifts not only in the museum, but also to take you below the glass sea, and ingeniously in the ship's funnel to allow wheelchair access to all decks on the ship.

> "Everyone should visit this ship. It is totally disabled-friendly and the staff are very helpful."
>
> **Donald Hillier, Dartford**

Two narrow, manual wheelchairs are available. In wet weather, the wooden deck can be slippery, and in some of the areas below deck the planking is uneven. You'll find disabled toilets on the ship itself and in the museum and café.

Food & drink ▶▶ The light and airy *Dockyard Café* serves delicious cakes and pastries that are prepared on the ship. You can enjoy your lunch and views of the floating harbour.

082 Thermae Bath Spa, Bath

Address: Hot Bath Street, Bath BA1 1SJ Website: www.thermaebathspa.com Telephone: 0844 888 0844 Hours: daily 9am–10pm; some facilities vary Dates: closed 1 Jan & 25–26 Dec Entry: fees vary depending on treatments, sessions and packages; 2-hour spa session in New Royal Bath [D]£12 [C]£12 [A]£24

Combining Georgian architecture with modern facilities, this state-of-the-art natural, thermal spa complex uses the flow of a million-odd litres a day of mineral-enriched hot water. Soothing and de-stressing, a visit here is a wonderful treat and great value.

The main focuses are New Royal Bath, designed by Nicholas Grimshaw, with its futuristic use of glass, and Cross Bath, just over the quiet, cobbled street. In New Royal Bath, you can indulge in the Minerva Bath, with its whirlpool, jet massage and gentle currents, and the open-air rooftop pool – delightful even on a cold day, and with magnificent views across the city. New Royal also has aromatherapy steam rooms and waterfall showers. Cross Bath, with its smaller open-air thermal pool, is housed in an adjacent building, constructed over the Cross Spring sacred Celtic site. Here, you can try out a wide range of spa therapies, including body wraps, massages, hot stones and dry flotation, as well as body care treatments and facials.

Thermae has generally good access credentials, as you might expect, though there's no dedicated car park. Getting to the entrance from the Blue Badge spaces (no time restrictions) in Beau Street means travelling over slabs and cobbles; alternatively, there is three-hour time limit parking near the building. An automatic door leads to reception, and lifts provide access to all levels. There's plenty of Braille signage inside. Two lightweight shower wheelchairs can be borrowed and there are accessible toilets and showers, but no hoists in the changing rooms. Steps with handrails take you into the water, and there are attendant-operated hoists to get you in and out of all the pools. Assistance chairs give access to the baths. The treatment rooms are a good size and some have raise-and-lower beds. Everything you might need – towels, robes, slippers – is available to hire and included in some of the packages. Some visitors prefer the privacy of the separate Cross Bath building, which has a disabled changing room and shower facilities and also assistance-chair access into the bath. Staff will take care of assistance dogs as they are not allowed pool side.

Food & drink ▶▶ *Spring's Café and Restaurant* has a varied menu. Eating here is an experience not to be missed, dressed in the same wet costumes and white robes as the other patrons. An extra 45 minutes can be added to your session to cover your eating time.

083 Steam Museum of the Great Western Railway, Wiltshire

Address: Kemble Drive, Swindon SN2 2TA **Website:** www.steam-museum.org.uk
Telephone: 01793 466646/466637 **Hours:** daily 10am–5pm **Dates:** closed 1 Jan & 25–26 Dec **Entry:** [D]£6.40 [C]free [A]£6.40 [3–16s]£4.25 [Con]£4.25

Many of the best steam locomotions in the world were built at Swindon's Great Western Railway Works, so Steam holds massive appeal for locomotive enthusiasts, but is an enjoyable place to visit for many other people too.

Set in the middle of the former Swindon Railway Works, this museum takes you into the world of the principal engineer, Isambard Kingdom Brunel, and those who built and drove the engines and travelled on the Great Western Railway. The GWR service was a benchmark for public transport in the middle of the nineteenth century and the GWR Works – at its peak – turned out more than one hundred new locomotions each year. As well as the big engines and the usual memorabilia and exhibits, the museum is populated by the figures of former railway workers – a few of the more than ten thousand people employed by the Works in the early 1900s. The evocative Works area of the museum gives a sense of day-to-day life for those employees, and is home to the great locomotive "Caerphilly Castle", displayed in all its gleaming glory – a fine example of the achievements of those staff.

This is a fairly accessible museum: the gravelled car park is right outside the main entrance and automatic doors lead into a large foyer, where you'll find the museum shop and café and access to the toilets. Wide doors lead into the museum itself, where all the exhibits are level, or accessible via ramps. There's a lift to a viewpoint over the museum and then an upper level with a view over the adjacent main line. There are three powered scooters available, but beware that their batteries may not have enough power for a lengthy visit to the museum. The video displays have captions and subtitles, and if you need any help the museum staff are happy to assist.

Food & drink ▶▶ The *Station Buffet* is small, but you can visit the café at Heelis House, the National Trust headquarters, just over two hundred yards from the museum – this is a quieter alternative than the places to eat in the nearby shopping outlet.

084 Avebury Stone Circle, Wiltshire

Address: near Marlborough SN8 1RF **Website:** www.nationaltrust.org.uk/main/w-avebury
Telephone: 01672 539250 **Hours:** stones no closures; museum & gallery daily Apr–Oct
10am–6pm, Nov–Mar 10am–4pm **Dates:** stones no closures; museum & gallery closed
24–26 Dec **Entry:** free access to the stones; museum and gallery [D]£4.20 [C]free [A]£4.20
[child]£2.35

Avebury Stone Circle

Avebury is a small village near Marlborough in Wiltshire, built in the middle of a huge
Neolithic (new stone age) henge, or stone circle – part of a complex of ancient settlements
dating back five thousand years.

As you pass the earthworks and standing stones on the main road running through
the village, you sense the site's significance: at the height of its importance it was the
Neolithic equivalent of St Peter's in Rome. The National Trust's museum has an interactive exhibition describing the history of the site and its reconstruction in the 1930s, while
the adjacent gallery exhibits many of the artefacts found during excavations in the area by
the archeologist Alexander Keiller. Although now a UNESCO World Heritage Site, and
one of the most important megalithic (giant stone) sites in Europe, many of the stones
are missing, taken to be used for building materials over the centuries or periodically
destroyed because of their pre-Christian origins. Out among the stones, you are free to
wander at will – visitors often remark about the special atmosphere, which becomes
particularly magical at dusk. Be aware that the grass can be long and sheep graze in the
area, so it can be messy.

Blue Badge holders can use the car park in the High Street; otherwise there is a pay and display National Trust car park 550 yards away. The village is flat but there are cobbled areas and some narrow pavements. Parts of the henge itself have level access to the stones, which you're free to get right up to. The Trust centre isn't very well signposted, but when you find it you'll discover its museum, gallery, café and toilets are all accessible.

Food & drink ▸▸ The vegetarian café at the visitor centre can cater for special dietary requirements and its cream teas are delicious. *The Red Lion* (☎01672 539266) pub in Avebury serves good food but doesn't have wheelchair accessible toilets. The accessible toilets next door close at 6pm.

085 Stourhead, Wiltshire

Address: Stourton, Warminster BA12 6QD **Website:** www.nationaltrust.org.uk/stourhead
Telephone: 01747 841152 **Hours:** house daily 11am–5pm; garden daily 9am–7pm or dusk
if earlier **Dates:** house closed Wed, Thu & 2 Nov–31 Mar; garden no closures **Entry:** garden
and house [D]£12.30 [C]free [A]£12.30 [5–17s]£6.10

Stourhead, a Palladian mansion owned by the Hoare family since 1717, has a superb garden with replica Roman and Venetian buildings and an extraordinary folly. The house contains a superb collection of painting and furniture and, together with the gardens, was given to the National Trust in 1946.

In 1902, fire destroyed a large part of the house, but most of the furniture and paintings were saved. Today, the highlights are the Regency library, the collection of Chippendale furniture and the remarkably tall Pope's Cabinet made for Pope Sixtus V in 1590 and recently restored. While the furnishings are undeniably beautiful, for many visitors the real draw is outside: Stourhead's grounds are a feast of colour for most of the year and deliberately designed to offer breathtaking views around the lakeside set-

Stourhead

ting. They are a consummate example of the eighteenth-century passion for landscape gardening – created in 1740 by Henry Hoare II, they earnt him the moniker Henry the Magnificent. There's a circuit around the lake that is just over a mile long, a two-mile path to the Alfred Tower folly, which stands 160 feet high (no wheelchair access to the top), and a three-mile circular route that takes in the deer park and an Iron Age fort.

From the disabled bays in the car park, there is a four-hundred-yard path to the house entrance. A free wheelchair accessible shuttle bus transports visitors between the entrance, restaurant and shop, the gardens, the house and finally the courtyard, which is home to an accessible toilet and *The Spread Eagle*, a pub. There are thirteen concrete steps into the house with no firm hand hold, but there is a stair climber available. It is very safe, although visitors need to be ready for a few bumps and jolts along the way. The stair climber has to be booked a day in advance, and can only be operated if trained staff are on site. Once you're inside, all the public rooms are on one floor and accessible. Outside, the way-marked cycle tracks and footpaths around the wider estate are accessible to walkers and powered scooters, with surfaces varying from gravel to grass and compacted woodland soil. Some parts are undulating and others get muddy in wet weather – manual wheelchair users will definitely need assistance. A double-seater powered scooter is available to borrow for one hour: only set off on it if you feel confident about driving.

Food & drink ▸▸ Foodies are spoilt for choice at Stourhead. The fully accessible restaurant by the entrance serves locally sourced produce – some even grown in the kitchen garden at the house. The cosy and splendid *The Spread Eagle* (℡01747 840587, Ⓦwww .spreadeagleinn.com) in the courtyard serves hearty lunches and evening meals – there is a two-inch threshold step but once inside all is level.

IDEAS ▸▸ ACTIVITY BREAKS

The Calvert Trust (Ⓦwww.calvert-trust.org.uk) runs accessible outdoor activity holidays at three centres in England: at Exmoor (℡01598 763221), Kielder in Northumberland (℡01434 250232) and the Lake District (℡01768 772255). Facilities vary at each centre, with each offering a slightly different mix of activities, from canoeing and caving to paragliding using a specially developed "aerobike".

Phab (℡020 8667 9443, Ⓦwww.phabengland.org.uk) is a charity that supports a network of over two hundred inclusive activity clubs throughout England and Wales. They also run summer camps and festivals for physically disabled children and fund special short breaks where young people of all abilities can enjoy adventurous outdoor activities together.

The Red Ridge Centre (℡01938 810821, Ⓦwww.redridgecentre.co.uk) is an outdoor education centre in Powys, Wales. Although typically hired out to groups for exclusive use, the centre also runs special weeks for individuals who need a carer to accompany them on holiday.

The Speyside Trust (℡01479 861285, Ⓦwww.badaguish.org) is a small charity based at the Badaguish Cairngorm Outdoor Centre, in Scotland. They provide respite care and assisted activity holidays for adults and children with learning and/or physical disabilities, and have four modern lodges that can be hired out.

086-087 Exmoor 21-Mile Drive and Lynton to Lynmouth Cliff Railway, Devon

Address: railway bottom station The Esplanade, Lynmouth EX35 6EQ; railway top station Lee Road, Lynton EX35 6HW **Website:** railway www.cliffrailwaylynton.co.uk **Telephone:** railway 01598 753486 **Hours:** cliff railway 10am; closing times vary between 5pm & 9pm depending on time of year **Dates:** cliff railway closed 6 Nov–13 Feb **Entry:** cliff railway [D] single £1.95 return £2.85 [C]single £1.95 return £2.85 [A]single £1.95 return £2.85 [child] single £1.10 return £1.85; all dogs single 50p return £1

On wild Exmoor, windswept moors give way to gentle wooded valleys, which in turn roll into handsome coastline. This 21-mile drive covers the best of it and will have you reaching for your camera again and again.

The drive takes a figure-of-eight route: you should follow signposts from Lynmouth through Watersmeet, Rockford, Brendon and Countisbury, back through Lynmouth and then past Lynton, Valley of the Rocks, Woody Bay, Martinhoe, Hunters Inn, Killington Lane and Barbrook, before ending the drive right where you started at Lynmouth. As you pass by the Valley of the Rocks you'll realise why this area is nicknamed England's "Little Switzerland" – there are dramatic rock formations in every direction and even a herd of wild goats. The drive towards Hunters Inn is via a single-track road along the cliff, with the woods on one side and the sea on the other. Pop a £1 toll in the honesty box along the way – the scenery is so dazzling you won't begrudge the fee. At Hunters Inn there are some basic disabled toilets (the male toilets have a two-inch step) by a National Trust shop selling lovely gifts and locally produced ice cream. From this spot you can embark on a one-mile wheelchair accessible trail to the rocky cove of Heddon's Mouth and back, although visitors on powered scooters can go a little further – ask for directions in the National Trust shop.

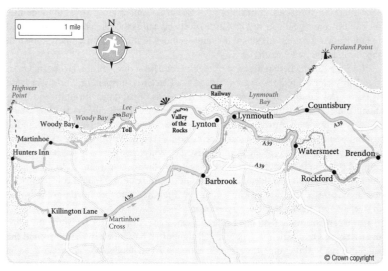

© Crown copyright

Back in the car, it's a straightforward drive back to Lynmouth, the seaside home of the water-powered cliff railway that travels back and forth to the cliff top at Lynton. This is a short but fun trip with exceptional views of the coastline. The Victorian carriages are wheelchair accessible, and small powered scooters are welcome. If you can manage a few steps you can get off at Lynton and enjoy a bite to eat while admiring the impressive coastal views. But pretty Lynmouth with its whitewashed cottages and charming gift shops is actually the more accessible place, so if you can't disembark and have to do the round trip back to the bottom, you won't miss out. There are three Blue Badge spaces in the Lynmouth car park, and the public toilets are by the Memorial Hall.

Food & drink ▶▶ At Lynton the *Cliff Top Cafaurant* (☎01598 753366) boasts panoramic views, excellent cream teas and has an accessible toilet. Or if you fancy tasty fish and chips in Lynmouth try *Fish on the Harbour* (☎01598 753600) or the *Esplanade Fish Bar* (☎01598 753798) – just ask for the ramp at the latter.

088–089 Sherborne Castle & Lakeside Gardens and The Sherborne Old Castle, Dorset

New Castle Address: New Road, Sherborne DT9 5NR Website: www.sherbornecastle .com Telephone: 01935 812072 Hours: Tue–Thu, Sat & Sun, bank holidays 11am–4.30pm; Sat castle interior 2–4.30pm only Dates: Mar–Oct Entry: castle and gardens [D]£9 [C]free [A]£9 [under 15s]free [Con]£8.50; reduced rates for garden only Old Castle Address: off the B3145, Sherborne DT9 3SA Website: www.english-heritage.org.uk Telephone: 01935 812730 Hours: daily: Apr–Jun & Sep 10am–5pm; Jul–Aug 10am–6pm; Oct 10am–4pm Dates: closed Nov–Mar Entry: [D]£3 [C]£3 [A]£3 [5–15s]£1.50 [Con]£2.60

Perched on a low hill, Sherborne Castle has an impressive lakeside setting and some very interesting historical connections. Sir Walter Raleigh originally tried to modernise the twelfth-century Sherborne Old Castle (the ruins across the lake), but instead decided to build a new home on the site of the hunting lodge in the Deer Park – now known to the locals as the "new" castle.

The State Rooms here reflect a variety of decorative styles – Tudor, Jacobean, Georgian and Victorian, and the castle was used as a Red Cross hospital in World War I and as the D-Day landing HQ in World War II. Details of paintings, furniture and ornaments can be found on information sheets in each room, via a Braille guide, or by asking the very helpful staff. After a dose of history, you can take a very pleasant walk in the grounds, pausing to feed the ducks. There's no marked disabled parking in the grassy car park, which can be problematic on a busy day. Wheelchair access to the castle is via a ramped side entrance, but if you can't manage stairs then access is limited to the ground floor as there's no lift. Outside, the courtyard next to the café and shop is cobbled, with a mat around the edge to make it a bit less bumpy. The paved paths around the grounds vary in steepness but there's usually a gentle option.

If you can take more than one castle in a day, it's very much worth visiting the ruins of Sherborne Old Castle too – only a well-signposted half mile drive away around the lakeshore road. At the ruins, the grounds, although grassy, tend to be compact and can be pretty much freely explored. On a sunny day, it's a serene spot to relax with a picnic, but be sure to position yourself so you can take in the enchanting views over the lake to Raleigh's former home. The car park here is a short distance from the ticket office, but it is possible to be dropped off closer to the entrance. You enter the castle itself via a sloping timber bridge, but after that all areas are level except steps to the chapel area of the ruins, and there are benches around to perch on.

Food & drink ▸▸ The *Walled Garden Restaurant* (☎01935 814345) at the pleasant Castle Gardens Nursery is conveniently situated on the drive between the two castles. It offers teas, coffees, home-made cakes, freshly prepared lunches and afternoon teas. There is access for wheelchair users via the rear entrance and there are disabled toilets.

090 Abbotsbury Swannery, Dorset

Address: New Barn Road, Abbotsbury DT3 4JG **Website:** www.abbotsbury-tourism.co.uk /swannery.htm **Telephone:** 01305 871858 **Hours:** 20 Mar–31 Oct daily 10am–5pm or 6pm (call to confirm); last entrance 1 hour before closing **Dates:** closed Nov–19 Mar **Entry:** [D]£9 [C]free [A]£9.50 [5–15s]£6.50 [Con]£9

The ballerina Anna Pavlova studied swans at Abbotsbury Swannery in the 1920s for her legendary role in *Swan Lake*. If you come in May or June you're likely to see fluffy cygnets all over the site. But there are plenty of swans all year round, together with a multitude of other birdlife – don't forget your binoculars.

Abbotsbury Swannery

Low fences throughout make it easy to get up close and personal to the birdlife. Along the trails there's plenty of information about birds, wildlife and the history of the swannery – established in the eleventh century by Benedictine monks to supply their dinner table. You'll also come across various display areas, a duck trap and a hide with a window at wheelchair user level. If you include a feeding time in your visit – either midday or 4pm – you can get hands-on experience feeding the swans while taking in an enthusiastic talk from the swanherd about the set-up. By the disabled car park is a willow maze, with a grass surface, which should keep you and any children entertained for a while, before you finally succumb to cakes in the café.

> "It is well worth visiting to see these magnificent birds. The disabled facilities are good but the shingle paths could be improved."
>
> **Rita Jones, Plymouth**

Abbotsbury is a twin-centred site where the café and shop are separated from the swannery entrance by around four hundred yards, so it pays to organise your visit if you have restricted mobility. Disabled parking next to the shop and café is effectively two bays in an adjacent lay-by. To reach the swannery, disabled visitors can drive the four hundred yard distance and park in the car park next to the entrance. There are two wheelchairs on loan on a first-come-first-served basis, so it's advisable to arrive as early as you can. The swannery has two accessible walks, totalling just under nine hundred yards in length, helpfully on packed gravel paths, although these can get a little deep and loose in the picnic area.

Food & drink ▸▸ The coffee shop has particularly good cream teas and local cakes, while the nearby *Ilchester Arms* (☎01305 871243, ⓦwww.ilchester-arms.co.uk) in the village serves lunch and evening meals and has an accessible twin room – helpful if you fancy an overnight stay.

091 The Blue Pool and Tea House, Dorset

Address: Furzebrook, near Wareham BH20 5AR **Website:** www.bluepooltearooms.co.uk **Telephone:** 01929 551408 **Hours:** grounds open 9.30am, teahouse, museum & shop 10am; closing times vary seasonally **Dates:** closed Jan–Feb & Dec **Entry:** [D]free (wheelchair users) [C]£5 (wheelchair user assistant) [A]£5 [5–14s]£2.50 [Con]£3.80; family tickets available

"It's never blue," says the redoubtable Miss Barnard, the owner of the Blue Pool, "it varies between green and turquoise." Whatever you decide the colour is from one moment to the next, the clay in suspension in this forty-foot-deep lake renders the water lifeless and unfit for aquatic plants or animals – or for that matter people swimming. But despite its inhospitable conditions, its striking appearance and tranquil surrounds undoubtedly make it worth a visit, if only to soak up the unique atmosphere.

This lozenge-shaped, two-hundred-yard-long jewel of the Dorset countryside, nestled in the forest, is utterly peaceful and features some substantial woods and heathland to explore. It also has a wonderful time-warped teahouse that, in terms of décor and fittings, has hardly changed since it opened in 1935. Once you've bought your tickets, and possibly had a look at the small museum of clay and clay-mining, head off around the fifteen-minute shoreline path encircling this Site of Special Scientific Interest. Keep your eyes open for various woodland mammals or, if you can identify them, a Dartford warbler or the exceedingly rare sand lizard.

There's plenty of parking at the entrance but no specific disabled bays. If the fairly steep slope to the ticket office looks too much, you can ask for the main gate to be opened and to drive all the way up to the teahouse. Three manual wheelchairs are available for loan. All the buildings have level or ramped access, although this may not be obvious to the casual observer, and the owners are very proud of the standard of their toilets. The red route around the pool is around half a mile long and wheelchair accessible, though the clay surface can get sticky in wet weather. Parts of the green route are accessible – including the adventure playground along the way – but you'll have to be able to manage stairs to get all the way around the circular route.

Food & drink ›› The teahouse serves coffee, lunch, afternoon tea and vibrantly coloured cupcakes in lovely china pots and cups. It is accessible via double doors that can be unbolted for wheelchair access.

092 Monkey World Ape Rescue Centre, Dorset

Address: Longthorns, Wareham BH20 6HH Website: www.monkeyworld.org Telephone: 01929 462537 Hours: Jan–Jun & Sep–Dec 10am–5pm; Jul & Aug 10am–6pm Dates: closed 25 Dec Entry: [D]£7.25 [C]free [A]£10.50 [3–15s]£7.25 [Con]£7.25

Neither a zoo nor originally a tourist attraction, Monkey World was set up in 1987 as a sanctuary dedicated to rescuing apes and monkeys that had been abused by their owners. The centre houses more than 240 primates and is an internationally respected conservation and captive-breeding centre.

Monkey World is an inspirational and fun place to visit. The dedication of the staff, the results they achieve and the affection they have for their charges are plain to see, and the enthusiasm is infectious. Many visitors come back regularly to check the progress of the primates they have adopted. Regular daily talks on eight of the species in the centre are given by the primate-care staff; printed versions of these are available on request. The centre was originally founded to care for chimps, and their four chimp groups are still the main attraction, along with three groups of delightful orang-utans, five species of superbly arboreal gibbons and seven species of monkeys, marmosets and lemurs. For visitors with visual disabilities, there are three life-sized sculptures of orang-utan, chimpanzee and marmoset heads available to feel.

There are nineteen disabled parking spaces – five on tarmac close to the entrance and the rest on gravel around the perimeter fence. Disabled visitors have to overcome many steep slopes, but 25 powered scooters are available to borrow and help make it all a lot more manageable. Book one in advance, and remember to bring along ID and £10 for the refundable deposit. The various collections in the 65-acre site are linked by winding paths and the signage is still not all it could be, so it is easy to get lost. However, the narrow and steep Woodland Walk is the only route that is inaccessible to wheelchair users.

Food & drink ›› Monkey World has a fast-food restaurant and a thatched kiosk for snacks.

093 The Donkey Sanctuary, Devon

Address: Sidmouth EX10 0NU Website: www.thedonkeysanctuary.org.uk Telephone:
01395 578222 Hours: daily 9am–dusk Dates: no closures Entry: free, though donations are
welcomed

Founded in 1969, the Donkey Sanctuary at Slade Farm House, Sidmouth, is a charity
providing a peaceful home for more than four hundred rescued and unwanted donkeys
on around 250 acres. You can meet the donkeys and enjoy the outstanding views from
the trails.

Start at the visitor centre, where you can pick up a map for £1 showing the various
trails. Staff can advise on the suitability of the trails depending on your abilities and
the weather, but the best ones for wheelchair users are usually A, C, F and G, which
mix paved, hardcore and grass surfaces and moderate slopes. Trail A, the 45-minute
central walk, goes down to the main yard and barn, where you'll find the older donkeys
– be aware that on wet days the grass can be hard work. Further on, you'll encounter
donkeys with special needs, the hospital and recuperation paddocks, and donkeys for
adoption. There are plenty of seats, resting areas, indoor and outdoor picnic areas and a
restaurant. Feeding donkeys is discouraged but bins are provided for you to leave suitable treats such as carrots. Trail C features the curiously unkempt-looking Poitou breed,
from France, and a maze. This is fun for children: you buy a sealed maze map from the
visitor centre for £1 and get your money back if you return the envelope unopened.
Most of the trails cross beautiful countryside and trails F and G have wonderful sea
views. As well as donkeys, look out for the mules and the recently acquired Canadian
miniature donkeys.

There is plenty of parking for Blue Badge holders just a few minutes from the visitor centre. A slight slope down to the centre can be avoided on your return by using
the level path via the adoption paddocks. The sanctuary's maps mark accessible toilets
and sheltering points on the various trails. Three manual wheelchairs are available – in
summer you should prebook. Dogs on leads are welcome. Ask at reception for Braille
booklets with information about the sanctuary and how to adopt a donkey – and to find
out whether the staff who have had BSL training are on site.

Food & drink ▸▸ A former donkey barn has been turned into the spacious, accessible
Hayloft Restaurant where visitors can enjoy light snacks, hot lunches, cake and cream tea
while observing the animals in the main yard.

094 Buckfast Abbey, Devon

Address: Buckfastleigh TQ11 0EE Website: www.buckfast.org.uk Telephone: 01364
645500 Hours: abbey Mon–Thu 9am–6pm, Fri 10am–6pm, Sun noon-6pm; intermittent
closures for prayers and services; shops and restaurants opening hours vary Dates: abbey
no closures; shops and restaurants closed Good Friday & 25–26 Dec Entry: free

Buckfast Abbey

This magnificent abbey with its tranquil gardens by the river Dart is a living monastery with a thousand-year history. A peaceful sanctuary, the abbey is home to a community of Benedictine monks who have always welcomed guests, and it attracts visitors from around the globe.

Buckfast Abbey was founded nearly a thousand years ago and stood for five hundred years until Henry VIII's dissolution of the monasteries. A community of Benedictine monks returned in 1882 to rebuild it on its medieval foundations. It was completed in 1938. The monks were gifted stone masons, as evidenced throughout the abbey. Don't miss the bronzes and stained-glass windows, the largest of which, at the rear of the abbey, seems to radiate light even on a dull day. The brothers lead a life of study, prayer and work. Their commercial acumen supports them well: in the abbey gift shop you can buy the famous Buckfast tonic wine, honey from the Buckfast hives, biscuits and jam. The Monastic shop, in a restored eighteenth-century mill, sells gifts made by the Buckfast brothers as well as by monks and nuns from across Europe, while the abbey bookshop is the largest religious bookshop in southwest England. Outside, the physic garden, sensory garden and lavender garden all boast interesting designs and unusual plants and herbs – and are as much for the benefit of the monks' work and leisure as for the pleasure of visitors.

The abbey is less than a mile from the A38, and has ample free parking. Most of the grounds, gardens and buildings, including the church and the restaurant, with its twelfth-century arch, are wheelchair accessible. Audioguides are available for the church, and you can get Braille and large print guides from the gift shop. Accessible toilets are situated at the entrance to the church and beneath the restaurant. The gift shops can be crowded in high summer.

Food & drink ▸▸ You can enjoy hot and cold food, cakes and cream teas in *The Grange* restaurant, which has a lovely view over the abbey and its gardens.

095–096 South Devon Railway and Totnes Rare Breeds Farm, Devon

Addresses: railway The Station, Dartbridge Road, Buckfastleigh TQ11 0DZ; Rare Breeds Farm, Mayhems Cottage, Littlehempston, Totnes TQ9 6LZ **Website:** www.southdevonrailway .co.uk; www.totnesrarebreeds.co.uk **Telephone:** railway 0845 345 1466; farm 01803 840387 **Hours:** railway peak season departs Buckfastleigh 10.45am, 12.15pm, 2.15pm & 3.45pm, Totnes 11.30am, 1pm, 3pm & 4.30pm; farm 10am–5pm **Dates:** closed Nov–Mar (with Christmas & New Year exceptions) **Entry:** combined entrance [D]£13 [C]free (if employed) [A]£13 [5–14s]£8.20 [Con]£11.90; separate tickets available

There's something about places run by enthusiasts that is incredibly alluring, and both the South Devon Railway and the Rare Breeds Farm draw you in because of the dedication of the staff and volunteers. Together they make for a very enjoyable day out.

At Buckfastleigh station staff happily get out the ramp for wheelchair and small scooter users to board the steam train. There's a bit of commentary on the thirty-minute journey which takes you along the beautiful valley of the river Dart, passing fields of happy looking cows and even a bank of pixies! Once at Littlehempston it's about one hundred yards along the platform and over the track to the Rare Breeds Farm. The welcome at the farm is instantaneous and visitors are encouraged to get hands on. Children will love the ample opportunities to feed, pet and closely observe many animals including owls, rescued hedgehogs, seaweed-eating sheep, chickens and goats. Visitors can go into some of the enclosures too. This is not a massive site, and the paths are level and typically surfaced with bark chippings or short grass. Knowledgeable staff will happily give blind and visually impaired visitors more information about the animals.

Back at Buckfastleigh station there's a miniature railway, an accessible railway museum and a shop selling gifts and kit for model train enthusiasts. There is disabled parking at the station. It is possible to visit the Rare Breeds Farm directly, but you'll have to pay to park in Totnes and then walk over five hundred yards along a cycle path to reach the site. There's an accessible toilet in the Buckfastleigh station restaurant and another at Littlehempston station. There are no toilets at the farm, so remember to use the one at the station when you arrive or you'll have a two-hundred-yard trip there and back.

Food & drink ▶▶ The *Garden Café* at the farm is accessible and serves local produce whenever possible. On the train, certain coaches now have wheelchair access to the buffet car, and at Buckfastleigh station *The Refreshment Rooms* are accessible and spacious.

097 Paignton Zoo, Devon

Address: Totnes Road, Paignton TQ4 7EU **Website:** www.paigntonzoo.org.uk **Telephone:** 01803 697500 **Hours:** opens daily 10am; closing time varies between 4.30–6pm, call ahead; last entrance one hour before closing **Dates:** closed 25 Dec **Entry:** [D]£10.35 [C]free [A]£12.50 [3–15s]£8.80 [disabled 3–15s]£6.95 [Con]£10.30 [disabled Con]£8.50

Paignton Zoo seamlessly blends education and conservation work with a happy environment for animals and visitors alike. It's a hilly site, parts of which can be difficult for people with limited mobility to deal with, but with more than three thousand animals, there is a lot to see, and you can easily fill a day here in the areas that are accessible.

Stick to the yellow trail if you want the most wheelchair-friendly route – it takes you from the main entrance to close-up views of flamingos and parrots, and then to a pair of lakes with islands populated by monkeys and gibbons. This yellow route also brings you to the animal encounter area – where you'll have the chance to see giant tortoises, red pandas, peacocks, porcupines, meerkats and kangaroos – and on to the impressive Reptile Tropics and the new crocodile swamp. A path winds through the swamp giving you face time with crocodiles above and below the water. Keep a look out, too, for the world's biggest snake, the reticulated python, usually curled up in one of the trees. The orange route is also reasonably accessible, and takes you to the African Savannah, where giraffes, elephants and the baby black rhino and its parents live. The pink route, however, is more difficult and has steps, though fortunately it only takes in a small part of the zoo.

While far from being one hundred percent accessible, the zoo has begun to consider the needs of wheelchair users when upgrading habitats and aims to make all new exhibits accessible. There are two free car parks, with plenty of disabled spaces, but the main one is on a slight incline while the overflow car park is more level but you do have to cross a busy road. There is a drop-off point right outside the entrance which you should use if you can. A £20 deposit is required for hiring manual wheelchairs and powered scooters, with a further £5 non-refundable charge for the latter. It's worth the fee as having the scooter will make all the difference to your day. However, you could also take the Jungle Express road train around the lakes, but you will need to be able to transfer onto a seat. Blind and visually impaired visitors can prebook a volunteer to escort them around the zoo. The shops located in the main entrance are fully accessible.

Food & drink ▶▶ Located in the heart of the zoo, *The Island Restaurant* has a full menu that includes good value Sunday roasts.

098 The Camel Trail, Cornwall

Address: Padstow, Cornwall Website: www.padstowcyclehire.com; www.trailbikehire.co.uk
Telephone: cycle hire shop 01841 533533; trail bike hire shop 01841 532594 Hours: camel trail no closure; cycle hire shop Jan–mid-Jul & Sep–Dec daily 9am–5pm; mid-Jul–end-Aug daily 9am–9pm; trail hire shop daily 9am–6pm Dates: no closure dates for camel trail; shops closed 25–26 Dec, call ahead to check for extra Christmas & New Year dates Entry: camel trail free; hire rates vary; booking advisable on peak dates

Starting from the beautiful setting of Padstow Harbour, the Camel Trail follows a disused railway line along the Camel Estuary. Along the way there's plenty of beautiful scenery and lots of places to stop for a well-earned pasty or pint.

Very popular with cyclists, the trail is a relatively level path with a compacted surface which you can follow to Wadebridge (five miles), or more ambitiously Bodmin (eleven miles), or even all the way to the end of the trail in Wenfordbridge (nineteen miles). Travel as far as Wadebridge and you're on the estuary, with sandbanks, muddy creeks and rocky shores. In winter you can expect to see wigeon, long-tailed duck and goldeneye, as well as divers, grebe and waders. Spring and autumn bring many migrant birds, while in summer the estuary hosts heron, little egret, cormorant, oystercatcher and several species of gull. If you're lucky you may also spot seals at play in the water. Beyond Wadebridge the route is increasingly wooded, before it emerges on the fringes of Bodmin Moor.

Designated parking spaces (£1 per hour) can be found in Padstow at the car park by Rick Stein's fish-and-chip shop. A RADAR-key-accessible toilet is behind this venue, and another is opposite the tourist information centre on the North Quay. The two cycle-hire centres at the start of the trail can offer wheelchairs, bikes with trailers and even, with advance booking, a wheelchair tandem – a rickshaw-like contraption with the wheelchair user riding up front in comfort, while a companion pedals behind. They also have maps and details of the trail.

Food & drink ►► Arrive early to avoid the queues at the famous *Stein's Fish & Chips* (Ⓦ www.rickstein.com), where there is a disabled toilet and very tasty food on sale. Alternatively, grab a Cornish pasty and watch the boats and birds pass through the harbour.

099 Eden Project, Cornwall

Address: Bodelva, St Austell PL24 2SG **Website:** www.edenproject.com **Telephone:** 01726 811911; access information 01726 818895 **Hours:** gates open summer daily 10am–6pm; winter daily 10am–4.30pm; later closing Fri–Sun, times vary seasonally; Eden opens 1 hour after gates; last entrance 90 minutes before closing **Dates:** closed 24–26 Dec; check website for maintenance closures **Entry:** [D]£16 [C]free [A]£16 [under 16s]£5 [Con]£8–11; discounts available online; family tickets available

The Eden Project's awe-inspiring scale only becomes apparent once you've passed the entrance, at the lip of this cavernous former clay mine. Standing in the landscaped grounds below are the vast, geodesic biomes – colossal, ecofriendly glasshouses – imaginatively and entertainingly showcasing the world's plantlife in all its diversity. Eden is a feel-good, botanical theme park, a registered charity that's low on tat and high on changing the world, and by any standards one of the UK's best family attractions.

The Mediterranean Biome features the sights and scents of warm temperate zones – the Med, the Cape in South Africa and northern California – with herb and vegetable gardens, fruit trees and a vineyard. The Rainforest Biome takes you on a trek through the jungles of Malaysia, West Africa and South America, where huge trees tower overhead, with exhibits on fair trade and deforestation. Don't miss the coffee, bananas and mangoes growing here, or the accessible interactive activities. The rainforest can get extremely warm and humid, but there are plenty of seats to rest on, and there's an air-conditioned refuge in the middle, where you can chill out if the heat gets too much.

> "Just amazing! I would go back one hundred times."
>
> **John Fisher, Barnsley**

Eden has excellent access: on arrival, marshals direct you to parking spaces. Apple Two car park, closest to the entrance and visitor centre, has Blue Badge parking and manual wheelchairs to borrow. Low-floored park-and-ride buses shuttle between the car parks and there are also buggies to transport people who have mobility difficulties. Toilets are also plentiful and accessible. There are two routes down to the Biomes – the one that goes over the bridge and down in the lift is the shortest, but you don't actually have to walk as you can take the land train there and back instead. There are slopes throughout the site, but these are mostly manageable and most of the few steps and steep gradients have alternative routes. For powered scooter users, most of Eden is a breeze. Eden's on-site scooters should be booked two weeks in advance if you're planning to visit during peak holiday times. Manual wheelchair users can get help from one of Eden's trained volunteers.

Food & drink ▸▸ There's excellent food at numerous accessible restaurants and cafés, where the bulk of the produce is local and organic.

100–101 Tate St Ives and Barbara Hepworth Museum & Sculpture Garden, Cornwall

Address: Porthmeor Beach, St Ives TR26 1TG **Website:** www.tate.org.uk/stives **Telephone:** 01736 796226 **Hours:** Mar–Oct daily 10am–5.20pm; Nov–Feb Tue–Sun 10am–4.20pm; last entrance 20 minutes before closing **Dates:** closed Mon in Nov–Feb; closed 24–26 Dec **Entry:** combined tickets [D]£4.50 [C]free [A]£8.75 [under 18s]free [Con]£4.50

Opened in 1993 in a striking modernist building, Tate St Ives showcases contemporary art, often focusing on the Cornish art scene that flourished through the middle of the twentieth century. If you love art, you'll want to go out of your way to visit; and even if you're not a natural art lover, you should visit, as it might just change your mind.

Tate St Ives is directly above the beach, giving it a delightful atmosphere, particularly in summer when it chimes with seaside noise. Inside the bright, spacious galleries, you'll find modernist pieces that were created in the immediate vicinity of St Ives itself, or around west Cornwall. Special exhibitions change three times a year. As well as exhibiting local artists, Tate St Ives runs an Artist Residency programme, supporting new talent by providing bursaries and studio space in the town and exhibiting the resulting works. The gallery runs a daily programme of events including free talks and activities, usually with an audio loop and occasionally with a BSL interpreter.

Access is good on the whole, with a ramp and a lift to every floor and recently installed disabled toilets. The wheelchair route between Tate St Ives and the Barbara Hepworth Museum and Sculpture Garden (which Tate also manages) is up a cobbled street, past numerous gift shops and galleries. At the museum, one ramp takes you into Hepworth's sculpture workshop, and another into the tranquil garden housing her works. If you're bringing a wheelchair, you need to call ahead to let them know (☎01736 791102). Tours for visitors with visual disabilities can be arranged, and there is an audioguide too. Short video clips downloadable from the website, feature BSL interpreters detailing visitor information, including opening times.

Food & drink ▸▸ *Tate St Ives Café* is a light, modern space with great views, and serves hot lunches, sandwiches, cakes and puddings with clotted cream.

View from the helicopter

102 Helicopter to the Isles of Scilly, Cornwall

Address: The Heliport, Penzance TR18 3AP **Website:** www.islesofscillyhelicopter.com
Telephone: 01736 363871 **Hours:** Mon–Sat several flights daily, times vary seasonally **Dates:**
no flights Sun **Entry:** return fees vary depending on season & length of stay [A]£96–185
[under 2s]£20–53 [2–15s]£60–105; assistance dogs free; scenic flights available

The longest established scheduled helicopter service in the world, from Penzance to the
Isles of Scilly, carries tourists to their holidays and offers scenic flights, as well as serving as
a lifeline for the islands' inhabitants.

The flight takes just twenty minutes to either St Mary's or Tresco, some 28 miles
southwest of Land's End. You soar at remarkably low altitude along the Cornish coastline,
with fabulous views of the castle-like monastery of St Michael's Mount, before heading out
over the sea, swooping over fishing boats and wave-battered rocks. To get the best view,
choose one of the single seats on the left-hand side; or, if you can manage the walk, choose
one of the two seats at the rear with curved windows, giving even better panoramas of the
stunning scenery. Heading back, you take in Land's End, the famous Minack Cliff Theatre
carved into the granite overlooking Porthcurno cove, and dozens of other beaches, coves
and villages. It's a hugely enjoyable, rather self-indulgent way to spend an hour or two: if
you can, try to give yourself a few days on the islands themselves, with their gardens and
idyllic beaches, and leave a little holiday money in Tresco or St Mary's.

The heliport building is fully accessible with a small refreshment area and accessible
toilet. It is located just five minutes from the train station, from where there is a regular
shuttle bus to the heliport – you need to be able to manage one step to access this vehicle.
For drivers, the heliport has a pay car park (£7 per day). There are five fairly steep steps
up to the helicopter. If you can manage these, your wheelchair can be taken with you to the
door; if not you're transferred into a narrow wheelchair, hoisted into the helicopter, and
then transferred into your seat on board the aircraft.

Food & drink ▸▸ The *Renaissance Café Bar* (☎01736 366277), situated in the Wharfside
shopping centre in Penzance, has views of the Harbour, St Michael's Mount and across the
Bay to the Lizard. It is fully accessible with a disabled toilet.

ISLE OF MAN

CUMBRIA

LANCASHIRE

MERSEYSIDE

GREATER
MANCHESTER

CHESHIRE

The Northwest

The Northwest

Once gritty hotbeds of industry, the northern cities of Liverpool and Manchester have truly moved with the times, developing into vigorous urban centres with distinctive cultural identities – and two of the northwest's most popular destinations. For those who prefer a slower pace, the spectacularly scenic Lake District offers respite and, while visitor numbers are always high, finding a dale to call your own still remains a possibility.

103 Theatre by the Lake, Cumbria

Address: Lakeside, Keswick CA12 5DJ **Website:** www.theatrebythelake.co.uk **Telephone:** 01768 774411 **Hours:** performance days ticket office 9.30am until after the evening performance; non-performance days 9.30am–8pm (some parts of building close at 5pm) **Dates:** closed 25 Dec **Entry:** ticket prices vary depending on seat and production [C]free

It may not be what you'd expect to find on the banks of Derwent Water, but Theatre by the Lake – a registered charity funded from the Arts Council Lottery Fund – has succeeded brilliantly in bringing the dramatic arts to a part of the country more commonly associated with bracing walks and cloud-shrouded landscapes.

You would be hard pressed to find a more beautiful setting, or such a relaxed atmosphere, at a theatre anywhere else in the country. Virtually everyone attending will be on holiday or a weekend break, and there is always a sprinkling of walkers arriving still wearing their deerstalkers and brandishing sticks – not your usual metropolitan theatre crowd. Opened in 1999, and since then expanded, the complex now houses two stages: the large Main House which seats four hundred visitors, and the one-hundred-seater Studio. Each summer season the company produces a series of works, with an intelligently interlocking programme that enables visitors to comfortably see several different plays over the course of a long weekend. In addition, there's a year-round repertory programme, and the theatre hosts a string of annual festivals, including literature, jazz and film.

Reaching the venue is easy: there's a huge car park at the theatre with a dozen or so disabled bays just outside the entrance, and a wheelchair is available to help with transfer inside. If organised in advance, auditorium seating can be removed to create wheelchair spaces. The facilites for disabled people are generally good, with accessible toilets on all floors – though the restaurant's accessible toilet is tricky to get to. Pre-performance touch tours of the set can be booked, while captioned and audio-described performances are scheduled for certain shows – details are listed on the website. Assistance dogs are welcome in all areas of the building. Alternative versions of the programme can be requested.

Food & drink ▶▶ You'll find a full pre-theatre menu upstairs in the light and airy *Friend's Gallery* where you can relax with a glass of wine while taking in the views of the lake.

104–105 Walls Drive Trail and Ravenglass & Eskdale Steam Railway, Cumbria

Address: railway Ravenglass CA18 1SW **Website:** www.lake-district.gov.uk; www
.ravenglass-railway.co.uk **Telephone:** railway 01229 717171 **Hours:** trail no closures;
railway check website for timetable **Dates:** railway check website for seasonal variations
Entry: trail free; railway unlimited travel for 1 day [D]£10.80 [C]£10.80 [A]£10.80
[5–15s]£5.40; dogs £1.50; family tickets available

Ravenglass is the only coastal village in the Lake District – a wonderfully quiet spot,
where mountain scenery gives way to coastline, a world away from the tourist hotspots
of Bowness and Ambleside. Following the undemanding Walls Drive trail takes you
through magnificent Cumbrian countryside, culminating at the site of some significant
Roman remains.

Ravenglass car park is large and has accessible toilets – it's an excellent base to set off
from and is clearly signposted on the only road that leads into the village. The beginning of the walk skirts the station of the Ravenglass and Eskdale Steam Railway: when
you leave the car park, head towards the railway bridge, and then follow signs to the
Roman Bath House. The path slopes slightly from the car park but quickly becomes
level and is compactly surfaced along the entire scenic trail. After around thirty minutes of smooth progress, you reach the ruins of Glannoventa – a huge Roman fort,
perhaps once one in a string of defences built along the northwest coast. Much has been
destroyed and, apart from earthworks, all that now remains is the Bath House, one of
the largest existing Roman structures in England. It's possible to get inside and look
around – the level grass surface is firm if a little muddy following heavy rain, and there
is a bench to rest on nearby.

Ravenglass & Eskdale Steam Railway

From Ravenglass to the Bath House and back is little more than a mile. The village is a small and accessible place with smooth level roads and pavements throughout – its huge natural harbour is well worth a look when you return. If you'd like to see more of the area, the steam railway winds seven scenic miles inland past craggy Muncaster Fell, views of the Scafell range and through the Eskdale Valley. The four locomotives in service have accessible carriages and ramped access on and off the train. Many of the charming stations en route have level access, but not all are manned. The line ends at the Dalegarth station near Boot, which has a new visitor centre. The full return journey takes one hour and forty minutes.

Food & drink ▶▶ The award-winning and recently restored *Pennington Hotel* (ⓦ www.penningtonhotels.com) in Ravenglass has views of the village and out to sea. It has level access and is only metres away from the village car park.

106 Windermere Lake Cruises, Cumbria

Address: Bowness, Ambleside **Website:** www.windermere-lakecruises.co.uk **Telephone:** 01539 443360 **Hours:** schedules vary seasonally; check website **Dates:** closed 25 Dec **Entry:** prices vary depending on route taken, check website

Windermere is not just England's longest lake, it is perhaps almost its most beautiful. Certainly the rugged majesty of the Lake District scenery is spectacular, and taking a cruise is a gentle way to appreciate it.

You might think boats and piers don't mix with disabled passengers, but these cruises can be a great experience, even for wheelchair users – all that is required is a little advance research so you can decide which journey will best fit your needs. The cruise company that operates all the boats on Windermere offers numerous choices of journey – starting from Bowness, Waterhead (for Ambleside) and Lakeside – on a wide variety of vessels, for varying length of times (a full round trip takes ninety minutes). This means a range of options is open to disabled visitors. When you take the *Swan* from Bowness to Ambleside, for example, you'll find pier access is excellent and a perfectly adequate ramp takes you on deck. There's no wheelchair access to the upper deck or to the downstairs bar and toilets, but there are outside seating areas at both bow and stern, and a wonderfully roomy saloon with fabulous views and a café and shop. All the cruises are delightful, and provide an unforgettable experience.

All the relevant waterfront areas are step-free and there's generally plenty of parking, though few designated spaces. Ticket offices are easily reached, with induction loops, and staff are usually helpful and informative. None of the boats have accessible toilets, but they are available at each of the three landing stops. Only a couple of the largest boats are fully wheelchair accessible, while others have walking access from the pier and some special cruises have commentaries. There are timetables and maps on the website but for specific disability information and advice, call the company ahead.

Food & drink ▸▸ Windermere is in the heart of the Lakes – so there are endless opportunities for great food. Try child-friendly *Sheila's Cottage* (℡01539 433079) in Ambleside.

107 Blackwell the Arts and Crafts House, Cumbria

Address: Bowness-on-Windermere LA23 3JT **Website:** www.blackwell.org.uk **Telephone:** 01539 446139 **Hours:** Apr–Oct daily 10.30am–5pm; Jan–Mar & Nov daily 10.30am–4pm **Dates:** closed 25–26 Dec **Entry:** [D]£6.50 [C]free [A]£6.50 [5–15s]£3.80

Blackwell, close to the banks of Windermere, was designed by architect MH Baillie Scott for Sir Edward Holt, a Manchester brewing magnate. Completed in 1900 as a prestigious holiday house, it's the archetypal Arts and Crafts home. Combined with its stunning location in the centre of the Lake District, it offers a tranquil, civilised step away from the nearby tourist crush.

The charitable Lakeland Arts Trust, which looks after Blackwell, has spent millions restoring the house after the ravages of unsympathetic previous owners, and the benefits are obvious in every room. So much of the extraordinary original interior remains in the house that it has become the focal point of the Arts and Crafts trail in the area. The library holds a specialist collection of books on the movement – call the curator in advance if you want to consult them. The shop has plenty to offer too, and there are changing exhibitions of art, ceramics and crafts throughout the year.

Blackwell has parking for about fifty cars, but it's best to arrive early at busy times. The house is spacious, so it is naturally very accessible. There are lifts to upper floors, and only a few rooms can't be reached by wheelchair due to the occasional short flight of stairs. Staff will show you a book of photographs of these areas so you can acquaint yourself with what has been missed. There are accessible toilets in the house and next to the tearoom.

Food & drink ▸▸ With home-made lemonade, cream teas and the "Sublime Pudding of the Day" advertised, you won't want to go further than the award-winning tearoom to eat, where the walls are adorned with quirky paintings, and the lake views are stunning.

108 Blackpool Tower, Lancashire

Address: The Promenade, Blackpool FY1 4BJ **Website:** www.theblackpooltower.co.uk **Telephone:** 01253 622242 **Hours:** daily opens 10am; closing varies seasonally and depending on venue & events; last entrance 1 hour before closing **Dates:** closed 25–26 Dec; variations for venues & events **Entry:** prices vary seasonally; online discounts available

Blackpool Tower and its ancillary attractions are the epitome of the British day at the seaside. Somehow, the tower seems to have survived its kitsch reputation and stood the test of time to retain its own ironic appeal.

Whatever the weather, there's plenty to see. The tower boasts much more than a trip to the top – although this can still take your breath away, especially if you do the Walk of Faith across the glass floor. The comfortable lift takes you over four hundred feet above the earth, where you can see straight down to the ground and as far afield as Wales and the Lake District. You can also enjoy the excitement of the traditional "Mookys Circus of Dreams" (depending on your mobility, you can even join a circus skills class) and the truly magnificent Victorian splendour of the tower Ballroom, where you can enjoy high tea while the dancing takes place. Alternatively, you can terrify the kids on the Jurassic Walk in the 3D Cinema or tire them out in Jungle Jim's Adventureland.

The tower has no dedicated parking of its own. There are plenty of spaces only two minutes away, in outdoor and multistorey car parks: both have designated spaces, but expect them to be very busy. If you'd rather arrive by public transport, note that the railway station is a ten-minute walk away, although bus and coach stations are closer. Sadly the trams are not accessible. Because of its Victorian origins, the tower is not particularly spacious or well lit, and accessible toilets are only available on levels one and five. All the attractions are accessible, though, with the exception of the ballroom balcony. Seating for disabled visitors in the circus is limited, so booking is essential. Wheelchair users are asked to visit with a helper.

Food & drink ▶▶ You don't need to leave the tower to eat, and there is plenty of choice: *Bickerstaffe's Buffet* serves pizzas and pastas, *Restaurant 1894* dishes up roasts and curries, and you can tuck into a slice of cake at the *Tower Coffee Company*.

109 RSPB Ribble Discovery Centre, Lancashire

Address: Fairhaven Lake, Lytham St Annes FY8 1BD **Website:** www.rspb.org.uk; www .fairhavenlake.com **Telephone:** 01253 796292 **Hours:** 10am–5pm **Dates:** closed 25–26 Dec **Entry:** free, with variations for some events

Less than seven miles down the coast from the razzmatazz of Blackpool, you'll find yourself in this oasis of calm on the Fylde Peninsula, between Lytham town and the sea. This is the ideal place to take the kids for a more edifying run-around in the fresh air before a trip to the tower.

The Ribble Discovery Centre at Fairhaven Lake (also known as Ashton Marine Park) is an education and observation centre on a 650-yard-long artificial lake, created by enclosing tidal sands and mud banks. The Ribble estuary is an important habitat for many species of birds, in fact it is the second most important estuary site in England – home to 250,000 birds at the height of the season. In the spring, redshanks and lapwings nest in the area, and at other times there are black-tailed godwits, pink-footed geese, wigeons and golden plovers. The centre organises bird walks and illustrated talks and runs a fully accessible shop, an education room with interpretation boards and sensory bird-call buttons, and CCTV to view the lake. Although funded by Fylde Council, the RSPB and corporate donations, it's not actually an official reserve, so hides and screens can't be constructed.

The lakeshore is very accessible for people with mobility problems. There's adequate parking, and a good, hard, level path all around the lake – this is less than a mile long and it usually takes about thirty minutes to get around it. There are some benches dotted at points along the way, and if you are wheelchair user, you can receive assistance from a volunteer if required. There is also a wheelchair accessible boat for water trips. The staff in the education facility try very hard to involve people with sensory disabilities and volunteers are on hand to attend to any specific requests. On your way around the lake, you'll come across an independent café and a RADAR-key-accessible toilet too.

Food & drink ▶▶ The café on the lake is accessible, but Fairhaven Lake is only a short walk from the seaside charm of Lytham, and a short drive from the bright lights of Blackpool, where there's lots of food to choose from.

THE NORTHWEST

110 Manchester United Stadium Tour and Museum

Address: Old Trafford Stadium, Sir Matt Busby Way M16 0RA **Website:** www.manutd .com **Telephone:** 0161 868 8000 **Hours:** daily 9.30am–5pm; tours every 10 mins 9.40am– 4.30pm **Dates:** tours not available on match days; museum closed on all weekend match days **Entry:** tour & museum [D]£12.50 [C]free [A]£12.50 [child]£8.50 [Con]£7.50–8.50

The Theatre of Dreams is certainly a dream destination for wheelchair users. It's accessible throughout and you don't have to be a Manchester United fanatic to enjoy the stadium tour or the museum.

Consistently a member of the top three richest clubs in the world, MUFC has money to burn, and it shows in the first-class facilities. Disabled visitors receive excellent customer service – stadium tours are simply arranged by phone, with helpful advice available. You're sure to be advised to book a slot early in the day, to avoid the bigger groups. The tour experience is remarkably accessible, and as comprehensive as you could wish for, covering the immaculate pitch, the changing rooms, players' tunnel and dug-out, plus the museum, with its Trophy Room, kit displays, and the Hall of Fame of the club's playing legends. The interactive archives are fascinating – the club has a very full history, with many stories of success to tell, but of course, there is also the Munich tragedy to be remembered. If you come for a match, you'll experience state-of-the-art disabled provision. It's impressive that the normal business of the stadium is as wonderfully accessible as the tour. Services for disabled supporters are second to none, with hundreds of wheelchair-plus-companion seats available, including forty with their own sockets for live match commentary.

On arrival, you'll be personally greeted and directed to a choice of disabled parking spaces. The excellent service continues throughout: at every step there are helpful staff, and everywhere is well lit, clearly signposted, smooth and step-free, with ramps or lifts where needed. Individual helpers are available too.

Food & drink ▶▶ The *Red Café* is completely accessible, and a good place to study your complimentary copy of the Disabled Supporter's Booklet. Always busy with fans, this comfortable and welcoming environment is open every day except match days.

111 The Royal Exchange Theatre, Manchester

Address: St Ann's Square M2 7HD **Website:** www.royalexchangetheatre.co.uk **Telephone:** 0161 833 9833 **Hours:** performance times vary **Dates:** closed 25 Dec **Entry:** variations depending on performance and seat [C]free

Situated within Manchester's vast former Cotton Exchange, the futuristic Royal Exchange Theatre demonstrates an electrifying mix of ancient and modern that works on every level. This is an exciting place to visit and the most prestigious theatre in the north.

Opened in 1976, most of the steel-and-glass structure of the Royal Exchange Theatre is suspended from four giant columns, erected inside what was once the largest trading hall in the world. Productions in the main theatre are enthralling, with its in-the-round design (the biggest in Britain) meaning every member of the audience feels a connection with the performers. Every season brings a mix of classics and new work, and there is always a mix of light and dark: 2010 promises diversity in the shape of the dystopian *Nineteen Eighty-Four* and the farcical *Charley's Aunt*, among many other productions. Together with the work of the innovative backstage crew, shows are always memorable. There is also a smaller studio space, where new and more experimental works are put on for short runs. With pre-performance jazz, Q&A sessions after some performances, and theatre tours, visits here are always accompanied by a sense of energy and enthusiasm. There is a very decent restaurant, bars, a shop and continually changing displays, all contained on one huge floor, which makes navigation very easy.

Arriving by car, you'll find twenty or more Blue Badge bays within two minutes of the theatre. Access to the building is by steps or a very comfortable lift. If the lift is out of action, use one of several others in the building. Staff make every effort to accommodate visitors with any type of disability. Wheelchair spaces in the main theatre are located on the second row (the fixed seating can be removed if booked in advance) with excellent unimpeded views. The first row of seats is moveable and low level, and can be removed (if they haven't already been booked) if your wheelchair is very large and can't fit in the second row space. The third row of seats is raised, so disabled visitors can enjoy the performance, comfortable in the knowledge they are not blocking the view for the patrons sitting behind them. Some performances are BSL-interpreted and most are audio-described. Studio seats are usually not reserved but an exception will be made if you make a request. There are plenty of accessible toilets.

Food & drink ▶▶ *The Round* is the perfect location for pre-theatre dining, lunch or dinner. You can have an excellent meal with friendly service, relaxed in the knowledge that your theatre seat is only yards away.

112 Manchester Velodrome

Address: National Cycling Centre, Stuart Street M11 4DQ **Website:** www.manchestervelodrome .com **Telephone:** 0161 223 2244 **Hours:** daily 8am–10.30pm; event times vary **Dates:** closed 25–26 Dec & bank holidays **Entry:** watching sessions free; sessions start from £5; event costs vary [C]free

After the cycling triumphs achieved by the TeamGB and ParalympicsGB cyclists in Beijing (including Darren Kenny's four paralympic gold medals), visiting the home of British cycling has become hugely popular.

Manchester Velodrome is England's only Olympic-standard indoor track, one of the fastest in the world, and the place where the conquest of world biking was planned and prepared. Built for the Commonwealth Games in 2002, and part of the Sport City complex, Manchester Velodrome is a huge structure, set on a spacious site, with no design compromises. Spectator seating runs all around the outside of the track. There's a large central space inside the track which can be used for other sports, and it's even possible to fit temporary seating here to watch basketball, for example, while the cyclists practise on the track. The velodrome offers cycling classes for all ages and abilities, and individuals with disabilities can contact the venue and discuss special lessons. Currently, anybody who can

Manchester Velodrome

ride a two-wheel bike and understand basic instructions will be considered for enrolment. At the time of writing, a new class for severely visually impaired people who need to ride a tandem was being developed. Five bikes had been donated, and instructors were being trained – the operation was planned to be up and running by Spring 2010. If cycling isn't your bag then you may want to visit for the National Badminton Championships, Paralympic Wheelchair Basketball or even the National Cheerleaders' Championships. And with the City of Manchester Stadium (home of Man City), the home track of one of the country's best athletics clubs, Sale Harriers, and the National Squash Centre of Excellence all across the road, you're in sporting heaven.

The Velodrome has huge parking areas with many spaces. There is level or slightly ramped access from outside to the main concourse. Around the track there are wheelchair and companion spaces that have superb views. RADAR-key-accessible toilets and retail facilities around the concourse are very accessible. For events in the centre of the track it is even possible to enter the Velodrome via an outside accessible ramped entrance which brings you out at the track centre. Alternatively, there's a lift from reception to get you there, though it is small.

Food & drink ▶▶ The café on site has three hot meal choices daily, and there is always a vegetarian option – but Rusholme's world famous curry mile is just a short drive away.

113 Knowsley Safari Park, Merseyside

Address: Prescot L34 4AN Website: www.knowsleysafariexperience.co.uk Telephone: 0151 430 9009 Hours: summer daily 10am–4pm; winter daily 10.30am–3pm Dates: closed 25–26 Dec Entry: [D]£9 [C]free [A]£12 [3–15s]£9 [Con]£9

Knowsley Safari Park, in the grounds of historic Knowsley House near Liverpool, is a conservation-led, drive-through wildlife sanctuary with active breeding programmes, where you can come face to face with all manner of exotic animals from emus to elephants. The main safari route is covered in your own vehicle, so there are no access problems there, while a reduced route, passing many of the paddocks, can be followed in a wheelchair or on a powered scooter.

Once you've entered the park, you can do the drive as many times as you like and are guaranteed close encounters with the impressive wildlife. Some of the rarest highlights include tigers, white rhinos, a pack of highly endangered African wild dogs, beautiful lechwe antelope, shy and exceedingly rare bongo antelope, scimitar-horned oryx, Père David's deer and two-humped Bactrian camels. The park also has less vulnerable species, such as lion, elephant, giraffe and wildebeest. If you drive through Monkey Jungle the encounter with the baboons may be a bit too close for comfort, as they clamber all over the vehicles, occasionally taking a souvenir away with them (there's a car-friendly route for visitors who would rather avoid them). In the pedestrian area, the Bug House has excellent, low displays, the upstairs Sea Lion Show has a ground-level side entrance, and the Giraffe House has easy access and viewing. If you're a meerkat fan, you'll love watching the on-site artist carving away to make little wooden sculptures of them – you can buy the finished article to take home as a souvenir of your day.

> "I find it difficult to walk, so this was a very good place for me because I could stay seated."
>
> **Mavis Reast, Fleetwood**

Arriving is no problem, as there is excellent signage and a huge amount of parking, though relatively few designated wide spaces. By the car park are two large, fully equipped accessible toilets with ramped access, and there are other accessible toilets around the site. In the pedestrian area, there are smooth, wide paths and lots of benches. Even the little land train has a special carriage for wheelchair users.

Food & drink ▶▶ *Oasis*, the large café-cum-restaurant is spacious, family-friendly and centrally located, but has fixed seating. Or you can take your chances with a picnic, under the watchful eyes of the monkeys who'll happily pinch your lunch!

114 The Albert Dock, Liverpool

Address: Liverpool L3 4BB Website: www.albertdock.com Telephone: visitor centre 0151 233 2008 Hours: variations depending on venue, check individually Dates: closed 25–26 Dec; check venues individually Entry: docks free; other venues vary, check individually

Originally redeveloped in the 1980s, the Albert Dock has become a major tourist attraction. The complex sits on the banks of the Mersey, with views, walks and grassy areas to play and picnic on.

On the back of Liverpool's status as European City of Culture 2008, the area is receiving huge investment. The Merseyside Maritime Museum and International Slavery Museum are both magnificent, with several floors of superb exhibits and installations in a converted dockside warehouse – they place Liverpool at the centre of the world's trading history and bring alive the great status of the port. Tate Liverpool is a nationally important gallery drawing visitors from around the world. And of course you can't visit

View to the Royal Liver building from the Albert Dock

Liverpool without paying homage to the Beatles – The Beatles Story doesn't disappoint. Finally, you could finish the day with a concert at the brand new Echo Arena, or a drink and some retail therapy in the Liverpool One entertainment complex.

There is designated outdoor parking plus a huge new multistorey, with lots of accessible spaces. The venues have many staff that try very hard to accommodate the needs of all visitors. The two museums are very accessible with plenty of lifts, accessible toilets and hearing loops, while great care has been taken with signage and information. Tate Liverpool has similar facilities, plus wheelchairs, BSL-interpreted tours and touch tours. The Beatles Story has lift access and portable ramps – the basement venue looks a little awkward at first, but it's a surprisingly comfortable and accessible place to visit. The Arena has wheelchair access and a choice of seats as excellent as you would expect from a new concert venue. Outside, there are a few challenges, including the occasional slight gradient, flagstones and cobbled surfaces, but the whole area is crisscrossed with hard paths, making all areas accessible.

> "The Albert Dock is a marvellous showcase of how work can be done to modernise heritage buildings."
>
> **Keith Porter, Milton Keynes**

Food & drink ▸▸ The choice of places to eat reflects the international history of the port – from the Pan American Club (☎0151 702 5840, ⓦwww.panam-venue.co.uk) to Indian food at the Spice Lounge (☎0151 707 2202, ⓦwww.spicelounge.uk.com), and a traditional boozing experience at The Pumphouse (☎0151 709 2367).

115 Catton Hall Shooting Ground, Cheshire

Address: Bradley Lane, Frodsham WA6 7EX **Website:** www.cattonhall.co.uk **Telephone:** 01928 788295 **Hours:** contact venue to book **Dates:** closed 25–26 Dec **Entry:** prices vary, clay-pigeon session from £45; quad-trekking from £55; minimum age 18

This is the perfect way to get rid of any pent-up frustrations – shoot them out of the sky. You can book a one-to-one session of clay pigeon shooting with an instructor, or shoot in a small group, and quickly become proficient at picking off the clays. It's surprisingly addictive.

If clay pigeons don't grab you, you might be interested in traditional archery, including longbow or crossbow, air rifle-shooting and falconry, which are also on offer. The club at Catton Hall doesn't offer special classes or facilities for disabled people, but the staff do all they can to help every visitor get involved. Positions for falconry, and targets for rifles and archery, are set up just outside the clubhouse, where the terrain is decent. Elsewhere the site is hilly, but there are solid paths and lots of willing helpers – although it's probably wise not to visit in bad weather. Visitors can hire quad bikes and if you are able to transfer from a wheelchair, have good balance and use the twist-grip controls, you can try some rough and wet cross-country quad-trekking, along a nine-mile route through the estate.

Whichever sport you choose, be sure to get directions from the website or study a map well before you set off, as Catton Hall isn't signposted in Frodsham, and can be very tricky to find. The site isn't perfect – there are steep slopes, but you can ensure level parking by calling ahead so staff can save you a suitable space. After an activity, you can relax in the huge shooting lodge (with a single step at the entrance but fully accessible inside) or sit out on the veranda and watch everyone else take their aim. At the time of writing, a new toilet extension was under way.

Food & drink ▸▸ The shooting-lodge has a large and airy restaurant, serving light snacks throughout the day and three-course evening meals.

116 Quarry Bank Mill and Styal Estate, Cheshire

Address: Styal, Wilmslow SK9 4LA **Website:** www.nationaltrust.org.uk **Telephone:** 01625 527468 **Hours:** check ahead for seasonal variations **Dates:** closed 24–25 Dec; check ahead for seasonal variations **Entry:** mill, apprentice house & garden [D]£13.50 [C]free [A]£13.50 [child]£6.70; parking £4

Quarry Bank Mill is one of the greatest industrial heritage sites in the UK, and home to the most powerful working waterwheel in Europe.

This former cotton factory is exceptionally well preserved – the National Trust conserves and manages the site. The ground floor exhibition charts the history of Quarry Bank, but it's not until you witness the waterwheel working, and hear the noise as it begins to drive the two looms, that you get a sense of what factory life must have been

Quarry Bank Mill

like. The four-storey Mill is the centrepiece of a visit, but also within the grounds is the Apprentice House – costumed guides give tours of this building that illuminate the sacrifices made by the children who worked in the factory. Disabled visitors can see the schoolroom, kitchen and parlour on the ground floor. The tour then moves upstairs to the inaccessible medical room and dormitory, but an audio link and book of photographs are provided for visitors who can't make it up there.

The National Trust is aware that access is tricky to some parts of the site and the friendly staff do all they can to provide assistance. It isn't possible to park by the entrances to the buildings, and the path from the car park is lengthy and steep – so the Trust runs a fully accessible shuttle bus to transport disabled visitors from their car to a handy, but part-cobbled, drop-off point by the admission kiosk. The bus is free and operates every thirty minutes between 11.30am and 3pm. There is a specially provided accessible entrance into the Mill, and inside more platform lifts allow access to each level, apart from the top floor gallery – to reach that you have to pop back to the accessible entrance, and then re-enter the building via a bridge on the south side. There are two wheelchairs available to borrow. If you visit in a powered scooter, be aware that some walkways are narrow and that the platform lifts may be out of bounds to you. Unfortunately safety limitations restrict too many wheelchairs being present on the site at one time. Braille and large print guides are available.

The wider Styal estate has extensive grounds, but there are many steep gradients to manage, and a powered scooter is required to explore fully. However, the recently opened eight-acre "Secret Garden", close to the Mill, is fully accessible for wheelchair users and incredibly picturesque.

Food & drink ▸▸ Head to well-heeled Wilmslow for a bite to eat. The fun *Chilli Banana* (Ⓦwww.chillibanana.co.uk) Thai restaurant has ramped access via the front of the King's Arms Hotel.

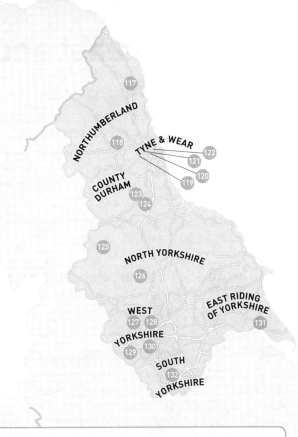

The Northeast and Yorkshire

The Northeast and Yorkshire

The northeast is full of cultural attractions, from the handsome university city of Durham and the vibrant, youthful Newcastle-upon-Tyne to the majestic fortresses that line the lovely Northumberland coast. Nicknamed "God's own county" for its rolling green hills and serene valleys, Yorkshire is Britain's largest county. The historic city of York is a major tourist draw, while the metropolis of Leeds and the craggy coastline around Whitby are just as diverting.

117 The Alnwick Garden, Northumberland

Address: Denwick Lane, Alnwick NE66 1YU Website: www.alnwickgarden.com Telephone: 01665 511350 Hours: daily Apr–Sep 10am–6pm; Oct–Mar 10am–4pm Dates: closed 25 Dec Entry: [D]£7.50 [C]free [A]£10 [child]1p only [Con]£7.50; prices include a £1 donation to the charitable trust that runs the garden

Twelve years ago, the Duchess of Northumberland set up a trust to transform an area of derelict wasteland into a spectacular contemporary garden – thankfully her vision was realised, and the Alnwick Garden has become the third most visited garden attraction in England.

But this is no typical country estate – in fact, with its colourful Cherry Orchard, meandering Bamboo Labyrinth and watery Serpent Garden, it feels more like a fantasy land. Water and light are used to theatrical effect at Alnwick: the huge central Grand Cascade is unlike any run-of-the-mill water features you may have seen elsewhere – its fountains and jets erupt on a spectacularly complex cycle, while visitors try to dodge them. Elsewhere there are places to paddle and a mysterious bubbling pool – it goes without saying you'll need to bring a change of clothing for children. The plants grown in the infamous Poison Garden require a special licence from the Home Office, and can only be viewed on guided tours. But perhaps the most enchanting feature at Alnwick is the Tree House – in this huge cedar, pine and redwood building, trees grow through the floor and wooden walkways lead outdoors into the surrounding treetops, while a roaring log fire keeps everyone cosy. One of the world's largest tree houses, it's a remarkably accessible structure.

> "We had a super day at Alnwick. Every area was perfectly accessible and there was so much to see that I almost used up the battery on my powered scooter."
>
> **Ishbel MacKinnon,
> Isle of Mull**

The Alnwick Garden

It seems that considerations for disabled visitors were at the forefront of design plans. Disabled parking is close to all the main buildings and garden features, so you don't have to trek for miles to get to the best bits and back again. The garden has smooth, solid surfaces although it is large, with some slight gradients. Powered scooters and wheelchairs are available – check out the scooter-use map available on the website. At the time of writing, the charitable trust was raising funds to construct an all-ability adventure playground as well as a Garden for the Senses where visitors would be encouraged to experience the sounds and smells of the raised beds and watercourses while blindfolded.

Food & drink ▶▶ The restaurant in the Tree House is a fairly pricey but magical place to eat. If you'd prefer something a bit cheaper, try *The Pavilion Café*, which is equally accessible and overlooks the Grand Cascade.

118 High House Farm Brewery, Northumberland

Address: Matfen NE20 0RG **Website:** www.highhousefarmbrewery.co.uk **Telephone:** 01661 886192 **Hours:** Mon–Tue & Thu–Sun 10.30am–5pm **Dates:** closed Wed; check ahead for Christmas & New Year dates **Entry:** [D]£4.50 [C]free [A]£4.50 [12–17s]£2 [Con]£4.50

Not far from Hadrian's Wall, this award-winning brewery is housed in converted, listed buildings on the two-hundred-acre High House Farm. It's a working farm, and visitors realise that on arrival, when greeted with all the traditional farmyard smells, but these are quickly swamped with the thick, hoppy scent of the brewing process.

Fourth-generation farmer Steven Urwin founded the brewery in 2003, and produces a constantly expanding range of seasonal beers. Ferocious Fred is an almost black ale, named after the farm's grumpy and boisterous bull, while Nettle Ale is brewed to a fourteenth-century recipe with comfrey and ginger replacing the hops. On the real ale tour, you can learn about the beer-making process, and sample some of these specialities too. Everything in the brewery is housed in one complex. Entering from the large car park you are directed up an external staircase, but you can enter independently downstairs, where there's a platform lift. Upstairs you'll find a large tearoom and a bar serving High House ales, and a spacious shop, with bottled ales and local delicacies. This is where you enter the brewery and the ale tour. A cut-away floor allows visitors to listen to the tour guide while overlooking the brewing equipment below – a real boon for disabled visitors because it provides a unique perspective, and allows you to avoid the hassle of navigating around the tanks. On the tour, walkers descend the staircase located here, to get a hands-on experience, and a platform lift is available so everyone can participate fully.

Outside, after the tour, there is a circular country lane walk, or a farm walk, though it's not recommended for wheelchair users because of the uneven surfaces and mud. The car park is large and level, but has loose shale that wheelchair users will need to take care with. The old shell of the building remains, but the interior has been cleverly modernised so, once inside, this is a surprisingly disabled-friendly place, and every element of the tour can be accessed. There's a good toilet, small ramps for occasional changes in floor levels, solid smooth wooden floors and lots of space.

Food & drink ▶▶ There is a very comfortable restaurant next to the visitor centre, serving hot lunches, hearty dinners and two-course hot suppers on some evenings. Keep an eye out for the traditional apple and raspberry crumble – perfect washed down with a pint of High House ale!

119 Derwent Valley Railway Path, Tyne & Wear

Address: behind Blaydon Rugby Club, Hexham Road, Swalwell NE16 3AD **Website:** www .durham.gov.uk (search under leisure and culture) **Telephone:** 0191 414 2106 **Hours:** visitor centre Mon–Fri noon–2pm, Sat & Sun noon–5pm **Dates:** closed 25–26 Dec **Entry:** free

The Derwent Valley Railway Path follows the disused railway line along an incredibly varied route past beautiful, wild countryside, historic parkland and reclaimed industrial sites.

This is a wonderful outdoor experience for people of all ages and abilities – there are some varying surfaces, but much of the path is level tarmac. The constantly changing views can be accredited to the fact that this isn't a simple, single trail, but actually a complex set of routes. It is straightforward to follow though: starting from the Swalwell visitor centre, you can follow the river along one of the wheelchair accessible paths (on each bank), through the park on the Derwent Walk. You'll travel through woods and meadows, circle lakes and ponds and cross the river. There is another visitor centre at Thornley Wood, and several accessible observation hides overlooking bird-feeding stations, ponds and wetlands – you could spot woodpeckers, sparrowhawks, badgers and even otters. The route travels through the release zone of the Northern Kite Project where 94 red kites were released between 2004 and 2006 – the colony is flourishing, and you'll see the birds circling and swooping in the sky. This is also an area rich in historical sites: along the railway line trail itself, you'll come across the Nine Arches Viaduct and Derwenthaugh Park (the site of the Derwenthaugh Coke Works and Crowley's

Ironworks), as well as older sites, including the nineteenth-century Axwell Hall, thirteenth-century Hollinside Manor and the Gibside Estate, which dates from 1620.

The Swalwell visitor centre has accessible parking, a disabled toilet and an information point. From there, you head off along eight miles of wide, tarmac paths (four miles out, four miles back) with virtually no gradients, and the option of a further network of more challenging footpaths. There is another accessible toilet just past the halfway mark at Thornley Woodlands Centre (also fully accessible). If this sounds too tough, or time is limited, note that shorter circular routes can be taken by crossing the river near Clockburn Lake or returning from the Nine Arches Viaduct, just before Thornley. Alternatively, you can pick up the trail at any of six accessible points from lay-bys on the A694.

Food & drink ▶▶ You'll need a flask of hot coffee to keep you going, but afterwards you can warm up with a gourmet cuppa at the fascinating *Pumphrey's Coffee Roasting Rooms* (☎0191 414 4510, ⓦwww.pumphreys-coffee.co.uk) in Blaydon.

120 BALTIC Centre for Contemporary Art, Tyne & Wear

Address: Gateshead Quays, South Shore Road NE8 3BA **Website:** www.balticmill.com
Telephone: 0191 478 1810 **Hours:** Mon & Wed–Sun 10am–6pm, Tue 10.30am–6pm **Dates:** closed 1 Jan & 25–26 Dec **Entry:** free

The BALTIC Centre for Contemporary Art

This huge "art factory" is stunningly located on the banks of the Tyne, housed in the old Baltic Mill – a Hovis flour mill opened in 1950. Right next to the Millennium Bridge, BALTIC boasts dazzling views of the Newcastle waterfront as well as a constantly rotating programme of progressive exhibitions.

The original postwar shell of the building has been kept and a cutting-edge structure fitted inside. The gallery floors are extensive, and exhibitions are on display generally for weeks or months at a time. There is no permanent collection – the emphasis here is on showcasing innovative and occasionally provocative art. Much space is given over to local artists and community projects, but works by famous names have previously been housed at BALTIC, including a retrospective of the conceptual work of Yoko Ono and a unique, electronically produced "visual music" exhibition by Brian Eno of Roxy Music fame.

Designated disabled parking is alongside the building and in other spots nearby. The entrance to BALTIC is reached by a rough brick ramp, so if you are in a chair, make sure your tyres are fully inflated. The staff seem to be well versed in the accessible features of the building, many of which are very good. The lifts to each floor are huge glass constructions; the shop is bright and easy to get around; the toilets are well designed; and walking sticks, powered scooters, manual wheelchairs and tri-wheel walkers are available to hire. There has recently been a marked improvement in the accessibility of the signage and written information in the building. Regular tours of the exhibitions can be BSL-interpreted if required and audio and Braille versions of the What's On guide can be provided, as can adapted computers and adult changing rooms (on request). An impressively comprehensive list of facilities for disabled people appears on the website.

Food & drink ▸▸ The ground floor *Café Bar* has plenty of accessible tables and chairs, a licensed bar and outdoor seating. But for great modern British food, and unrivalled views of the city, try the highly rated restaurant *Six* on the BALTIC rooftop.

121 The Sage Gateshead, Tyne & Wear

Address: St Mary's Square, Gateshead Quays NE8 2JR **Website:** www.thesagegateshead .org **Telephone:** 0191 443 4661 **Hours:** daily 9am–9pm; performance end times vary **Dates:** closed 25–26 Dec **Entry:** building free; prices vary depending on performance & seat

Designed by Norman Foster, the remarkable Sage Gateshead sits high above the Tyne, like a great soap bubble of steel and glass. Built to be the northeast's premier concert venue, it hosts music events from classical to rock, from brass to jazz and from folk to soukous.

The now iconic outer shell houses three major spaces. Hall One is a 1700-seater, state-of-the-art concert hall with extraordinarily good acoustics, capable of showcasing the Northern Sinfonia and a solo artist equally well. Hall Two is smaller and more experimental – a ten-sided space with many movable seats where the stage can be reconfigured and even transformed into a dancefloor. The third venue, the Northern Rock Foundation Hall, is a rehearsal and participation space. The Sage is a fine, enlivening place to attend a performance – in 2010, acts including Don McLean and Katie Melua will showcase their talents there.

There's Blue Badge parking right outside the front door and an abundance of properly designated disabled spaces around the outside. All of them lead to simple, level access to the building. The whole structure is open, uncluttered and free of steps. Whether in toilet changing areas (plenty of accessible toilets on every level), loops, venue audibility, ease of movement from one point to another, or low surfaces in retail areas, designers have clearly given access issues careful thought, and put their decisions into practice. It's a very welcoming space, too, with positive, well-informed staff. A full access guide is available online or from the venue. If there's one – relatively minor – criticism to be made, it's that the coordinated design results in some dark areas and occasionally poor colour contrast that won't be helpful for visually impaired visitors.

Food & drink ▸▸ Outside the auditoria, a very large public concourse houses the *Sir Michael Straker Café*, bar, chill-out areas and shops: sit down with a coffee or a beer and survey the brilliant view.

122 Seven Stories: The Centre for Children's Books, Tyne & Wear

Address: 30 Lime Street, Ouseburn Valley NE1 2PQ **Website:** www.sevenstories.org.uk
Telephone: 0845 271 0777 **Hours:** Mon–Sat 10am–5pm, Sun 10am–4pm **Dates:** closed 25–26 Dec **Entry:** [D]£4.50 [C]£4.50 [A]£5.50 [child]£4.50 [Con]£4.50

This very special and unique centre – a registered charity whose trustees include Quentin Blake and Philip Pullman – brings books alive for children. Not a conventional bookshop, nor a library, Seven Stories uses every technique possible to provoke children's imaginations and involve them in the wonder of books and reading.

The lowest floor of this converted warehouse is home to the Creation Station, with various activities aimed at school groups. There is a light and airy café on level 2, where a gradual slope takes you to the well-designed reception on level 3, with its dropped counter, hearing loop, and spaces to sit. And this is where you'll find a wonderful, colourful bookshop, with displays and activities in abundance. But the fun really starts on the next few floors: there are exhibitions on a century of children's fiction, from Toad Hall to Pooh Corner, and mischievous characters in Up to Mischief with Horrid Henry. Original manuscripts and artwork are on display too; talks are occasionally given by authors and illustrators; and the magical roof area is a space for storytelling and dressing-up. Seven Stories isn't just for children – but for anyone who enjoys reading.

Unfortunately, car parking is a problem: there are no designated spaces and the streets in the area are narrow and busy. If you don't want to battle with this, the yellow Quaylink bus is highly recommended – it gets you to within a two-minute walk or push of the centre. Once you're here, you'll find the building interior – designed for children, and with DDA-compliancy in mind – is very accessible. There are low levels, wide passageways for pushchairs, bright colours and lots of contrast: features that work well for children and adults alike. There's a large lift to all levels, though you may need a lot of patience, as it's in constant use with buggies.

Food & drink ▸▸ The fully accessible *Cool Cat Café* serves child friendly and healthy dishes that are named after famous children's books. Head into Newcastle if you'd prefer something more sophisticated.

123 Low Barns Nature Reserve, County Durham

Address: Witton-le-Wear, Bishop Auckland DL14 0AG **Website:** www.durhamwt.co.uk
Telephone: 01388 488728 **Hours:** reserve daily 9am–4.30pm; visitor centre Mon–Fri
10am–4.30pm, Sat & Sun 10am–4pm **Dates:** closed 1 Jan & 25 Dec **Entry:** free; car park
£2.50

Low Barns Nature Reserve is in a secluded location in West Durham. Based around three old gravel lakes in a meander of the River Wear, it affords easy access to many types of habitat and wildlife – for such a small area there is incredible diversity here.

Visitors regularly see roe deer, stoats and even otters on the circular walk around the lakes. Starting from the visitor centre, this walk is less than two miles long, but has an option to detour to one of the observations hides. There are four hides in all, giving you great views of Marston Lake with its islands and marshes; West Lake with its reed beds and wet pasture grazed by Exmoor ponies; and the ancient Alder Wood. There is a butterfly garden, coot pond, observation tower, a wonderful boardwalk through the reed beds and also several winter-feeding stations that attract a huge variety of birds. Look out for brilliant kingfishers and, in summer, even migrant pied flycatchers.

This is a very accessible site. There is tarmac parking (which was being extended at the time of writing) and an accessible toilet. Paths are level and firm, with few gradients, though they can get muddy and have some patches of loose chippings filling puddle areas – powered scooters will have no trouble, but manual wheelchair users may need assistance. The paths that lead to the hides are inclined, but well surfaced, while the boardwalk is flat and wide. All the hides are spacious, with low windows. The only inaccessible feature is the observation tower, but a video link is provided if you can't manage the climb.

Food & drink ▸▸ The visitor centre has a very welcome coffee shop, which is run by volunteers. Otherwise you'll have no problem finding a lovely local pub in the local Witton, Crook and Bishop Auckland areas.

124 Locomotion: National Railway Museum, Shildon, County Durham

Address: Shildon DL4 1PQ **Website:** www.locomotion.uk.com **Telephone:** 01388 777999
Hours: Apr–Oct daily 10am–5pm; Oct–Apr daily 10am–4pm **Dates:** closed 1–2 Jan & 22–31
Dec **Entry:** free, with variations for some events

The very accessible Locomotion is an extension of the National Railway Museum in York. Railway buffs will be keen to explore Britain's railway heritage in detail, but most visitors will enjoy just wandering among these magnificent engines.

The museum is made up of seven restored buildings and a brand-new structure, all on the site of Britain's first passenger transport line that was opened in 1825. Some of the vehicles on site are almost two hundred years old. At reception, videos and models help you plan your visit and you're then free to explore the site – you can see the goods and parcel offices, the station and the coal drops, all of which have interactive info points. And as well as the engines, you can watch the restoration work that is taking place, or try your own skills as a railway worker. The Travel Challenges feature presents the impact of transport on the environment – it's interesting, but if the edu-tainment gets too much, there are picnic areas and space for children to play.

Most of the buildings are clustered together near the car parks, and are all accessible. There are smooth paved and tarmac pathways between all buildings. The only separate building – the new structure that houses the main museum collection – is a ten-minute walk away on flat tarmac, although a wheelchair accessible bus also makes the journey every few minutes. Everything visitors can see is on one level, and surrounded by acres of space. The shop, toilets and café are all perfectly accessible. In fact, the only thing you may not manage in a wheelchair is a trip on the old steam train. Staff are extremely keen to help where they can, and are constantly trying to improve accessibility. Work is under way to create wheelchair access onto an old railway coach and a Braille pack of museum information has recently been produced.

Food & drink ▸▸ The *Platform 7 Café* is in the same new space as the main museum collection, so you can enjoy lunch in comfort, with space and a view of the magnificent locomotives. Try the brilliant Royal George Sausages.

125 The Wensleydale Creamery, Yorkshire

Address: Gayle Lane, Hawes, Wensleydale DL8 3RN **Website:** www.wensleydale.co.uk
Telephone: 01969 667664 **Hours:** Mon–Sat 9.30am–5pm, Sun 10am–4.30pm **Dates:** closed 25–26 Dec **Entry:** [D]£2.50 [C]£2.50 [A]£2.50 [child]£1.50; shops free

Wensleydale – the inimitable Yorkshire cheese – is still made in the heart of the Yorkshire Dales. The Wensleydale Creamery may be a commercial factory but it prides itself on the authenticity of its cheeses, and the local ingredients and traditional recipes it uses. So if you like the crumbly stuff half as much as Wallace and Gromit do, this visitor centre is worth a visit.

First produced by French Cistercian monks living in the Dales, surprisingly Wensleydale started life as a blue cheese – you can learn all about these monastic origins in the museum. Other farmhouse kitchen and agricultural exhibits reveal just how gruelling life in the Dales once was. Across a level yard from the museum is the creamery itself, with a viewing area where you can watch the cheese-making process – from the pasteurisation of the fresh milk that arrives every morning to bandaging the cheese for drying. The factory doesn't operate every day, so call ahead to check before a visit. The best time to see the factory in action is between 10am and 3pm. Wensleydale has to mature in a cold, dark store for four to six months before it's ready to be sold: of course you can buy some in the creamery's specialist cheese shop. All the different varieties – from oak smoked and sheep's milk to ginger and cranberry – are available for you to sample. You can even pick up honey roast pork sausages produced from pigs fed on the creamery's very own whey.

Although awe-inspiring, an undulating journey through the rolling hills and vales of the Yorkshire countryside might leave some disabled visitors apprehensive about accessibility at the creamery. There is no need for concern though – in fact the one-storey site is level and there are six disabled parking spaces close to the reception. The museum, viewing gallery, café and restaurant are all wheelchair accessible, and there is one free manual wheelchair available. The site is compact, and seating is dotted around, but the gift and cheese shops can get rather busy, leaving some tight spaces to navigate – so try to avoid those areas at peak times.

Food & drink ▶▶ *The Buttery* has dramatic views over the Dales and serves a signature dish – the Ultimate Ploughmans, a stodgy affair with five creamery cheeses accompanied by a pint of Yorkshire Ale.

126 Fountains Abbey and Studley Royal Estate, Yorkshire

Address: Ripon, near Harrogate HG4 3DY **Website:** www.fountainsabbey.org.uk **Telephone:** 01765 608888; textphone 18001 01765 608888 **Hours:** main buildings Mar–Oct daily 10am–5pm; Nov–Feb 10am–4pm; deer park daily dawn–dusk **Dates:** closed 24–25 Dec **Entry:** main buildings [D]£8.25 [C]free [A]£8.25 [5–15s]£4.40 [Con]£8.25

Studley Royal estate, tucked in a wooded valley, is a hidden gem. Most visitors come for the soaring, eight-hundred-year-old ruins of Fountains Abbey, Britain's most complete Cistercian foundation, but the estate, laid out in 1720, includes the beautiful, formal Water

Fountains Abbey

Gardens, the wide open spaces of the Deer Park, and more than twenty listed buildings, including the Jacobean mansion of Fountains Hall.

The abbey is close to the West Gate and easily visited in an hour or two. But stunning as it is, it makes up only a fraction of the Studley Royal park, whose eight hundred landscaped acres are a joy to visit and, with a picnic, could easily fill a day. At any time of year, wheelchair exploration is a delight, thanks to smooth, hard paths everywhere, including a recommended wheelchair route from the West Gate, through the abbey and all around the Water Gardens. There are some gradients, but your workout is rewarded with some stunning, often unexpected views. Throughout the year, special events highlight the park's unique features: floodlit walks around the ruins by night together with appropriate music (shivers and ghosts guaranteed), classical concerts and firework displays using the abbey as a backdrop, open-air Shakespeare, and theatre groups. Once a year, you can even join a free floodlit drive-through of the estate for disabled drivers – this is a very popular event, so keep an eye for dates, and book as early as you can.

West Gate car park has about sixty free, disabled spaces and accessible toilets. The abbey itself is accessible with some small ramps – take the usual care on uneven, grassy surfaces – and almost all of the other main buildings boast good access. Only Fountains Hall, in fact, presents a real problem, with lots of unavoidable steps. If you want the accessible facilities at the visitor centre, you'll have to negotiate a very steep hill down to the abbey and formal gardens. Fortunately, a fully accessible mini-bus is laid on to ease this journey – a superb facility. If you only want the abbey and Water Gardens, arrive at the West Gate entrance, where access is relatively flat.

Food & drink ▸▸ The visitor centre restaurant serves excellent local and seasonal food in spacious, comfortable surroundings. You'll find the same selection at the *Studley Tearoom* with added superb views of the park.

127 IMAX Cinema at the National Media Museum, Yorkshire

Address: Bradford BD1 1NQ **Website:** www.nationalmediamuseum.org.uk **Telephone:** 0870 701 0200 **Hours:** museum Tue–Sun 10am–6pm; IMAX daily 10am–late, show times vary **Dates:** museum closed Mon except bank holidays and school holidays; closed 25–26 Dec **Entry:** museum free; IMAX tickets vary depending on film

The National Media Museum is a fabulous, accessible destination, with eight floors of exhibitions, cinemas, simulators and galleries on photography, film, TV, animation and science. It provides a wonderful day out for children in particular, but is a great experience for everyone.

Seeing a movie in the blissfully accessible, giant-screen, 3-D IMAX cinema – the chief attraction – is an absolutely staggering experience with real wow-factor, leaving you goggle-eyed in your seat, and applauding wildly at the end. The rest of the museum, with the exception of a couple of simulators, is equally accessible, with widespread Braille and tactile labels, plus a number of staff who can sign. Highlights – especially appealing to kids – include the blue-screen interactive studios that allow you to read a

TV news bulletin or ride a magic flying carpet. Exhibitions planned for 2010 include *Immersion*, a study of how video games, horror films and virtual worlds have affected how we engage with everyday life.

Thanks to Bradford's busy one-way system and poor signage to the parking, the museum can be tricky to reach, and some of the disabled parking bays are on a slope, so it is best for wheelchair users to visit with a companion. Once inside, though, it would be hard to improve upon. At the IMAX Cinema, access is perfect and completely level: a very wide, comfortable back row is fully dedicated to wheelchair users and their companions, and offers some of the best views in the house. Headphones are provided for those with hearing impairments. The museum café has lots of room, low counters and moveable seating throughout.

Food & drink ▸▸ The very accessible café serves the usual range of excellent soups, sandwiches and cakes, while the *PictureVille Bar* deals in drinks and cold snacks.

128 Royal Armouries, Yorkshire

Address: Armouries Drive, Leeds LS10 1LT **Website:** www.royalarmouries.org **Telephone:** 01132 201999 **Hours:** daily 10am–5pm **Dates:** closed 24–26 Dec **Entry:** free

Light, airy and spacious, this state-of-the-art exhibition space houses an extensive range of arms and armour from ancient hunting weapons to the present day. More than 8500 exhibits from the national collection, formerly in the Tower of London, are displayed over five floors in a series of themed galleries. You'll know already if it takes your fancy, but less enthusiastic visitors usually leave enlightened and impressed too.

The Royal Armouries is not just weapons in cases; there are interactive displays and a number of audio presentations in each of the galleries as well as film shows and special events. Daily presentations, from April to October, include horse shows, jousting bouts and falconry, all taking place in the nearby outdoor Tiltyard. Visitors can also visit the horses and birds in the menagerie between the Tiltyard and the Craft Centre – the latter area home to a gunmaker, armourer and wardrobe mistress. One gallery is dedicated to oriental weaponry – you won't miss the full body-armoured Mughal elephant. The central part of the museum is ground floor only, so there's a great view up to the roof. At each level, glass walkways link the galleries on either side, and crossing them is not for the faint-hearted.

There are six free disabled parking spaces next to the Tiltyard and further (paying) bays in the nearby multistorey car park. The entrance is across a level, paved area and, once you're inside, access between each level is via one of the four lifts, though be warned these can be extremely busy at peak times. There are four manual wheelchairs available to borrow. There are accessible toilets throughout. The displays are well lit, although some of the printed descriptions are hard to read and there's only limited Braille labelling. In addition to plentiful seating, there's the bonus of portable gallery stools.

Food & drink ▸▸ *The Bistro* is located just inside the entrance and offers a good variety of refreshments, while the café on the second floor has a more limited choice. There's also a picnic area on the fourth floor with drinks and snack machines.

129 Standedge Tunnel, Huddersfield Canal, Yorkshire

Address: Waters Road, Marsden, Huddersfield HD7 6NQ **Website:** www.standedge
.co.uk **Telephone:** 01484 844298 **Hours:** visitor centre daily 20 Mar–Sep 10am–5pm;
Oct–7 Nov 10am–4pm; short trips every hour Mon–Fri 11am–3pm, Sat & Sun 10am–4pm
Dates: closed 8 Nov to 19 Mar **Entry:** visitor centre free; short trips [D]£4 [C]free [A]£4.50
[5–15s]£3.50 [Con]£4; prices vary for through trips

Fully accessible canal boats make short voyages into the Standedge (pronounced Stan-nige) tunnel. At over three miles long, and six hundred feet deep, Standedge is Britain's longest waterway tunnel, drilling deeper beneath the hills than any other.

You can take your place in a glass-roofed boat for a fascinating trip into the Huddersfield Narrow Canal, entering the torch-lit darkness beneath the Pennines. This extraordinary journey and mode of transport was part of the fabric of the British economy in the nineteenth century, and knowledgeable enthusiasts and locals do a great job of keeping the history alive. The tunnel opened in 1811 – having taken seventeen years to construct – and was mostly lined with brick, but left as bare rock in places. As you pass through you can still see the footmarks on the tunnel roof where men would "walk" the boat along by lying on the top of the cabin. Look out, too, for the connections to the three parallel rail tunnels, only one of which is still in use. The typical visitor journey is 550 yards into the tunnel and back again – this takes about thirty minutes.

There are four designated Blue Badge spaces at the small visitor centre car park, right by the tunnel entrance. You should buy your tickets for short boat trips from the adjacent Tunnel End Cottages. The modern glass-roofed boats can be boarded and disembarked comfortably from the inside dock. The boat dimensions are governed by the tunnel's width, so call ahead if you think there may be issues with your wheelchair or powered scooter. Some boats are permitted to go all the way through the tunnel, either

IDEAS ▶▶ TOURS AND TRIPS

British Tour Plans (☎01623 511210, ⬤www.britishtourplans.com) is a bespoke road-trip planning service that can cater for disabled travellers. Send details of where you want to go, any specialist interests and what the nature of your disability is and they will supply an itinerary with places to visit, accommodation and turn-by-turn driving directions. They check access for all accommodation and any recommended attractions. Charges start at £195 for a typical five to ten day tour.

Chalfont Line (☎01895 459540, ⬤www.chalfont-line.co.uk) offers escorted holiday services to slow walkers and wheelchair users. They offer door-to-door transport, assistance with baggage and a Personal Assistance service. They run coach tours around Britain and can organise tailormade holidays in London and the surrounding areas.

Vitalise (☎0845 330 0149, ⬤www.vitalise.org.uk) provides group holidays in the UK and overseas for people with visual impairments. Sighted guides provide assistance throughout the trip. Tours on offer range from city breaks to outdoor activities. They also run holiday centres (see box p.171).

under their own diesel power or when towed – if you do this journey, you'll need to be able to climb steps at the far end. If you can do that, also bear in mind you'll have to walk, or get a taxi, back to your car. Whatever you choose to do, make sure you complete your visit with a tour of the fully accessible visitor centre, where you can learn in fascinating detail about the race to connect east and west under the Pennines.

Food & drink ▶▶ There is a roomy café in the visitor centre for snacks, drinks and views, and in good weather tables are set outside for an even nicer experience.

130 Yorkshire Sculpture Park

Address: West Bretton WF4 4LG **Website:** www.ysp.co.uk **Telephone:** 01924 832631
Hours: grounds & ysp centre daily Apr–25 Oct 10am–6pm; 26 Oct–28 Mar 10am–5pm
Dates: closed 24–25 Dec **Entry:** free; car park £4

Set in five hundred acres of the eighteenth-century Bretton Estate, the Yorkshire Sculpture Park (YSP) displays contemporary sculptures out in the open. Mixing culture with fun and outdoor invigoration makes this a great, if sometimes surreal, place to visit.

The park's woodland glades and open spaces roll down towards a large lake and provide a unique home for dozens of sculptures, including pieces by Barbara Hepworth and huge bronze works by Henry Moore. The Access Sculpture Trail, almost nine hundred yards from the main car park, is a sensory landscape area of the park, developed to be accessible to everyone, and focusing on scent, touch, sound and texture. In addition, there are several indoor galleries in the centre – the Bothy, Garden and new Underground Gallery – where you can enjoy sculpture regardless of the weather. The huge Longside Gallery is in a converted riding school at the southern end of the park.

Yorkshire Sculpture Park

There isn't a direct, hard-surface footpath to it, and the shuttle bus isn't wheelchair accessible, so you'll have to drive over if you want to visit – the car park is exclusive to Blue Badge holders.

An excellent YSP map displays accessible routes through the wider Bretton estate – many of the paths are wheelchair accessible, but some are wire-meshed and there are hilly areas to deal with. The long route across the estate, in particular, is not recommended because the surface can be slippery. There are three powered scooters to borrow, and a donation towards their maintenance is requested. But you can drive around the park as much as you need. The main entrance and car park are on the north side of the park, outside the village of West Bretton, but free Blue Badge bays and accessible toilets are available at all of the YSP car parks. All the indoor galleries and the visitor centre, shop and café near the main entrance are fully accessible.

Food & drink ▶▶ The wheelchair accessible restaurant in the visitor centre has glorious views over the park – the food is delicious and fairtrade whenever possible.

131 The Deep, Yorkshire

Address: Princes Dock Street, Hull HU1 4DP **Website:** www.thedeep.co.uk **Telephone:** 01482 381000 **Hours:** 10am–6pm; last entrance 5pm **Dates:** closed 24–25 Dec **Entry:** [D]£8.95 [C]free [A]£8.95 [3–15s]£6.95 [Con]£7.50

With its sharply pointed front end, and slick grey aluminium exterior, the landmark building that houses The Deep is distinctly shark-like in appearance – aptly so, because this huge aquarium houses more than forty sharks and 3500 other fish.

As well as a visitor attraction, The Deep is an educational and conservation charity, equipped with impressively high-tech, interactive displays. You are taken on a descending journey to underground levels, exploring from the early beginnings of sea life to todays oceans, and from the warm waters of the tropics to the icy Antarctic. At every level, the giant tanks contain an array of species, from teeming, coral reef-dwellers of the tropics to the strange creatures of the coldest depths. You can get up close and personal with all the residents, be they beautiful, ugly, timid or downright scary. Children are kept busy the whole time: watch out for the interactive Magic Pool on your way round, and check the website for news of 3D films and seasonal events. The highlight for visitors of all ages is the breathtaking ride in the world's only underwater lift, back up to the ground floor, through the main tank, home of the sharks. Daily dive shows take place, when the sharks are fed by hand – thrilling!

Access around the whole site is excellent. To start with, arriving is easy – the car park has twelve disabled spaces, right next to a designated disabled entrance. Powered scooters, wheelchairs and walking frames are available free of charge, but it's wise to call ahead to book. There are seating areas on each level – but be warned that descending between each level involves making your way down two ramps, which can be crowded at busy times. The lift is wheelchair accessible, but if it is not suitable for you, be aware that you can't head back up the ramps either, so the only options available are to take the stairs, or ask for assistance using the staff exit. Lastly, on several dates throughout the year, "quiet days" are organised, when the audio system is turned down, the lighting turned up and a BSL-trained member of staff delivers a signed presentation.

Food & drink ▶▶ *Observatory Café* has moveable furniture and impressive views over the Humber Bridge and estuary. On Friday and Saturday evenings visitors can dine with the sharks in the award-winning *Two Rivers* restaurant.

132 Magna Science Adventure Centre, Yorkshire

Address: Sheffield Road, Templeborough, Rotherham S60 1DX **Website:** www.visitmagna .co.uk **Telephone:** 01709 720002 **Hours:** daily 10am–5pm **Dates:** closed some Mon, call to check; closed 1 Jan, 24–27 Dec & 31 Dec **Entry:** [D]£9.95 [C]free [A]£9.95 [5–15s]£7.95 [Con]£8.95; discounts available online

Magna has four huge interactive pavilion structures built inside the shell of what was once one of the biggest steel mills in the world. The thread that runs through the vast centre (550 yards long and twelve storeys high) is the demonstration and celebration of science, and particularly the ear-splitting heavy industry of the north, which is now largely historical. Everything at Magna is on a monumental scale.

The four pavilions represent the four elements: earth, air, fire and water, each one housing themed collections of experiments and demonstrations. You can operate a JCB, blast a rock face, fire a super-soaking hose, shine searchlights and engage in masses of hands-on gadget adoration. Together with the extensive play areas Sci-Tek and Aqua-Tek, which also welcome people with disabilities – not to mention the fun to be had from zip wires, abseiling, bungee-jumping and dodgems – there's enough here to occupy most families for a long day. And to remind you what it's all built upon, at regular intervals they fire up the steel mill's original arc furnace for The Big Melt, in a ground-shaking, post-industrial, multimedia spectacular.

> "Three generations of my family visited Magna and we all enjoyed it."
>
> **Ian Littler, Stockport**

The designated parking spaces aren't wide enough to be compliant and are unmarked, so if possible, get dropped off at the entrance. Once you're inside Magna, the site is superb for visitors with mobility problems. The incredible scale means it never gets crowded, even when more than a thousand people are here at once – so you'll have no problem navigating in a wheelchair. Portable seating is available at reception to help you if visiting on foot. A huge, slightly sloped reception area (with an excellent low section) leads to lifts, and the pavilions are connected by long, wide walkways with a perfect metal surface. Make sure your mobility scooter has fully charged batteries – you could cover miles in a visit – and if you're coming in winter be sure to dress warmly. Braille signs indicate the toilets and stairs, but visually impaired visitors may struggle with the low light in much of the building. While some of the interactive exhibits have subtitles, in general visitors with hearing impairments may find the empty, echoing spaces distracting. Some areas have strobe lighting effects.

Food & drink ▶▶ The very modern, glass-fronted *Fuel Restaurant* is wheelchair accessible and reasonably priced, but has atmospheric subdued lighting.

Wales

ISLE OF ANGLESEY

CONWY

FLINTSHIRE

DENBIGHSHIRE

WREXHAM

GWYNEDD

POWYS

CEREDIGION

PEMBROKESHIRE

CARMARTHENSHIRE

MERTHYR TYDFIL

BLAENAU GWENT

MONMOUTHSHIRE

NEATH PORT TALBOT

RHONDDA CYNON TAF

CAERPHILLY

TORFAEN

NEWPORT

SWANSEA

BRIDGEND

VALE OF GLAMORGAN

CARDIFF

Wales

Cross the border into Wales and you'll find an untamed land with a captivatingly different character. Here mountains thrust skywards from the wild and windswept landscape, crossed by spectacularly scenic roads and railways. Though scarred by the impact of a once thriving mining industry and the aftermath of its demise, the region displays a forward-looking spirit, with Cardiff, the world's youngest capital, leading the way.

133 Techniquest Cardiff

Address: Stuart Street, Cardiff Bay CF10 5BW **Website:** www.techniquest.org **Telephone:** 029 2047 5475 **Hours:** Mon–Fri during term time 9.30am–4.30pm, Sat, Sun & non-term time 10am–5pm **Dates:** closed 1 Jan & 24–26 Dec **Entry:** [D]£5 [C]free [A]£7 [4–16s]£5 [Con]£5; planetarium £1.30

Committed to making learning fun, accessible and exciting, Techniquest is a hands-on interactive science centre for the whole family. The museum's have-a-go approach makes it an exciting place for children and young people.

Based in a large Victorian building, a space once used for engineering work, Techniquest is full of light and space – perfect for scientific illumination. Visitors can try their hand at launching a hot air balloon or damming a river. The ground floor has science-based games installations, including explanations of how oil rigs and submarines work, why yachts sail and how hydrogen-fuelled rockets are launched. There's even a colony of leafcutter ants, which are fascinating to observe. The exhibits are labelled with easy-to-understand information under helpful headings like Try This and What's Happening? MusicQuest – where you can find out about the science of music and sound, dance on a giant xylophone, and use the whispering dishes to send messages – is on the mezzanine. Techniquest has its own one-hundred-seat science lecture theatre, a laboratory for experiments and workshops, and a Planetarium where you can discover the stars and view the sky as it will be on the night of your visit. There are plenty of seasonal workshops – kids will really enjoy the "spooky science" that takes place at Halloween.

There are eight free disabled parking spots at the front entrance to Techniquest and eighteen disabled bays in the nearby car park. Once inside, there's step-free access to all public areas, places to sit down, and a café. The lecture theatre has very steeply raked seating, but there are seats down at the front, and space for wheelchairs, and there are similar facilities in the planetarium. The accessible toilet is roomy, as is the lift.

Food & drink ▶▶ Techniquest's café is small – there are plenty of bars, restaurants and ca-fés in the Mermaid Quay area, including the spacious *Mimosa Kitchen and Bar* (☎029 2049 1900, ⦿www.mimosakitchen.co.uk).

134 Wales Millennium Centre, Cardiff

Address: Bute Place, Cardiff Bay CF10 5AL **Website:** www.wmc.org.uk **Telephone:** ticket office 0870 040 2000 **Hours:** box office performance days Mon–Fri 10am–performance end, Sat & Sun 11am–performance end; non-performance days Mon–Fri 10am–6pm, Sat & Sun 11am–5pm **Dates:** closed 25 Dec **Entry:** building free; performance prices vary [C]free

Wales Millennium Centre

The award-winning Wales Millennium Centre has a commitment to engaging with the disabled community which is as impressive as the building's iconic design.

Since opening in 2004, the centre has become a world-renowned venue for the arts, but it is also an inclusive meeting place for the local community. The magnificent Donald Gordon Theatre hosts art events ranging from hip-hop to ballet, opera to musicals, and contemporary dance to stand-up comedy. There are workshop and studio sessions, behind-the-scenes tours, and free daily performances on the foyer stage. Also in demand are the pre-show touch tours, which explore the building's intentionally varied use of tactile materials and reliefs – the centre is as memorable to the touch as it is to the eye. You may come here to see the Welsh National Opera or the BBC Orchestra of Wales. And also resident is Touch Trust, which provides creative touch-based music, art and dance activities for people with profound and multiple disabilities. It has a large disabled toilet and changing rooms with a hoist and large changing table. Phone ahead to book a session.

> "The hearing loop system helped make the experience at the Wales Millennium Centre very enjoyable."
>
> **Gwyn Kemp-Philp,
> Newport**

WALES

Theatres can be tricky places for disabled people, but here every effort has been made to make the venue as welcoming and accessible as possible. The centre has eighteen disabled parking bays, all under cover, and bookable in advance. There are automatic doors at all entrances, lifts, and level access to all areas. Accessible toilets are dotted throughout and the auditorium has accessible seating and wheelchair access on every level. There are induction loops in all key public areas; audio-described, BSL-interpreted and captioned performances are available; and signage and directions around the building are given in large clear type and raised text – in both Welsh and English Braille.

Food & drink ▶▶ This is a truly public building, where people can come and go as they please to meet, eat and enjoy. The lounge bar and restaurant *ffresh* serves pre-show meals, or you can relax with a coffee at *Crema* or in the *Hufen* ice-cream parlour.

135 RSPB Conwy Nature Reserve, Conwy

Address: Llandudno Junction, Conwy LL31 9XZ **Website:** www.rspb.org.uk/reserves /guide/c/conwy/index.asp **Telephone:** 01492 584091 **Hours:** 9.30am–5pm (coffee shop 10am–4.30pm, or 4pm in winter) **Dates:** closed 25 Dec **Entry:** members free, non-members [D]£2.50 [C]£2.50 [A]£2.50 [5–15s]£1 [Con]£2.50

Conwy RSPB Nature Reserve is the perfect place to get back to nature. The estuary is home to many varieties of birds; the star species to tick off here are black-tailed godwits, shelducks and, with a bit more difficulty, water rails poking about furtively in the reeds. It is a fascinating place to visit, even for ornithological novices.

At Conwy you'll find an impressive mix of untamed nature – including serious winds off the estuary – and decent access for all, which is a difficult trick to pull off. The boardwalk is superb, taking you straight into the reeds in perfect safety on an absolutely level wooden track. The main tracks are firm and hard, generally smooth, with only slight gradients, and well drained so puddles rarely muddy the issue. The looser-surfaced more distant trails can be difficult in poor weather though, and the boardwalk can get slippery when wet. In rain, it's sensible to visit RSPB Conwy using a powered scooter, although updates are posted on the notice board when conditions get particularly challenging. The hides and screens are solidly constructed with hard floors, all adapted for the comfort of wheelchair users with wide doorways, plenty of turning space and viewing points at various heights.

Although most RSPB nature reserves would claim to offer what Conwy does, the staff here are enthusiastically trying to improve accessibility at all times and are helpful, without being fussy. The newly built visitor centre has a welcoming reception area (with low counter and knee recess) and a well-laid-out shop with spacious aisles and low displays. There are plans to improve the more remote trails as well as the car park surface and to provide more than the current three designated disabled spaces, although the car park is already huge.

Food & drink ▶▶ A teatime queue outside a café serving fish and chips is about the best recommendation you can get, so don't hesitate to try *Harbour View* (☎01492 581156) on Glan Y Mor Road.

136–137 Llanberis Lake Railway and National Slate Museum, Gwynedd

Address: Llanberis LL55 4TY **Website:** www.lake-railway.co.uk; www
.museumwales.ac.uk **Telephone:** railway 01286 870549; museum 01286 870630 **Hours:**
railway check website for departures; museum daily Easter–Oct 10am–5pm; Nov–Easter
Sun–Fri 10am–4pm **Dates:** railway check website for seasonal variations **Entry:** railway
[D]£7.20 [C]£7.20 [A]£7.20 [3–15s]£4.50 [Con]£6.70, family discounts available, dogs £1;
museum free

From its terminus at the National Slate Museum at the foot of Mount Snowdon, this
miniature steam train carries passengers on a round trip through breathtaking scenery.
It chugs through Llanberis, with its distinctive candy-coloured houses, and then doubles back to follow the shore of Lake Padarn and take in spectacular views of Snowdon,
before returning to its starting point.

Kids will adore the journey aboard a genuine steam train through rolling countryside, and, luckily for them, the sixty-minute trip also includes a stop at a lakeside picnic
spot (Cei Llydan) with an excellent children's play area and a woodland centre. You
can also break your journey at Llanberis High Street and catch a later train back. The
vintage steam engines that haul the train coaches along were salvaged from the nearby

Llanberis Lake Railway

Dinorwic slate quarries – contemplating their original purpose is good preparation for a visit to the National Slate Museum. Since the quarry closed in 1969, this site has been given over to telling the story of the miners' working lives and the Welsh slate industry with a range of engaging displays and video presentations. The exhibition areas are level and easily accessible with wide doorways and spacious interiors; there's also a lift up to the impressive water wheel that once powered much of the machinery.

There are six Blue Badge parking spaces in nearby Padarn Country Park with paved routes leading to the museum, whose slate and gravel paths can occasionally prove challenging for wheelchair users. Away from the main pathways, watch out for the train tracks, used in the past by the slate quarry trucks, that crisscross the site – staff can provide assistance for wheelchair users. Make your way through the café complex to reach the train station – note that on your return you'll pass back through the ticket office, shop and café. The conductor will help with a ramp that permits easy access to the partially adapted carriage, which has fold-up seats to accommodate all types of wheelchairs and scooters, and windows offering an unobstructed 360-degree view.

Food & drink ▸▸ The *Caffi'r Ffowntan Café* is a good size and serves hot and cold food and drinks.

138 Llangollen Wharf, Denbighshire

Address: Wharf Hill LL20 8TA **Website:** www.horsedrawnboats.co.uk **Telephone:** 01978 860702 **Hours:** Easter–Oct trips every 30 minutes daily 11am–4pm **Dates:** Easter–Oct **Entry:** horse-drawn [D]£6 [C]£6 [A]£6 [child]£3; family tickets available

If you want a complete break from modern life, what could be nicer than a trip on a horse-drawn canal boat? Peace and quiet, superb Welsh scenery and not even the noise of an engine to disturb the tranquillity.

The Horse Drawn Boat Centre offers 45-minute trips along the Llangollen canal, on purpose-built passenger boats, with simple but excellent ramped access for wheelchair users. Several wheelchairs can be accommodated on each boat, so there's no need to book, and you can choose whether to sit in the open air or under cover. If you want to do the two-hour motor-barge trip across the aqueduct, you'll need to drive to another wharf (or be able to make the bus transfer) and get onto a non

> "The path that runs alongside the single track waterway over the viaduct is fine to walk across, as long as you aren't scared of heights!"
>
> **John Blair, Fleet**

wheelchair accessible boat. If you can get there, and negotiate four steps onto the boat, the crew will welcome you and make every effort to assist you into position. Besides the boats, the well-maintained canal has excellent, level towpaths, providing the ideal country walk for anyone with limited mobility.

Although Llangollen Wharf is superb, getting to it can be challenging. There is next to no signage in the town centre or on main roads, and there's no proper on-site parking for anyone – space for two or three cars on a steep slope, but nothing designated for disabled people. The best option is to be dropped off at the wharf and park the car

Llangollen Wharf

elsewhere. There is a schoolyard nearby which can be used outside school hours, and there's on-street parking and ample parking in the town centre. And the hilly nature of the area can't be avoided; there is no flat way to approach the place. But don't let any of these approach issues put you off – once you're enjoying the journey, your perseverance is amply rewarded.

Food & drink ▶▶ The famous and fully accessible tearooms are adjacent to the canal, where the horse-drawn boats are boarded.

139 Centre for Alternative Technology, Powys

Address: Machynlleth SY20 9AZ **Website:** www.cat.org.uk **Telephone:** 01654 705950 **Hours:** daily 10am–5.30pm or dusk if earlier **Dates:** closed 4–10 Jan & 23–28 Dec; cliff railway closed Nov–Mar **Entry:** [D]£8.40 [C]£6.40 [A]£8.40 [5–15s]£4.20 [Con]£7.40; rates reduced in winter

Occupying the site of a disused slate quarry near Machynlleth, with stunning views over the surrounding hills, the Centre for Alternative Technology – Canolfan y Dechnloleg Amgen – is a leading international institute for the development of practical solutions to the world's environmental challenges.

This is a charity, supported by huge enthusiasm from staff and volunteers; the vitality and energy of CAT is refreshing. Visitors meander alongside the resident poultry and ducks, while volunteers lead guided tours and staff busily tend the display gardens and organic vegetable beds. As you make your way along the trail around the site, you will want to get involved. An audioguide is available to help you explore, and learn more about the impressive working demonstrations of sustainability in action at CAT – everything from wind, solar and water power to organic growing via waste and recycling is covered. There are some fascinating examples of low-energy ecological building to take in too.

You arrive either on the two-hundred-foot-high, wheelchair accessible, water-powered cliff railway, or from the disabled parking at the top of the site. The paths taking you round CAT have been widened and levelled as far as possible to improve wheelchair access, though the nature of the site means some are unavoidably rough, and a couple of them are too steep for wheelchairs. You can call ahead to book a free powered scooter, and the centre is packed with so many things to take in, if you have to miss a couple of them, you'll still have been very well served. If you feel inspired to start reducing your impact on the planet, there's a good shop, with an excellent range of books and eco-friendly goods, and a very helpful information service at reception.

Food & drink ▶▶ With so much to see, CAT's wholefood restaurant allows for a welcome break – many of the ingredients in the hearty, home-made vegetarian meals are organically grown on site.

Centre for Alternative Technology

Red Kite

140 Gigrin Farm, Red Kite Feeding Station, Powys

Address: South Street, Rhayader LD6 5BL **Website:** www.gigrin.co.uk **Telephone:** 01597 810243 **Hours:** summer daily 1–5pm with feeding at 3pm; winter daily 1–4pm with feeding at 2pm **Dates:** closed 25 Dec **Entry:** [D]£4 [C]£4 [A]£4 [5–15s]£1.50 [Con]£3

Gigrin Farm in Powys became the Red Kite Feeding Station in 1993, following a request from the RSPB. The daily feeding of the birds – often hundreds of pairs – is an extraordinary sight and an increasingly popular attraction.

The site is a working farm, so unsurprisingly access isn't perfect, but significant efforts have been made, and it is worth the effort to see this natural spectacle. Visitors can head to several kite-viewing hides just before feeding time, and watch as a quarter of a tonne of beef is distributed to the waiting birds which have flown in from the surrounding countryside. What follows is a riot of colour and noise as the kites – resplendent-looking raptors in chestnut, white and black plumage – vie with other birds for the food that has been scattered, and perform natural aerobatics that have become an entertaining feature of the visit.

> "If you are patient, you are rewarded with the fantastic sight of red kites and buzzards feeding only ten yards away."
>
> **Stephen Walker, Witney**

If you're lucky, you may also see buzzards, which often land to feed on the ground. The well-stocked shop is worth visiting, but the information and display area is in a separate two-storey building: the ground floor is split level, but has two separate entrances that allow access to the whole of the lower floor. Although steps to the upper floor leave some displays out of bounds to wheelchair users, they present no deterrent to the main

WALES

153

event – seeing the kites being fed.

Gigrin Farm is accessed by a single-track tarmac road. There are no disabled bays, and in fact no formal parking area, and the space available is on a gentle gradient. The main area between the buildings has been tarred and there are no access problems across it or into any of the buildings, all of which have level access. If you need to, you can ask the staff for permission to park in one of the four spaces adjacent to the ramped entrance to the viewing hides. The accessible hides have designated low viewing points for wheelchair users.

Food & drink ▸▸ When it's your feeding time, try the wheelchair accessible *Carole's Cake Shop and Tearoom* (☎01597 811060) on West Street in Rhayader.

141 Craig-y-nos Country Park, Powys

Address: Pen-y-Cae, Swansea Valley SA9 1GL **Website:** www.breconbeacons.org
Telephone: 01639 730395 **Hours:** daily 10am, closing varies seasonally, times displayed in car park **Dates:** closed 25 Dec **Entry:** free; car park £2.50, free to Blue Badge holders

Craig-y-nos boasts a far more starry history than you'd expect from a country estate within the borders of the Brecon Beacons National Park. Adelina Patti, a Victorian opera superstar, bought Craig-y-nos castle and parkland in 1878 and spent a fortune developing it to entertain famous friends like the Crown Prince of Sweden.

Craig-y-nos is advertised as a country park, but it's actually a wooded valley, and feels surprisingly like a private garden. Adelina oversaw the extensive landscaping that transformed these forty acres into her personal pleasure grounds. As you gaze out at the avenues of rhododendrons, and the remains of the formal path circling the lake, it's not hard to imagine her revered guests taking a leisurely stroll before returning to the castle to enjoy a performance in her private theatre. The castle is rarely open nowadays, but it's the lush grounds that are the real draw anyway. Bound by the River Tawe, the land is also crossed by another, smaller river, the Lynfell; for those want to spend some time by the water's edge, a wheelchair accessible picnic bench sits in a perfect spot by the bridge across the Tawe. There's the lake too, and an easy ten-minute circular walk takes in the fish pond. This is the most accessible route, but if you want to press on, there is a longer, more undulating trail around the estate – but note that some of the paths are uneven and not clearly marked. There are rest seats though, and a sign directs wheelchair users along an alternative route back under the splendid rhododendron arch.

The car park is on a sloping site. There are two designated parking spaces by the main entrance, conveniently close to the disabled toilets and restaurants. If you drive down to the bottom of the car park, you'll find two more disabled spaces by the entrance to the trails, where you'll come across an excellent, large scale, tactile map to help you decide which route to take. The visitor centre is currently closed, and there seem to be no plans to reopen it. If you'd like to sit indoors, look for a small study room near the main entrance – it's basic, but warm and affords excellent views over the fish pond.

Food & drink ▸▸ The *Unusual Food Company* run the café at Craig-y-nos – at the time of writing, they were due to relocate to a refurbished restaurant on the site, early in 2010.

WALES

IDEAS ▶▶ CARAVANS AND CAMPING

Invercoe Highland Holidays (☎01855 811210, ⓦwww.invercoe.co.uk) lies at the heart of the stunningly beautiful valley of Glen Coe in Scotland. As well as an excellent shower block with accessible facilities, there is a laundry room with washer/dryer and a covered picnic area for BBQs and stoves.

Hadrian's Wall Camping and Caravan Site (☎01434 320495, ⓦwww .romanwallcamping.co.uk), less than half-a-mile away from some of the best preserved sections of the wall, is a quiet site nestled in a valley of rolling green hills. There is one disabled toilet and electric pumps are available for air beds.

Old Cotmore Farm (☎01548 580240, ⓦwww.holiday-in-devon.com), on Devon's southernmost peninsula, is popular with families and has 22 acres of parkland. The tidy amenities block has an excellent family/disabled shower room with baby-changing facilities.

Pencelli Castle (☎01874 665451, ⓦwww.pencelli-castle.com) is located at the heart of the Brecon Beacons National Park. Two large family/disabled rooms are on site.

For more ideas, check out **Caravanable** (ⓦwww.caravanable.co.uk), a website that lists caravan and camping sites offering a minimum of ramped access shower, basin and toilet facilities.

142 Pedalabikeaway Cycle Centre, Monmouth

Address: Hadnock Road, Monmouth NP25 3NG **Website:** www.pedalabikeaway.co.uk **Telephone:** 01600 772821; access information 01989 770357 **Hours:** times vary seasonally, check ahead **Dates:** dates vary seasonally, check ahead **Entry:** variations depending on bike [C]free

Pedalabikeaway aims to open up the countryside for cyclists of all abilities. It rents out all sorts of bikes, from tandems and tricycles to adapted bikes for people with disabilities and their companions, and directs you onto marked trails or guided tours, from easy family rides to more challenging routes.

From the Pedalabikeaway centre in the attractive town of Monmouth in southeast Wales, close to the border with England, it's possible to follow the course of the River Wye for four miles along a picturesque cycle trail which is part of the Peregrine Path. The first section of the trail takes you along a lane for approximately one mile. Alternatively, bikes can be relocated to a small car park where the traffic-free section begins. The linear route is fairly level and passes through the stunning countryside of the Wye Valley and on to the village of Symonds Yat in the Forest of Dean (see p.93). The friendly and extremely helpful staff are on hand to assist and there is plenty of room to practise before setting out on the trail.

The Duet bicycle is ideal for riders who are not able to pedal themselves. It has a supported seat at the front and a conventional bike at the rear for an able assistant. A side-by-side tandem is also available and would suit riders with sensory disabilities. Both bicycles are surprisingly stable and a great deal of fun to ride. There's a designated

WALES

toilet on site, with a shallow step, which also doubles as a changing room. The Forest of Dean Centre (see website), just a short drive away, also has several adapted cycles but please note the start of the trail here involves negotiating steep slopes and crossing a busy road.

Food & drink ▶▶ The *Saracens Head Inn* (☎01600 890435, Ⓦwww.saracensheadinn .co.uk) situated on the river in Symonds Yat is a good place to refuel before the return journey. It offers a seasonal lunch menu and lighter snacks from 12 to 2.30pm daily.

143 National Botanical Gardens of Wales, Carmarthenshire

Address: Llanarthne SA32 8HG **Website:** www.gardenofwales.org.uk **Telephone:** 01558 668768 **Hours:** 29 Mar–31 Oct 10am–6pm; Nov–end-Mar 10am–4.30pm **Dates:** closed 25 Dec **Entry:** [D]£6.50 [C]free [A]£8 [5–16s]£4 [Con]£6.50; family tickets available

These wonderful gardens, within easy reach of the A48, are set in the grounds of Middleton Hall and incorporate the 440-acre Waun Las National Nature Reserve. Remains of the estate, such as the Double Walled Garden, coexist with the site's twenty-first-

National Botanical Gardens of Wales

century buildings and features, making this a varied and often surprising day out.

The wide Broadwalk, skirted on either side by stunning herbaceous borders, leads from the entrance up to the calm Mirror Pool and the award-winning Great Glasshouse. Norman Foster's remarkable design, the largest single-span glasshouse in the world, houses a vast array of Mediterranean and Southern Hemisphere flora. Other highlights include the Apothecaries' Garden; the Wallace Garden, which focuses on plant breeding; and William Pye's striking water sculpture, the Scaladaqua Tonda. The garden as a whole encourages visitors to consider not only the extraordinary beauty of the thousands of plant species on display but also their ecological significance. Anyone eco-minded will be particularly drawn to the Living Machine water recycling facility, the biomass boiler plant and the organic farm. For youngsters, there's the Roots & Shoots Adventure Zone and events throughout the year such as the "Grape Escape" micro-raft run.

The garden is straightforward to get around, and well laid out if not level in all places. Eight different audioguides accessible by mobile phone are on offer and, at weekends, there's a Land Train circular tour which takes a wheelchair. There are sixteen disabled parking spaces by the main entrance – the door isn't powered but staff at the ticket desk will provide assistance. Scooters and wheelchairs are available free of charge if you book in advance. Finally, there's a regular shuttle buggy service to take you from the entrance to the Stable Block and Great Glasshouse, but check operating times as this is staffed by volunteers.

Food & drink ▸▸ There are two lovely places to eat on the site, *Seasons Restaurant* and *The Mediterranean Café*, but both these venues can get very busy – alternatively, there are plenty of places in the grounds where you can sit and picnic.

144 National Waterfront Museum, Swansea

Address: Oystermouth Road, Maritime Quarter SA1 3RD **Website:** www.museumwales .ac.uk/en/swansea **Telephone:** 01792 638950 **Hours:** daily 10am–5pm **Dates:** closed 1 Jan & 25–26 Dec **Entry:** free

The National Waterfront Museum tells the proud story of industry and innovation in Wales, through the changing lives of the people involved. Stressing the international importance of Wales as "the world's first industrial nation", the museum links the past to the present using fabulous interactive technology.

The museum building is impressive – a massive brick ex-dockside warehouse, enhanced by a modern slate and glass wing. The exhibits are set out in fifteen categories, including energy, people, the day's work, coal and metals, and each area has its own soundscape, evoking the theme. Real lives are featured throughout: there are poignant photos of miners from the local Tower Colliery and personal accounts of young people working in new industries like IT and design. The achievers category focuses on the careers of famous Welsh women and men, like Tanni Grey-Thompson, David Lloyd George and Aneurin Bevan. And the connection between culture and history is brought home by examining how lives and work have been linked to Wales' changing industrial heritage. If you plan to visit, be sure to check the website for the

WALES

packed events schedule – there are science lectures, interactive "Gener8 days" for budding engineers, a market selling local produce, and even wine-tasting. Most of the events are free.

The museum makes a big effort to be inclusive. There are five disabled bays right outside and Blue Badge parking in the street. There are more disabled spaces in the car park by the adjacent leisure centre – if you take your parking ticket into the museum you'll recieve a partial refund. You can't hire powered scooters at the museum, but there is a Shopmobility in the shopping centre opposite. All entrances and interconnecting doors are operated by large push buttons, and there are places to sit, disabled toilets, changing facilities, and a children's play area. All areas and some displays have interactive touch-screens, complete with audio description, texts in Welsh and English, and real-time BSL interpretation.

Food & drink ▶▶ You can picnic in the lunch room, or eat in the museum café, but if you explore along the waterfront and in the city centre, you will find plenty more options.

WALES

Scotland

Scotland

Support for devolution from the rest of the UK comes and goes, but Scotland has highlights enough to stand out regardless. Handsome Edinburgh plays on its history but is also a vibrant modern city, while Glasgow bubbles with energy and vigour. The Highlands' often jawdropping beauty can be easier to reach than you think – while the likes of the Falkirk Wheel and Dundee Repertory Theatre remind you there's life away from the classic draws.

145 The Royal Yacht Britannia, Edinburgh

Address: Ocean Drive, Leith EH6 6JJ **Website:** www.royalyachtbritannia.co.uk **Telephone:** 0131 555 5566 **Hours:** daily Jan–Mar & Nov–Dec 10am–3.30pm; Apr–Jun & Oct 10am–4pm; Jul–Sep 9.30am–4.30pm **Dates:** closed 1 Jan & 25 Dec **Entry:** [D]£10.50 [C]free [A]£10.50 [5–17s]£6.75 [Con]£9

Permanently berthed at Ocean Terminal in Edinburgh since going out of service, the Royal Yacht *Britannia* is one of the city's newest tourist attractions. Having played host to kings, princesses and heads of state, it's now open to the hoi polloi to follow in their footsteps.

Whether or not you're a fan of royalty or things naval, visiting *Britannia* is a very interesting experience and much has been done to make it a barrier-free attraction, with ramps installed where needed. Once you're on board, you can access everything from the bridge to the engine room. The running commentary brings the ship to life, telling stories of its crew through the years. Although it was only decommissioned in the Nineties, it's surprising how dated the fittings and décor are – far from lavish, *Britannia* is really rather frugal by what one presumes are the standards of modern luxury yachts.

Ocean Terminal is a modern mall, and from the ample accessible car parking on multiple levels, you have a level push (and a lift) to the *Britannia* ticket office. If you can manage stairs, you will find access to other decks straightforward, while if you have more restricted mobility, use the ramps back into the building, where you take the lift to the next level. The maintenance staff on board will happily assist, for instance if you require a push up a ramp. A 21-language audio description device can be set for visually impaired enhanced description and for those with learning difficulties; the lifts have Braille controls.

Food & drink ▸▸ The *Royal Deck Tea Room* was launched in 2009 – the food is a cut above the norm, a Braille menu is available and the views stretch over the Forth to Fife. The immaculately dressed staff only add to the delightful atmosphere.

146 The National Gallery of Scotland, Edinburgh

Address: 1 The Mound EH2 2EL **Website:** www.nationalgalleries.org **Telephone:** 0131 624
6200; parking 0131 624 6550 **Hours:** Mon–Wed & Fri–Sun 10am–5pm, Thu 10am–7pm
Dates: closed 25–26 Dec **Entry:** free, with variations for major exhibitions

Right in the heart of Edinburgh, just off Princes Street, lies the National Gallery Complex, whose three interconnected buildings house the Royal Scottish Academy, the Weston Link (a shopping and eating centre) and most notably the National Gallery of Scotland. The gallery is home to the national collection of fine art, which, for its size, equals any other gallery in the world.

Masterpieces from Raphael, Titian, El Greco, Velázquez, Rembrandt and Rubens vie for attention with Impressionist works by the likes of Monet, Cézanne and Degas and Post-Impressionists including Van Gogh and Gauguin. The Gallery also houses Antonio Canova's stunning sculpture *The Three Graces*. And above all there's a comprehensive display of Scottish painting, with all the major names, including Allan Ramsay, David Wilkie and William McTaggart represented. Perhaps the best-known painting is Sir Henry Raeburn's *The Reverend Robert Walker Skating on Duddingston Loch*, popularly known as *The Skating Minister*. The whole collection is superbly displayed in an impressive Neoclassical building, whose recent refurbishment involved the bold use of colour. The deep maroon walls might sound dark and dreary but clever use of light creates an airy, luminous atmosphere. Keep an eye out for visiting exhibitions which augment the already stunning

The National Gallery of Scotland

collection. Recently featured artists have included Goya, Warhol and Damien Hirst.

Parking can be tricky in the city centre but there are four dedicated Blue Badge bays in a pedestrianised area right outside the gallery. If you wish to take in the National Portrait Gallery and the Dean Gallery as well, you can use the regular, free, accessible bus that links all three. Since the refit, the National Gallery complex is fully accessible over all levels, and even has voice-activated lifts. There are two BSL trained staff on site – contact the Education Department for information on BSL and touch tours.

Food & drink ▶▶ *The Gallery* is a restaurant and café in the modern Weston Link. Sit back and enjoy an excellent three course lunch, and views over Princes Street Gardens.

147 The Scottish Parliament, Edinburgh

Address: opposite Holyrood House EH99 1SP **Website:** www.scottish.parliament.uk **Telephone:** 0131 348 5000; equality team 0131 348 6838 **Hours:** tours times vary seasonally, check website **Dates:** tours times vary seasonally, check website **Entry:** guided tour free

It took more than three hundred years but Scotland finally got its own parliament. On a groundswell of popular support, self-rule over most domestic affairs was devolved back to Edinburgh in 2002. Catalan architect Enric Morales was the designer of the legislature building. Sadly he died before completion but he left a formidable legacy, and a now iconic structure, behind.

Occupying a prime site at the foot of the imposing rocky outcrop of Arthur's Seat and right next to the Palace of Holyrood, Scotland's parliament building is a remarkable realisation of Morales' vision and of Scotland's view of itself as a nation. The plan of the building resembles tree branches and leaves to symbolise the growth of Scotland, and the lines of the building's footprint are evident as you move around. And as well as incorporating various Scottish architectural traits, such as the crow-step feature of Edinburgh tenement gables in the windows in the MSPs' offices, Morales doffs his cap to Charles Rennie Mackintosh too. Extensive use of glass bathes the entrance hall in light, which enhances the concrete vaulted ceiling, replete with the abstract Scottish saltire or diagonal cross motif. Where possible, local wood and stone have been used to enhance this unique, and accessible, structure.

You can come along and see government in action – by taking in either a debate in the chamber or a discussion in the committee rooms – but do call ahead to prebook, particularly if you want to ensure there is BSL interpretation. If you are simply curious about the architecture of the building you can undertake the tour instead. The whole parliament building is accessible throughout, with the debating chamber alone capable of accommodating sixty wheelchair users. Six dedicated parking places across from the front door of the building immediately make you feel good about the whole place, though be prepared for an airport-style security shakedown on entering. The public gallery, committee rooms, café and crèche are all fully accessible, and in a slew of disabled toilets, one even has an adult changing facility. Communication facilities are excellent; the parliament staff welcome calls using the RNID Typetalk service.

Food & drink ▶▶ In the bright café you can enjoy traditional Scotch Pie and Beans.

148 Culloden Battlefield Visitor Centre, Highlands

Address: Culloden Moor, Inverness IV2 5EU **Website:** www.nts.org.uk/culloden **Telephone:** 0844 493 2159 **Hours:** Apr–Oct 9am–5pm; Nov–Dec & Feb–Mar 10am–4pm **Dates:** closed 25–26 Dec **Entry:** [D]£7.50 [C]free [A]£10 [under 18s]£7.50 [Con]£7.50

16 April 1746 was a decisive day in British history: the date of the last battle fought on British soil, when 7000 crown troops swiftly and bloodily defeated Bonnie Prince Charlie's Jacobites. The Battlefield centre is a Highlands must-do and a gem – one of the most fascinating attractions of its kind and accessible to all.

The new centre's natural building materials and sympathetic architecture ensure it blends with its environment. The well-crafted displays are presented through vocal and tactile description, as well as by traditional glass-case presentation. The staff are very helpful, doling out advice, directions and tickets, and some give historical talks in period costume. Hand-held electronic guides (included in ticket price) enhance the experience, particularly while touring the battlefield outside. Using GPS, the guides beep when you arrive at points of interest to give you the background detail. You won't need a beep to notice the Cumberland Stone – the giant boulder that's supposed to mark the spot where the Duke of Cumberland took up his position to direct the battle.

There are fourteen Blue Badge spaces, and it's just a short stroll or push to the entrance to the centre, which has level access throughout. A rooftop viewing area can be accessed by an external ramp, which is not too steep (1:21) but rather long, so some wheelchair users may need a push. It's worth the effort of getting up there though – this has the best view of the grounds. On the battlefield itself, hard-surfaced paths are pushable but undulating in places; again, wheelchair users may need help. Accessible toilets are just inside the visitor centre entrance and there are wheelchairs to hire.

Food & drink ▸▸ Culloden Battlefield is pretty much out on its own, so the in-house catering is the only option available – luckily the light-filled restaurant is very pleasant.

149 RSPB Loch Garten Osprey Centre, Highlands

Address: off the B970, 10 miles from Aviemore **Website:** www.rspb.org.uk/reserves **Telephone:** 01479 831476 **Hours:** daily Jun–end Aug 10am–6pm **Dates:** closed end Aug–end May **Entry:** [D]£2 [C]free [A]£3 [under 16s]50p [Con]£2; family tickets available

The RSPB's Osprey Centre – near the spot, nestling in mature pine forest, where these stunning raptors returned to breed in Scotland – is a mecca for birdwatchers and a favourite with Bill Oddie.

The small, well-appointed Osprey Centre teems with viewing slots and equipment, with some binoculars and telescopes set low for wheelchair users. You get great views of the osprey nest through these, as well as opportunities to scan for the myriad small birds feeding nearby, including, if you're lucky, chirpy Scottish crossbills, and punk-headed crested tits. While the centre doesn't have facilities for people with sensory disabilities, enthusiastic staff are happy to describe the action, and numerous audio and video feeds from the osprey nest bring the atmosphere close up. Further afield in the surrounding Abernethy forest, you can see highly endangered capercaillies, roe deer, common lizards and even otters.

The centre is extremely well signposted from the A9. There are two dedicated parking spaces near to the reception and toilet block, but those with more limited mobility are permitted to drive the last 330 yards to the door, and park right outside the centre. Otherwise visitors can follow a gently undulating and well-compacted path to the centre – a chance to take in the hyperactive red squirrels that appear as if on cue. A gentle ramp takes you inside, where all is on one level and fully wheelchair accessible. The unisex adapted toilet – an eco-friendly composting contraption – is by the car park. If you need to borrow a wheelchair, you can call ahead to book. Any other advance queries can be answered by Richard Thaxton, a permanent member of staff on site in season. The centre has been awarded the Visit Scotland Gold Award for Green Tourism in 2010, and it deserves it – the sights, sounds and smells of the wilderness will stay with you long after a visit.

Food & drink ▸▸ There's nothing more than a tea machine on site, which gives you a perfect excuse to tuck in to Cairngorm Mountain Hare or Highland Lamb at *Anderson's Restaurant* (℡01479 831466, Ⓦwww.andersonsrestaurant.co.uk) in nearby Boat of Garten.

150 Cairngorm Sled-Dog Centre, Highlands

Address: Moormore Cottage, Rothiemurchus, Aviemore PH22 1QU **Website:** www .sled-dogs.co.uk **Telephone:** 07767 270526 **Hours:** tour 2.30pm; advance booking required for tour and safari **Dates:** 25 Dec **Entry:** tour [D]£8 [C]free [A]£8 [child]£4 [Con]£5; safari [D]£60 [C]free [A]£60 [child]£40 [Con]£40

In the Cairngorms National Park, the Cairngorm Sled-Dog Centre offers sled-dog safaris, on winter snow or muddy track. This is once-in-a-lifetime exhilarating experience, but you'll need to be robust to do it.

Alan and Fiona Stewart, who own and run the centre, are totally committed to their sport and their dogs – some of which have competed in the 1150 mile Alaska Iditarod. The Stewarts live in the beautiful forest of the Rothiemurchus Estate and have around forty dogs – all competitive, working animals but also friendly and affectionate. The safaris are undertaken on a two-seater or six-seater sledcart. The dogs sense the excitement in the air when they're going out and their rising anticipation brings the noise level up correspondingly. Before you know it you're hurtling along forest tracks at speeds of up 24 miles per hour – pretty impressive for dog power. The Stewarts' passion for their dogs is matched by their passion for the environment: not only will you have a truly memorable day, but you'll come away enriched by, and more knowledgeable about, the world we live in.

Even in good weather, this is no countryside jolly, but a true wilderness experience. Little specific provision is able to be made for people with disabilities, but the Stewarts will do anything and everything they can to include anyone who wants to take part in this unique adventure. A CD commentary is available. Unless you are super fit, you may want to take an experienced helper, to assist you with transfers and the like. You invariably get very wet and muddy, so warm, waterproof clothing is a must. If you love nature in the raw, and are up for being cold, wet and thrown about, you'll love it.

Food & drink ▸▸ A couple of miles back towards Aviemore is the Rothiemurcus Visitor Centre (☎01479 812345). Beautifully set in an old schoolhouse, its restaurant has a menu that is as lovely as the location.

151 Loch Insh Watersports, Highlands

Address: Kincraig, Kingussie PH21 1NU **Website:** www.lochinsh.com **Telephone:** watersports 01540 651272 **Hours:** watersports daily 8.30am–5.30pm; call ahead for other activities **Dates:** no closures **Entry:** prices vary for individual activities, call ahead for details

Sailing on Loch Insh

Set on the shores of an idyllic loch among the sugar-lump peaks of the Cairngorms, Loch Insh Watersports is perfectly positioned. Out of the loch pours the River Spey, tumbling into the Cairngorms National Park and into bottles of whisky. If you enjoy water sports, just messing around on the water, or simply great views, you could easily entertain yourself and the family for days here.

At Loch Insh, you can enjoy the adrenaline of some adventurous activities, especially in good weather, or just relax with a "nip" in the café-bar-restaurant. Just a short drive from the main A9 artery the loch is easily reached, and has accessible accommodation (excellent-value lodges from four-berth upwards), plenty of facilities and a host of activities on offer. The Loch Insh Activity Centre offers water sports (kayaking, canoeing, river trips, row boats and pedalos); sailsports (sailing and windsurfing); winter sports (skiing and boarding); and even more activities, including mountain biking, archery, orienteering, sledging, fishing, raft-building and multi-activity days. The centre has a silver Green Tourism award and has been operating here for nearly forty years, and makes full use of its location and reputation. If you only have time for a short visit, you can take a one-hour wildlife tour on the loch, visiting the RSPB's Insh Marshes Nature Reserve on the hunt for osprey, goldeneye duck and other birds.

Both the main entrance and the craft shop (a short distance across the car park) have ramped access, and plenty of space to move around. There are disabled parking spaces beside the door of the *Boathouse Restaurant*, and accessible toilets just inside the entrance. The jetties and loch shore are all accessible by wheelchair, via a sloping, hard-surfaced path which runs down to the beach. The team at Loch Insh will happily assist with boarding any craft, including the boat for the wildlife tour.

Food & drink ▸▸ The on-site *Boathouse Restaurant* (☎01540 651394) has ramped access and serves hot meals, light bites and snacks throughout the day. Book in advance for a table with loch views on the accessible balcony.

152 Cairngorm Funicular Railway and Ski Centre, Highlands

Address: Cairngorm by Aviemore, PH22 1RB **Website:** www.cairngormmountain.org.uk **Telephone:** 01479 861261 **Hours:** railway Easter–end Oct daily 10am–4.20pm; trains run every 30 minutes; check ahead as times vary; ski season times vary **Dates:** closed most of Nov & 25 Dec **Entry:** funicular [D]£8.25 [C]free [A]£9.50 [child]£6 [Con]£8.25; for ski school lesson prices enquire through website

Cairngorm Mountain Railway and Ski Centre is literally the pinnacle of Scotland's tourist industry – a wheelchair accessible visitor centre with viewing decks, shop and bar-restaurant – in the heart of the Highlands, at almost 3600 feet.

Thanks to climate change, the centre has had to reinvent itself as a year-round attraction. The fully accessible funicular whisks you up in eight minutes with ever-changing views. The vistas and sunsets from the restaurant and viewing decks are amazing – you might even catch sight of some of the resident reindeer. Have a look at the exhibition recounting the mountain's history, enhanced by tactile exhibits, including fur samples of the local wildlife and audio description accompanying the film show. If you can tear yourself away from the mountaintop, the all-abilities trail around the Wild Mountain Garden, back at car park level, is also worthwhile, with many plants indigenous to the area.

In the ski season, the mountain is home to Disability Snowsport UK (☎01479 861272, ⓦwww.disabilitysnowsport.org.uk), who specialise in getting people onto the pistes, with a full range of adaptive equipment. They offer all levels of instruction, usually one-to-one, from complete beginner onwards, to enable people with almost any disability to ski and snowboard.

There are eight allocated parking bays at the bottom station and a lift to the ticket hall.

> "The views at the top are spectacular, regardless of whether you visit in summer or winter."
>
> **Jean Elliott, Shotts**

Bear in mind that the weather can be very changeable in the Highlands and regardless of the time of year you should always be prepared with warm clothing. Even in mid-summer it can snow at the summit. In winter you should call ahead to check on conditions as the car park can be snowed in and the funicular subject to reduced or cancelled services. The four floors of the top station are fully wheelchair accessible.

Food & drink ▸▸ At the *Ptarmigan Restaurant* you can enjoy your lunch over spectacular views – this is the highest place to eat in Britain. On Thursdays during July and August, it hosts the highest of Highland Flings, accompanied by an extensive buffet.

153 Nevis Range Mountain Experience (Aonach Mor Gondola), Highlands

Address: Nevis Range, Torlundy PH33 6SQ **Website:** www.nevisrange.co.uk **Telephone:** 01397 705825 **Hours:** summer season daily 10am–5pm; peak summer Jul–Aug daily 9.30am–6pm; ski season Mon–Fri 9am–sunset, Sat & Sun 8.30am–sunset **Dates:** closed for annual maintenance mid-Nov–mid-Dec; other closures only in strong winds **Entry:** return ticket [D]£7 [C]free [A]10.50 [5–17s]£6 [Con]£9

Aonach Mor, situated in the Nevis Range and a short distance from Scotland's highest mountain Ben Nevis, is the location of Britain's only mountain gondola.

The gondola is open year-round, and transports visitors up 2150 feet, to a restaurant, Scotland's highest snow-sports area and, of course, dramatic views of the mountain, loch and glen landscape. The slopes are abuzz with skiers and boarders in winter, and offer options for both beginners and experts. An adaptive ski instructor is available for anyone with a disability interested in skiing, though this should be arranged in advance. The upper chairlifts above the gondola don't operate in summer, to protect the sensitive vegetation. The site also has World Cup mountain-biking trails, and forest tracks that are navigable by the more adventurous disabled visitor, if they're not too muddy. The downhill tracks are only open from mid-May to mid-September though the cross-country trails near the base station are open year round. Bikes can be hired on site, but unfortunately no adapted bikes are available. If you are interested in downhill biking, try to arrange it through Rough Riderz (ⓦwww.roughriderz.co.uk) which has

Nevis Range Gondola

hand-controlled downhill quad bikes. Beneath the restaurant, the Mountain Discovery Centre has information about the Nevis range's flora and fauna, but access is via a flight of stairs.

The gondolas are able to accommodate wheelchairs up to 23.6 inches wide, but if yours doesn't fit, transfer onto the gondola seat is quite easy. They also have a narrow chair, which can be wheeled up the ramp, into the gondola by the helpful staff (your own chair can go up with you). The restaurant is accessible by a steep ramp from the outside of the building, just fifty yards from the gondola arrival point, though in winter this may mean a short journey through snow. Its balcony-cum-viewing deck has one small step down to it.

Food & drink ▶▶ The *Snowgoose Restaurant* is right at the top, but space is limited and assistance dogs are not permitted. For something more luxurious try the local seafood at the *Crannog Restaurant* (℡01397 705589) lochside on Fort William town pier.

154 Pitlochry Festival Theatre and Explorer's Garden, Perthshire

Address: Port-na-Craig, Pitlochry PH16 5DR **Website:** www.pitlochry.org.uk **Telephone:** admin office 01796 484600; box office 01796 484626 **Hours:** check website for performance dates and times; theatre and box office daily summer 10am–8pm; winter 10am–5pm; garden 10am–5pm **Dates:** check ahead for Christmas & New Year variations **Entry:** tickets vary depending on performance and seat [C]free; gallery free; garden £3

The Pitlochry Festival Theatre offers more than performances. Visit for backstage tours, an art gallery and the Explorer's Gardens, which will delight horticulturalists.

The theatre offers year-round evening performances, and regular matinées, but even without seeing a performance, you could spend a few hours here enjoying a tour, the gallery, or simply the beautiful setting. On the banks of the River Tummel, the extensive garden and woodlands tell the story of the Scottish Plant Hunters who travelled the globe in search of new plants and trees. The gardens have a network of tarmac paths, steeply graded in places, but step-free. The stone outdoor theatre is rarely used for performances, but it's an interesting spot to visit. If you want to learn more about the trees and plants, take one of the garden tours on offer – they last about ninety minutes. You need to book ahead, and if you make them aware of any particular requirements, staff will try to accommodate your needs.

The modern theatre is a short walk – just less than a mile – across a suspension footbridge from the attractive centre of Pitlochry town. This is a step-free route, albeit steep in places. If you'd prefer to avoid the hills, it's better to drive to the theatre, where plenty of accessible parking is available by the entrance – with striking views across the valley. The venue welcomes disabled visitors: there's good access into the building, four wheelchair spaces in the auditorium and free tickets available for carers. Tours of the backstage area, including the Green Room, are available, and can be conducted as a "touch-tour" that even covers the set. Audio tours or audio-described performances are available on demand (book in advance if possible), and a hearing loop and IR system is fitted in the theatre. The art gallery is mostly accessible, though about a quarter of it is upstairs without lift access. There are plans to refurbish the theatre in the next few years and further improve accessibility.

Food & drink ▶▶ *Festival Restaurant, Café and Bar* offers a lunch and evening menu, with a buffet for matinees. And right beside the theatre, the *Port-na-Craig Inn & Restaurant* (℡01796 472777, Ⓦw+ww.portnacraig.com) sits on an idyllic position on the banks of the river.

155 Dundee Repertory Theatre, Dundee

Address: Tay Square DD1 1PB **Website:** www.dundeereptheatre.co.uk; www
.scottishdancetheatre.com **Telephone:** 01382 223530 **Hours:** check website for
performance dates and times; box office performance days Mon–Sat 10am–7pm, non-
performance days 10am–6pm **Dates:** no performances on Sun & Mon; closed 1–2 Jan &
25–26 Dec **Entry:** tickets vary depending on performance and seat [C]free

Dundee, situated on the banks of the River Tay on the North Sea coast, was once known for the three "Js" – Jute, Jam and Journalism. It also has the dubious honour of having been Britain's last whaling port. Much has changed since those days: it's now a bustling university town with a thriving arts scene, at the centre of which is the Dundee Rep.

This is the only full-time repertory theatre surviving in Scotland, with six permanent acting staff. The auditorium has 450 seats – a generous arena for a provincial theatre. Whether commissioning new works or adapting the classics, the productions here are widely acknowledged to be among the finest in Scotland. The theatre has received several prestigious TMA (Theatrical Management Association) awards in recent years, including two in 2007 for the musical *Sunshine on Leith*. In 2010, the ensemble is booked for performances as varied as the macabre *Sweeney Todd* and the Grimm Brothers' magical tale *The Elves and the Shoemakers*. As well as regular productions by the ensemble cast, there's stand-up comedy, touring productions and seasonal favourites like panto, too. Dundee Rep is also home to the innovative and inclusive Scottish Dance Theatre, which not only has performances that include dancers with a disability, but also encourages other disabled people to try out dance. Caroline Bowditch is a wheelchair user, a dancer and the theatre's "Agent for Change". If you're interested to hear about dance workshops, or opportunities, contact Caroline on ☎01382 342600 or ✉cbowditch@dundeereptheatre.co.uk.

Be aware of the brown road signs that direct you to the theatre from the outskirts of Dundee – they will take you to parking that is a lengthy uphill push away from the theatre. It's better to plan your own route (or call ahead for directions), and arrive early to secure one of the two dedicated bays near the front doors. Access to the theatre – purpose-built and opened in 1982 – is generally very good, with ramped access from the front, a lift to the auditorium, and disabled toilets in the upper bar and restaurant. In the auditorium, the dedicated seating areas afford excellent views of the stage, and all disabled visitors are well catered for. Some audio-described and BSL-interpreted performances are available, while pre-performance touch tours can be organised before audio-described matinées.

Food & drink ▶▶ The upstairs bar has lift access and serves interval drinks, but on the ground floor you can enjoy lunch or dinner in the very good, unpretentious bar-restaurant. Both venues are fully accessible.

156 Callander to Strathyre Trail, Perthshire

Address: Callander FK17 **Website:** www.incallander.co.uk **Telephone:** tourist board 01877 330342 **Hours:** no closures **Dates:** no closures **Entry:** free

Because of the spectacular environment, the strenuous push from Callander to Strathyre – a nine-mile-stretch of Sustrans' NCN Route Seven – is particularly recommended to fit and experienced wheelchair users. Splendid scenic contrasts between Loch Lubnaig and the Strathyre Forest, are set off by the distant mountain peaks.

The small, pretty town of Callander lies on the edge of the Trossachs, fifteen miles west of Stirling. The Station car park behind the *Dreadnought Hotel* – towards the north end of Callander main street – is a good starting point, with disabled parking spaces and accessible toilets. From there follow the NCN Route Seven signs towards Strathyre. Continue for just less than a mile, until you come to the A821 at Kilmahog, which you need to cross with care, remembering to shut the gate behind you. The trail now follows the old railway line and, after 2.7 miles, you reach the southern end of Loch Lubnaig, and the trail then stays close to the west shore of the 3.7 mile-long loch. Towards the north end of the loch, the path begins to climb gently and then goes more steeply uphill. The surface remains good but manual wheelchair users are likely to need strong assistance. After two hairpin bends, you get to a wonderful loch viewpoint. About half a mile further, you cross a narrow, twenty-yard-long wheelchair accessible, suspension bridge and a short while later you reach Strathyre.

Along the largely traffic-free trail, there are accessible toilets at Callander's large car park (six disabled spaces); after five miles at the Strathyre Forest Cabins visitor centre; and finally after eight miles at Strathyre forest commission car park, at the northwest end of the loch, whose RADAR-key-accessible-toilet, however, is not always very clean.

The whole trail, which is part of the National Cycle Network's Route 7: Lochs and Glens: Glasgow to Inverness (www.sustrans.org.uk), has a hard-packed, wheelchair-passable cinder surface, though can be muddy in parts following wet weather. It is likely you'll need a fit assistant for some of the steeper sections. The gates along the cycle route are wheelchair friendly, but if you are using a hand-cycle you will probably need assistance to open them. Rest seats are sporadically dotted along the route.

Food & drink ▶▶ The *Lade Inn* (☎01877 330152, ⓦwww.theladeinn.com) at Kilmahog, about a mile north of Callander and just off the route, has ramped access and has won good food and green tourism awards.

IDEAS ▶▶ FINDING ACCESSIBLE ACCOMMODATION

Accessatlast (☎01772 814555, ⓦwww.accessatlast.com) has a database of properties (UK and international), searchable via requirements such as hoists, grab rails and BSL interpreters. Many properties have been visited on behalf of accessatlast.com and/or reviewed by users. Those with full assessments have a good level of access detail.

Action for Blind People (ⓦwww.actionforblindpeople.org.uk/holidays) is a charity that runs four hotels, specifically adapted for those with visual impairments. They are fitted with talking alarm clocks, facilities for assistance dogs, Braille books and audio-described videos.

Disabled Holiday Info (ⓦwww.disabledholidayinfo.org.uk) has a database of UK hotels and other accommodation, searchable via an extensive choice of requirements – from ground floor rooms to accessible cutlery. It also provides advice on accessible attractions (see Useful Contacts p.193).

Holiday Access Direct (☎01502 566005, ⓦwww.holidayaccessdirect.com) pulls together links and advice on booking holidays and finding places to stay. The main focus is overseas holidays and flights but it does cover accommodation and services in the UK. A team of disabled travel experts can help you with specific queries.

Holidays For All (☎0845 124 9973, ⓦwww.holidaysforall.org) is a consortium of leading disability charities and specialist tour companies offering a variety of services from accessible hotels to fully supported residential centres. Some of the members are listed in this box.

Livability Holidays (☎08456 584 478, ⓦwww.livability.org.uk) owns and operates two hotels and several self-catering properties around the UK, all fully accessible with hoists and wheel-in showers.

Matching Houses (ⓦwww.matchinghouses.com) organises home swaps based on the premise that if your access needs match another member's, then their home will be accessible to you. Online sign-up is free and is required, even to do a preliminary search.

Responsible Travel (☎01273 600030, ⓦwww.responsibletravel.com) has hand-picked accommodation in England, Scotland and Wales that is not only accessible, but also ethical. Go to the "Special Requirements" section and select "Disabled Travel" from the drop-down menu.

Vitalise (☎0845 345 1970, ⓦwww.vitalise.org.uk) runs five holiday centres in the UK offering respite care and hires out two accessible self-catering lodges in Cornwall. The company also organises group holidays (see box p.141).

157 The Steamship Sir Walter Scott, Perthshire

Address: Trossachs Pier, Loch Katrine, by Callander FK17 8HZ **Website:** www.lochkatrine.com
Telephone: 01877 332000 **Hours:** Apr–Oct departs Trossachs Pier to Stronachlachar Pier
10.30am; scenic cruise departs Trossachs Pier 1.30pm & 3pm **Dates:** no cruises Nov–Mar;
other closures in bad weather **Entry:** single [D]£10 [C]£5 [A]£10 [under 16s]£7 [Con]£9;
return [D]£12 [C]£6 [A]£12 [under 16s]£8 [Con]£11; scenic cruise [D]£10 [C]£5 [A]£10
[under 5s]50p [5–15s]£7 [Con]£9

The SS *Sir Walter Scott* is over one hundred years old, and after a £1.4 million refit is looking good for another century. Visitors can board this delightful little ship for a journey
across Loch Katrine, amid the stunning lochs and mountains of the Trossachs.

Loch Katrine – which has been the source of Glasgow's drinking water since 1900 – is
only an hour from the city. The vessel carries passengers six miles across the loch, from
the home port of Trossachs Pier in the east, to Stronachlachar Pier in the west. Built at
Dumbarton, and named after the writer Sir Walter Scott (whose poem "The Lady of the
Lake" was set around Loch Katrine), the ship was then dismantled and transported over-
land to its home – a serious feat of logistics in 1900. Today the ship is still steam-powered,
but by eco-friendly bio-diesel instead of coal; if you're a fan of machinery, look for the
engine room, which is visible from the windows on deck level. Whether passengers soak
up the views out on deck, or stay comfortably seated inside the cabin, this is a wonderful
experience. The surrounding area is perennially popular with cyclists – if you'd like to do
some exploring, hire a golf buggy to tour the paths around the loch.

There are six dedicated parking spaces close to the amenities at Trossachs Pier – the
toilets, booking office and restaurant are in easy pushing distance. You may have to
queue to board, but there's plenty of historical information on the walkway walls to
keep you entertained. Visually impaired visitors may benefit from the live crew commentary. There is level access onboard. Improvements to this already very accessible
ship continue and the team is striving to make it a totally seamless visit for any disabled
visitor. Remember that sailings are subject to the weather – always call ahead.

Food & drink ▶▶ The homely *Anchor's Rest* is accessed by lift from the car park and is an
ideal way to start or finish your visit. On chilly days, lunch in front of the open fire is
the ideal way to end a visit.

158 The Falkirk Wheel, Stirlingshire

Address: Lime Road, Tamfourhill, Falkirk FK1 4RS **Website:** www.thefalkirkwheel.co.uk
Telephone: 08700 500208 **Hours:** visitor centre daily Apr–Oct 9.30–6pm; Nov–Mar Mon–
Wed 11am–3pm Thu–Sun 10am–4.30; check website for boat departures **Dates:** closed
1–2 Jan & 25–26 Dec; check ahead for maintenance closures **Entry:** boat trip [D]£8 [C]free
(if essential) [A]£8 [3–15s]£4.25 [Con]£6.75

The Falkirk Wheel is the world's first and only rotating boat lift – it was built in 2001, to replace eleven locks at the junction of the Union and Forth & Clyde canals, allowing vessels to move between the two waterways and cross Scotland from east to west.

This unique visitor trip, which lasts about an hour, starts as you roll off the boardwalk onto a wheelchair accessible boat. The boat then slowly motors into the lower gondola of the wheel and is gently lifted 115 feet up to the Union Canal, where it floats off again. The views as you rise are magnificent – on a clear day you can see for at least fifty miles – with Fife to the east, Argyll to the west, and gorgeous vistas of the Forth Valley in between. The rotating wheel itself looks like a double-headed Celtic Axe: a twenty-first-

> "I was delighted to find out that, not only could I visit this marvellous piece of engineering, I could actually go on the wheel too."
>
> **Patricia Irving, Oxford**

century innovation that links two essential elements of the industrial revolution. What adds to the fascination is that the linkage happens via the Roman era – once you're at the top, your boat crosses an aqueduct, passes through the 590-foot-long Roughcastle Tunnel, and then sails beneath the Roman Antonine Wall and into the upper basin. It then descends back to your starting point. Audio handsets and a tactile model are available, and there is on-board commentary too.

Disabled visitors (only) can avoid a ten-minute push from the main car park – up a hill and across a lock – by ignoring the brown heritage signs on the approach. Instead, head towards Falkirk town centre, and from that point follow the yellow signs that will direct you to a disabled drop-off point, and seven parking spaces outside the visitor centre. On entering the arc-shaped glass and aluminium complex, you're immediately struck by the scale of the operation. The bottom basin appears to be a natural amphitheatre – in fact it was once a quarry – but don't feel daunted, because the paved area all around is level and allows for comfortable pushing.

Food & drink ▸▸ After the trip try the delicious soup or home baking in the bright and easily accessible café, which also serves as an exhibition space. Thanks to the glass roof, you can eat and watch the spectacle of the wheel rearing up into the sky above you.

159 Gliding with Walking on Air, Kinross-shire

Address: Scottish Gliding Centre, Portmoak Airfield, Scotlandwell, near Kinross KY13 9JJ **Website:** www.walkingonair.org.uk; www.scottishglidingcentre.co.uk **Telephone:** 01592 840222 **Hours:** flying day is Fri, other dates possible by prior arrangement **Dates:** all year, but most frequently in spring and summer **Entry:** 15–30-minute trial flight £40

Walking on Air is a charity, set up to allow people with disabilities and a sense of adventure to soar the thermals using a modified glider. The club uses the Gliding Centre facilities at Portmoak Airfield, and the clubhouse has panoramic views of Loch Leven.

The Chairman of Walking on Air, Steve Derwin, is passionate about flying and the opportunities it offers for integration, enabling people with disabilities to participate on equal terms with the rest of the community. Go along for a trial flight and experience the adrenaline rush of the launch and landing, the almost spiritual experience of being up high as you soar quietly above the mountains, and the mesmerising views of the

Walking on Air

peaks' powdered summits and the lochs far below, sparkling like jewels. Gliding seems to make everyone a bit poetic. The club welcomes visitors and new members, and even if you're not sure about actually flying yourself, you're welcome to come along to meet the enthusiastic members, watch others fly and enjoy a very relaxing day out. For flying, they have a two-seater K21 training glider, known as "WA1", with hand controls fitted front and back. The Scottish Gliding Union has converted one of their gliders, as well, in case WA1 is out of action.

The Scottish Gliding Union has gone all out to support Walking on Air, both with willingness and enthusiasm to incorporate disabled people into its membership and with specific, accessible facilities. There's plenty of accessible parking on a hard-packed cinder surface, and developments are planned for a dedicated disabled car park. The clubhouse has ramped access, with restaurant and overnight accommodation (accessible though not specifically adapted). There's also a converted caravan at the launch point, with ramped access and a disabled toilet and shower.

Food & drink ▶▶ The home-made food at the clubhouse restaurant is great value: the full breakfast should set you up for a flight, and you can calm your nerves at the licensed bar afterwards.

160 The Titan Crane Clydebank, West Dunbartonshire

Address: Garth Drive, Queens Quays, Clydebank G81 1NX **Website:** www.titanclydebank .com **Telephone:** 0141 952 3771 **Hours:** Fri–Mon 10am–5pm **Dates:** closed Tue–Thu; closed 6 Oct–1 May **Entry:** [D]£3 [C]free [A]£4.50 [5–16s]£3 [Con]£3

The Titan Crane helped build world-famous ships, including the *Lusitania*, HMS *Hood* and the *Queen Mary*, survived the blitz and industrial decline, and is now a visitor attraction.

The Titan, like a colossal toy crane, has a box-girder construction and is 150 feet tall. Its viewing platform provides a stunning panorama up and down the river Clyde as well as views of the comings and goings at Glasgow airport. A 45-minute tour offers a running commentary on the former shipyard's past, pointing out the remains of the slipway, down which the likes of the *QE2* and *Britannia* were once launched, but is now little more than a few rotting planks sticking out of the river. Video presentations play inside and outside the crane's winding house, and sepia-tinted photos and films of a bygone age tell the story of the yard in good times and bad.

A bus that can be accessed by platform lift takes you on a short tour to the base of the crane, where you disembark and are transported in a couple of minutes by glass lift to the viewing platform. Up at the top, there are sets of fixed binoculars, two of them at a lower position, ideal for wheelchair users. There is a single, free, disabled parking space at the booking office with gently ramped access to the ticket office and shop, and there is an accessible toilet in the waiting area. The site is open to the elements, so it's best to wear warm clothes, even on a fine day.

Food & drink ▶▶ Hot drinks and light snacks are available at the shipyard, but if you'd rather eat somewhere less exposed, be aware that the closest restaurants are just less than a mile away in the Clydebank Shopping Centre.

161 House for an Art Lover, Glasgow

Address: Bellahousten Park, 10 Dumbreck Road G41 5BW **Website:** www .houseforanartlover.co.uk **Telephone:** 0141 353 4770 **Hours:** Apr–Sep Mon–Wed 10am–4pm, Thu–Sun 10am–1pm; Oct–Mar Sat–Sun 10am–1pm **Dates:** check ahead as venue is used for functions **Entry:** [D]£3 [C]£3 [A]£4.50 [under 16s]£3 [Con]£3

Legendary Scottish architect and artist Charles Rennie Mackintosh drew up plans for the House for an Art Lover in 1901, but it wasn't built until the 1990s; consequently this elegant house boasts all the hallmarks of a Mackintosh creation with the accessibility of a modern building.

The architects charged with its construction worked closely from the original designs. Mackintosh pioneered the Art Nouveau movement in the UK, and the building is emblematic of his desire to make the functional beautiful. Inside, all his signature designs are present – the high-backed chairs with their robust right angles, the softly tinted stained glass and, of course, the iconic Mackintosh rose. The grand Main Hall was designed for entertaining, and all the other main rooms radiate from it. The rose motif is evident throughout the intimate Dining Room, but it's the bright Music Room that really dazzles – bathed in natural light from the huge windows that lead onto the terrace, and featuring an ornate baby grand piano, the room is breathtaking. The computers in the Interpretation Room use twenty-first-century technology that Mackintosh could only have dreamt of – it's used mainly as a study suite, but it's a fascinating facility for all visitors to use. The souvenir shop is stocked with gems and is a great

The Music Room at House for an Art Lover

place to pick up gifts – you can buy Mackintosh-styled jewellery, as well as prints of his original work.

Only two levels of the four-storey building are open to the public – outside there is a ramp up to the house, and one down to the café, and a lift between floors inside. To save the effort of going uphill, enter via the café, and leave from the upper floor. There are four disabled parking spaces available in the staff car parking area, and disabled toilets are on the ground floor. The house has been designed with access in mind – some rooms are less spacious than others, but all surfaces are smooth. Staff are available if you need any assistance. The excellent audio sets are induction loop compatible. Only yards away from the house are the tranquil Victorian Walled Gardens – particularly worth a look at in high summer when the sweet peas are in bloom.

Food & drink ▸▸ *The Art Lover's Café* on the ground floor serves coffee, cakes, three course lunches, and everything in between – the food is sublime.

162 Scottish Football Museum, Glasgow

Address: Hampden Park G42 9BA **Website:** www.scottishfootballmuseum.org.uk
Telephone: 0141 616 6139 **Hours:** Mon–Sat 10am–5pm, Sun 11am–5pm **Dates:** museum closed when international matches are played; closed 1–2 Jan & 25–26 Dec **Entry:** museum [D]£3 [C]£3 [A]£6 [5–16s]£3 [Con]£3; stadium tour [D]£3 [C]£3 [A]£6 [5–16s]£3 [Con]£3; combined tickets available

Housed within Hampden Park Stadium (home of Queen's Park FC and the national side) is the Scottish Football Museum – or the Hampden Experience as it bills itself.

Glasgow is inextricably linked to the beautiful game and all the highs and lows, and notorious rivalries of Scottish football are recorded here. From the moment of your arrival at the imposing front of the stadium you're drawn deep into this world. While there are numerous items of tactile statuary and full-size artefacts, like old turnstiles and seating, the exhibits are far from dusty museum fare. Several times a year in Glasgow, two massive clubs – Rangers and Celtic – square up to decide bragging rights for their supporters. But this support is often marred by controversy, with both teams of followers being long associated with religious intolerance. To its credit, the museum does not shy away from such topics, but also dwells on the massive benefits the game brings. Audiovisual displays throughout recount anecdotes and tell the stories of the players, pundits and fans. Memorabilia from each era of football is everywhere, from the origins of the game in the Corinthian clubs of the nineteenth century to the present day. There are daily guided tours of the stadium at 11am, 12.30pm, 2pm and 3pm between November and March, and at 3.30pm from April to October – except when there is a match on.

The two-thousand-bay car park has plenty of disabled spaces, and there are also two Blue Badge spaces adjacent to the door. Visitors have to keep their eyes peeled for a tiny sign directing them to the disabled access point. This is essentially a controlled entry system which is also in service on match days – unfortunately there can be a delay with someone arriving to open the door for you, and the stadium staff are aware this service could be improved. If you don't want to risk a wait, you can enter via the main door, but you have to push up a fairly lengthy ramp. Inside, the seamless ease of access makes the museum a real pleasure to visit. It's a bit of a tardis, too, with more to discover around each cleverly constructed corner. The staff live and breathe football and are happy to inform and assist in any way they can. Magnifying glasses are available for viewing the displays. The shop is in the same large area as the café, while accessible toilets are situated in the corridor outside.

Food & drink ▸▸ The spacious café serves everything you'd expect, from freshly made salads to the Scottish football terrace favourite – meat pie with a cup of Bovril!

163 The Abbotsford Trust, Roxburghshire

Address: Abbotsford, Melrose TD6 9BQ Website: www.scottsabbotsford.co.uk Telephone: 01896 752043 Hours: Mar–Oct Mon–Sat 9.30am–5pm; Sun additionally 15 Mar–May & Oct 11am–4pm; Jun–Sep 9.30am–5pm Dates: closed 1 Nov–second Mon in Mar Entry: [D]£3.50 [C]free [A]£7 [child]£3.50 [Con]£3.50

Nestled on the banks of the river Tweed, Abbotsford is blessed with a stunning setting – it's easy to see how the romantic Borders landscape inspired Sir Walter Scott to become such a prolific novelist.

When the young Scott arrived at Abbotsford, the estate was a good deal more basic than the baronial pile and stunning formal gardens you see there today. He developed extensively, decorating lavishly with the proceeds from a career as an internationally

successful writer. Disabled visitors make their way into the house via the original main entrance. There is a lot to take in, from the imposing, dark-panelled entrance hall, to the armoury which is packed with military objects collected by Scott. But literary fans will be most over-awed by the study, where Scott worked on books including the Waverley novels, and the Library, where thousands of priceless volumes line the walls, still in the order that Scott arranged them. The small chapel, tearoom, shop and accessible toilets are on the floor below.

Abbotsford isn't a perfectly accessible site but the charitable trust that manages the estate is aware of its limitations, and is working hard to raise the substantial funds needed to make improvements, including building a new visitor centre. In the meantime, the staff are happy to provide any assistance you might need if you visit unaccompanied. The tricky bits are outside – you need to be prepared for some loose, deep and lengthy gravel paths as well as steep ramping at the entrance. The four disabled parking spaces are available via the private/staff entrance. Inside it's much easier to explore, and lightweight portable stools can be borrowed. To get to the lower floor, wheelchair users will have to exit the building and re-enter at the other side of the house – but if you ask to be let in through the "post room" door, you'll avoid some pushing. The gardens are quite steep and gravelled, but there is some seating dotted around.

Food & drink ▸▸ The modern tearoom is bright and spacious – it serves delicious, home-made hot drinks, sandwiches and soups as well as cakes and scones.

Northern Ireland

Northern Ireland

Northern Ireland has many areas of immensely beautiful countryside. Its main outdoor attractions – such as the Giants Causeway – are dotted around the coastline, while inland are the spectacular Mourne Mountains. The largest city is fast developing Belfast, a high-energy place full of grand buildings, as well as trendy shops and bars.

164 Ulster Folk and Transport Museum, County Down

Address: Cultra, Holywood BT18 0EU **Website:** www.nmni.com/uftm **Telephone:** 028 9042 8428 **Hours:** Mar–Sep Tue –Sun 10am–5pm; Oct–Feb Tue–Fri 10am–4pm, Sat & Sun 11am–4pm **Dates:** closed 25–26 Dec; closed Mon except bank holidays **Entry:** combined tickets [D]free [C]free [A]£7.50 [5–18s]£4 [Con]£3.50; separate site tickets available

Although billed as one attraction, you actually get two museums for your money when you visit the Ulster Folk and Transport Museum. At the Folk Museum, you can sample Irish life as it was a century ago: Ballycultra is a re-creation of a town with thirty authentic buildings, whilst the Rural Area focuses on farming life at the turn of the century. It's all brought to life by costumed staff, daily demonstrations of crafts like basket weaving and the scent of traditional soda bread cooking over a peat-burning stove. Some of the buildings may be inaccessible for wheelchair users, but enthusiastic guides are on hand to describe the premises and the lives of the folk who lived or worked there. A limited number of powered scooters are available free of charge for Shopmobility or Disabled Ramblers Association licence holders, but should be booked in advance.

The award-winning Transport Museum celebrates all things vehicular. It's one of the largest transport collections in Europe and a must-visit for transport buffs. But it's a great place for a family day out too – you can travel from the steam age to the jet age, testing your skills in the latter on an impressive flight simulator. Ireland has been a major innovator in the technology of rail transport, and this is reflected by the impressively restored collection of historic locomotives, carriages and wagons. Visitors will come across a world-renowned exhibition about the Belfast-built *Titanic* and the museum is also the only one in the world to feature a collection of Irish-built cars, among them the DeLorean, which shot to fame in the movie *Back to the Future*. Displays, photographs and audio exhibits are pulled together seamlessly to create a compelling experience for any visitor. The Transport Museum is indoors, and split across two sites. You can drive from one car park to another as you visit the museum. There are a few wheelchairs for visitors to borrow. The ramp system is good and only two areas are inaccessible to wheelchair users. In both cases, though, viewing areas allow you to see the exhibits.

Food & drink ▸▸ The Folk Museum's *Ballycultra Tearoom* serves hot and cold meals, while in the Transport Museum part of the park, the *Midland Kiosk* is the place to grab a snack. In good weather, the beautiful grounds are perfect for a picnic.

165 The Odyssey Complex, Belfast

Address: 2 Queen's Quay BT3 9QQ **Website:** www.odysseyarena.com; www.theodyssey
.co.uk **Telephone:** arena box office 028 9073 9074; arena box office textphone 028 9073
9174; W5 booking line 028 9046 7790 **Hours:** check website for performance dates and
times; arena box office Mon–Fri 10am–7pm, Sat 10am–5pm; W5 Mon–Thu 10am–5pm, Fri
& Sat 10am–6pm, Sun noon–6pm **Dates:** arena box office closed Sun; W5 closed 24–26 Dec
Entry: arena variations depending on performances and seats; Belfast Giants [D]£8 [C]£8
[A]£14 [5–15s]£8 [Con]£8; W5 [D]£6.80 [C]free [A]£6.80 [3–16s]£4.90 [Con]£5.40

You don't have to wait very long to get a rainy day in Belfast, and when you do, it's a perfect time to visit the city's "Millennium Project", the Odyssey Complex – although there are enough events and activities going on here to fill days worth of visits.

Part of the Laganside development (see p.182), Odyssey has quickly established itself as one of Belfast's main entertainment venues. The Odyssey Arena has ten thousand seats, is home to the Belfast Giants ice hockey team and stages performances by some of the world's biggest acts: Rod Stewart, Mark Knopfler and Leona Lewis are all secured for 2010. There is no such thing as a bad seat at the Odyssey Arena – great views of the ice rink or stage are guaranteed. There are six dedicated viewing areas available for wheelchair users, and assisted hearing headsets are available, so make the box office staff aware of any requirements – they can also brief the events stewards about your needs. Events lists in alternative formats can be requested by calling ☎028 9076 6000.

In the wider Odyssey Complex, there is even more to experience, all under the same roof as the arena, and all activities are fully accessible. You'll find an indoor bowling arena with ramped access and a cinema that you can reach by lift. But the big draw is W5, a discovery museum with over 180 interactive exhibits, aimed at kids of all ages. The attraction tries to answer five very important questions: Who, What, Where, When and Why? If your kids are inquisitive enough to want to know where electricity comes from, or how to beat a lie detector, then they'll love this place, and it will entertain them for hours.

> "W5 is a great accessible, hands-on science facility. It's an especially fun place for children, and you'll find that the staff are well trained and helpful."
>
> **Anthony Barclay, Carrickfergus**

The car parking spaces closest to the building are reserved for Blue Badge holders, but are available on a first-come, first-served basis. All the designated bays are within fifty metres of the entrance, with just one crossing and no steps to negotiate. There is lift access to the two upper levels of the complex, with level access throughout the ground-floor area. Accessible toilets are on all levels, there are low-level counters at the box office and many of the retail outlets, while the recently improved signage is clear.

Food & drink ▸▸ The complex is home to bars, cafés, restaurants and even a nightclub. A branch of *La Tasca* (☎028 9073 8241, ⓦwww.latasca.co.uk/belfast) serves tasty and affordable tapas. This restaurant has lift access, a disabled toilet (although small and with only one grab rail), and can provide large print menus if requested in advance.

NORTHERN IRELAND

166–168 Laganside: St George's Market, St Anne's Cathedral and Waterfront Hall, Belfast

Address: St George's Market 12–20 East Bridge Street BT1 3NQ; St Anne's Cathedral, Donegall Street BT1 2HB; Waterfront Hall, 2 Lanyon Place BT1 3WH **Website:** www .belfastcity.gov.uk/stgeorgesmarket; www.belfastcathedral.org; www.waterfront.co.uk **Telephone:** waterfront box office 028 9033 4455 **Hours:** market Fri 6am–2pm, Sat 9am–3pm; cathedral Mon–Fri 10am–4pm; waterfront check website for performance dates and times **Dates:** market closed Sun–Thu; cathedral closed Sat and after Sun services; check individual websites for Christmas & New Year closures **Entry:** free to public spaces; waterfront tickets vary depending on performance and seats

Belfast first grew on the banks of the River Lagan, and the now revitalised Laganside represents the vibrant Belfast of the new millennium. This vast area of waterside redevelopment takes in the Odyssey Arena (see p.181), Lanyon Place, the Cathedral Quarter, Custom House Square, Donegall Quay and the famous St George's Market.

Right across this showcase regeneration zone there are plenty of addresses to see and be seen at, and always a long list of events taking place. Laganside has a multitude of public arts spaces – indeed there is usually live music being played at St George's Market while locals scour the Saturday stalls. Open Fridays and Saturdays, St George's is Ireland's largest covered market, and has a disabled toilet (RADAR key required), and level access throughout. The atmospheric Saturday Food and Garden Market is really worth a visit if you fancy splashing out on the very best of Belfast's fresh food produce.

Little more than half a mile away, St Anne's Cathedral lies at the heart of the magnificent Cathedral Quarter. The cathedral was consecrated in 1904, but its most eye-catching feature was added just a few years ago. The Spire of Hope is a 54-metre-high steel spike that sprouts skywards from the cathedral roof, designed to "point to Heaven" – it's an addition that has divided local opinion. There is ramped access to all sections of the cathedral, except one small area that is accessible only via a few steps. Back outside, the cobbled streets of the Quarter can make it more difficult to negotiate than other areas of Laganside, but it's well worth doing so.

Despite the historical significance of the Cathedral Quarter, Laganside is best symbolised by its flagship development, the Waterfront Hall. As well as classical music concerts, this venue hosts many other events that will perfectly top off any day out in the area. In 2010 these will include acts as diverse as Pendulum, Status Quo and The Beach Boys. The purpose-built venue is well equipped for disabled visitors, and when lit at night the glass walls of the public areas are a glamorous sight.

Laganside doesn't have one central car park, but there is parking near each main site. Surprisingly, though, the modern Waterfront Hall doesn't have its own disabled parking – the nearest accessible spaces you'll find are in the multistorey car park attached to the Hilton Hotel on Lanyon Place, but you can get dropped off in front of the Waterfront building. Most of the pavements in the Laganside area are level, although there's a bit of a gradient as you approach the waterfront at Donegall Quay and exit Lanyon Place towards Belfast's main railway station. Staff at the venues are invariably helpful.

Food & drink ▸▸ In the local pubs, you'll find music and entertainment to suit prac-

NORTHERN IRELAND

tically any taste, from contemporary at *The John Hewitt* (☎028 9023 3768, ⓦwww
.thejohnhewitt.com) to traditional Irish at the *Duke of York* (☎028 9024 1062) – both
located in the Cathedral Quarter. Right on the waterfront, *The Edge* (☎028 9032 2000,
ⓦwww.at-the-edge.info) is a laid-back restaurant with great food, good disabled facilities and superb views. There is a Blue Badge spot outside the main entrance, but you
may need help with the heavy front doors.

169 Grand Opera House, Belfast

Address: Great Victoria Street BT2 7HR **Website:** www.goh.co.uk (equipped with
Browsealoud) **Telephone:** box office 028 9024 1919; stage door 028 9024 0411; box
office textphone 028 9027 8578 **Hours:** check website for performance dates and times;
box office Mon–Fri 9am–8pm, Sat 10am–6pm **Dates:** box office hours may vary on bank
holidays **Entry:** prices vary depending on performances and seats; a free seat is available for
essential carers

Grand Opera House

First opened in 1895, the Grand Opera House is one of Belfast's oldest and best-loved venues. From serious drama to the inevitable Christmas panto, the schedule is packed throughout the year – but whatever performance you choose, you are guaranteed a grand evening. The bill for summer 2010 boasts stage favourites from the heartwarming *Calendar Girls* to the bloodcurdling *The Woman in Black*.

The theatre closed at the height of the "troubles", and only reopened in 1980 when it became the focus of city centre renewal. And in 2006, a new performance space – the Baby Grand – was developed. The Main Auditorium in the old part of the building is magnificent: the original décor has been well maintained, and the atmosphere is intimate and relaxing. Most areas are wheelchair accessible and seating is spacious and comfortable with ample legroom. In the Baby Grand, all wheelchair spaces are in the front row. Staff offer excellent and reassuring one-to-one customer service. When you book, make them aware of your access needs to help them find the most appropriate seating for you – they can also keep your details on record to ensure they're fully appraised for your next visit. All the cafés, bars and restaurants are wheelchair accessible, so you are free to kick off your evening in style with a pre-show meal or cocktail.

Accessible parking is available in the multistorey car park behind the *Europa Hotel* and opposite the side entrance to the venue – this is approximately two hundred metres away, but some paths on the approach are uneven in places. The main entrance is level and a lift takes you to all other floors. Accessible toilets with grab rails and low level mirrors are on every level, except up in "the gods". Make sure you state when booking if you are planning to visit in a powered scooter. Colour contrast is excellent throughout and visitors with assistance dogs can be reassured the acoustics are not too intrusive. Audio described, signed and captioned performances are available for most productions, and some staff have had BSL training. Brochures are available in different formats on request.

Food & drink ▶▶ *Luciano's Café Bar* in the foyer serves snacks, coffee and pastries, while the *Hippodrome Restaurant* on the third floor offers more substantial meals. If you fancy a drink in the interval, try the circle or Baby Grand bars, but be prepared for crowds.

NORTHERN IRELAND

IDEAS ▶▶ MORE ACCESSIBLE MUSEUMS

The Beacon Museum (☏01946 592302, ⓦwww.thebeacon-whitehaven .co.uk) in Whitehaven, Cumbria, tells the story of the town, its harbour and its shipbuilding history. It's a family-friendly museum, and was built to be fully accessible. The facilities are excellent – all five floors are wheelchair accessible, the video presentations are subtitled, the signage is tactile, and the views from the telescope on the top floor are amazing.

Imperial War Museum, London (☏020 7416 5000, ⓦwww.london.iwm.org .uk) has step-free access via the park entrance, folding stools can be borrowed and staff are on hand to help. In 2010, the Terrible Trenches exhibition will help children understand about life for soldiers during World War I.

Museum of Science & Industry (☏0161 832 2244, ⓦwww.mosi.org.uk) in Castlefield tells the story of Manchester's scientific and industrial past. Don't miss the Victorian Sewer with its authentic smells. Although the site is historic – home to the world's oldest surviving passenger railway – the listed museum buildings are linked by smooth paths and there are lifts on site.

170 Ulster Museum, Belfast

Address: Botanic Gardens, Stranmillis Road BT9 5AB **Website:** www.nmni.com/um
Telephone: 028 9044 0000 **Hours:** Tue–Fri 10am–5pm, Sat 1–5pm, Sun 2–5pm; closed on
Mon except bank holidays **Dates:** closed 24–26 Dec **Entry:** free

Ulster Museum

The Ulster Museum doors were reopened to the public in October 2009. £17 million pounds and three years of development work have transformed this museum into a shiny, engaging and highly accessible place to visit.

The striking new 23-metre-high atrium floods the museum with light. Two more floors have been added, along with glass and steel walkways leading visitors into the art, history and science galleries, which tell the story of the evolution of Ireland, from Jurassic times through to recent political history. But it isn't just Irish history that is covered and must-see exhibits vary wildly in subject. On your hit list should be the gleaming collection of gold coins and jewellery rescued from the Spanish Armada fleet shipwrecked on the Giant's Causeway; Takabuti, an Egyptian mummy brought to the museum in 1835; the twentieth-century haute couture fashion collection; and the ever-popular Peter the Polar Bear, whose home is the impressive Window on our World display tower. The three new interactive Discovery Zones – nature, art and science – are especially entertaining for children.

Disabled visitors can move round this refurbished space with ease. There are six Blue Badge spaces available in the designated disabled car park, and ramps lead into the stunning entrance hall. In this spacious reception area you'll find the two main lifts, and elsewhere there are three additional self-operating lifts, which provide alternatives to the staircases in the old part of the building. There are plenty of disabled toilets on site. Visitors with sensory disabilities can call ahead to organise free personal guided tours.

Food & drink ▶▶ The brand-new museum restaurant overlooks the lovely Botanic Gardens next door, or you can eat your own packed lunch in the picnic room on the ground floor if the weather keeps you from venturing outside.

NORTHERN IRELAND

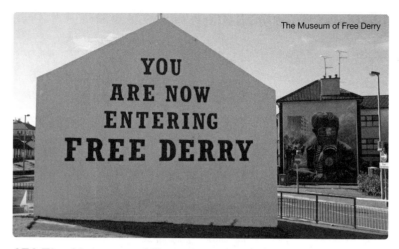

The Museum of Free Derry

171 The Museum of Free Derry, County Londonderry

Address: Bloody Sunday Centre, 55 Glenfada Park, Derry BT48 9DR **Website:** www
.museumoffreederry.org **Telephone:** 028 7136 0880 **Hours:** Mon–Fri 9.30am–4.30pm, Sat
additionally Apr–Sep 1–4pm, Sun additionally Jul–Sep 1–4pm **Dates:** closed 25–26 Dec **Entry:**
[D]£3 [C]£3 [A]£3 [10–16s]£2 [Con]£2

Located in an area known as the Bogside, the Museum of Free Derry is right on the door-
step of history – the Bogside played a key role in the "troubles" that beset Northern Ireland
from the late Sixties onwards. In fact, on the museum's reception desk you can pick up a
map that shows where thirteen civilians were shot dead by the army on the day in 1972
that is now known as Bloody Sunday – no place of death is more than a stone's throw
from the museum's front door.

The museum was established in 2006, and sets out to offer an explanation of what hap-
pened on that infamous day – it is an engaging and informative place to visit and attracts
visitors from all over the world. The tour briefly outlines the history of Derry in the run-up
to the start of the "troubles", and then moves on to detail the day itself, and the immediate
aftermath of the event. The story is told on around thirty exhibition boards while touch-
screen computers allow access to collections of photographs, never before seen in public.
Audio taken from amateur footage filmed between 1968 and 1972 is played at one stage
of the exhibition, and you can watch the film itself as you approach the end of the tour.
But perhaps the most illuminating part of a visit here is outside: the Bogside Artists'
murals are painted on many of the walls near the museum. To fully appreciate the murals and the events they depict, view them after you have seen the museum exhibits. The
Bloody Sunday Monument is only metres away too.

Visitors should be prepared for a few difficulties outside: some of the pavements are
uneven and finding a parking space can be tricky, as the museum is close to a residential
area. There aren't any dedicated disabled bays, but there are some spaces right outside
the museum and a few more on the main street adjacent to the museum. The makeshift

ramp to the museum entrance is very steep, and doesn't have a hand rail – wheelchair users may find it difficult to self-propel to the door. Inside it gets much easier though, with level access throughout and a spacious disabled toilet equipped with grab rails. The displays are highly visual, so deaf and hard of hearing visitors will find the museum largely accessible. The text on the exhibition boards is reasonably bold, but visually impaired visitors may struggle with some white text. Staff are on hand to provide assistance and answer questions.

Food & drink ▶▶ *Café Grianan* is close by on William Street, and serves well-priced snacks. £3.50 will buy you a delicious, fresh and huge sandwich. There is ramped access at the entrance, but remember to use the disabled toilets before you leave the museum, as there aren't any here.

172 Belleek Pottery Visitor Centre, County Fermanagh

Address: 33 Main Street, Belleek BT93 3FY **Website:** www.belleek.ie **Telephone:** 028 6865 9300 **Hours:** Jan–Feb Mon–Fri 9am–5.30pm; Mar–Jun Mon–Fri 9am–5.30pm, Sat 10am–5.30pm, Sun 2–5.30pm; Jul–Oct Mon–Fri 9am–6pm, Sat 10am–6pm, Sun noon–6pm; Nov–Dec Mon–Fri 9am–5.30pm, Sat 10am–5.30pm **Dates:** closed Sat & Sun in Jan & Feb, also Sun in Nov & Dec; closed 1–4 Jan, 17 Mar & 24–31 Dec **Entry:** [D]£2 [C]£2 [A]£4 [over 12s]£2 [Con]£2

Shop at the Belleek Pottery Visitor Centre

Originally set up by a landowner to provide employment for locals suffering the after-effects of the potato famine, the Belleek factory has been producing pottery for over 150 years – longer than anywhere else in Ireland – and its products are exceptionally popular.

The Belleek International Collector's Society has 7500 loyal members worldwide and many own hundreds of pieces of the trademark porcelain. You don't have to be an avid fan to enjoy the visitor centre – anyone can appreciate the craftsmanship on show. If you are keen to get collecting though, you can make a start in the spacious showroom, which has some exclusive pieces on sale, but visit the museum first to brush up on the history of the products. A bell signals loudly that visitors should gather together for the factory tour – when you hear it, head to the reception (deaf or hard of hearing visitors can be reassured that tour times are printed on entry tickets). It takes about thirty minutes to see everything behind the scenes – you'll witness working moulds being made and liquid slip being poured; watch designers painstakingly shape the intricate floral designs; feel the heat in the kiln firing area; and finally admire the work of the artists as they delicately paint the porcelain. You can chat to some of the craftspeople, and might even have the chance to get your hands dirty.

There are six Blue Badge spaces directly in front of the visitor centre, and the disabled toilets are roomy. The tour route only goes through areas that have been refurbished in the last decade, so it is a level journey all the way around. The guides are keen that everyone gets the best possible view, and chairs are provided for visitors on foot to rest at many of the stop points. Wheelchairs are available, but they can be rather hard-seated – take a cushion along for comfort!

Food & drink ▸▸ The *Belleek Tearoom* serves good-quality lunches on fine Belleek crockery. It's split-level, but you can specify that ground-floor seating is required. If you'd rather bring your own food, use one of the tables on the grassy area outside.

173 Peatlands Park, County Armagh

Address: 33 Derryhubbert Road, Dungannon BT71 6NW **Website:** www.ni-environment.gov.uk/peatlands **Telephone:** 028 3885 1102 **Hours:** park daily Easter–Sep 9am–9pm; Oct–Easter 9am–5pm; visitor centre daily Easter–Sep 10am–6pm **Dates:** visitor centre & railway closed Oct–Easter; park closed 25 Dec **Entry:** park free; railway [D]£1 [C]£1 [A]£1 [under 5s] free [5–15s]50p [Con]£0.50

Peatlands Park is the first of its kind in the UK – a ten-thousand-year-old peatland, opened to the public to raise awareness of environmental issues in this kind of habitat. Home to a wide variety of wildlife including waterfowl, butterflies, moths, lizards, newts and frogs, much of the park is protected as a National Nature Reserve and an SSSI (Site of Special Scientific Interest).

A leafy driveway leads into the woodlands and wetlands, and accessible paths connect the car park to the central area of Peatlands, where a visitor centre, railway, shop and toilets are based. You'll find an education centre with an interesting low-environmental-impact design here too. And immediately surrounding these buildings is a grassy area with picnic benches, an orchard and a small lake. You can make your way from here along the ten-mile network of waymarked trails, or tour the open bog area from the comfort of the visitor train. The narrow-gauge railway used for the original turbary, or turf cutting, has now been opened up to the public and is fully accessible. If you're a fan of surreal entertainment, visit on the last Sunday of July in 2010, when the park will be hosting the bizarre, but increasingly popular, Bog Snorkelling Championships.

The Parkside Walk is the only tarmac trail at Peatlands and is just under a mile long, while a boardwalk loop around the Bog Garden is also wheelchair accessible. The other trails have mixed surfaces of wood chip, boardwalk and gravel, so are heavy going for unassisted wheelchair users, but are just about suitable for powered scooters. A limited number of rough-terrain scooters can be borrowed by Shopmobility or Disabled Ramblers Association licence holders, but should be booked in advance. Call ahead, too, if your mobility is very restricted, as you may be able to arrange vehicle access further into the park.

Food & drink ▶▶ There aren't any cafés or restaurants at Peatlands, so if you think you'll get peckish, bring along a picnic. There are many picnic tables to choose from.

174 Armagh Planetarium, County Armagh

Address: College Hill, Armagh BT61 9DB **Website:** www.armaghplanet.com **Telephone:** 028 3752 3689 **Hours:** check website for seasonal variations **Dates:** check website for seasonal variations **Entry:** shows [D]£5 [C]£6 [A]£6 [child]£5 [Con]£5; exhibition area £2; family tickets available

Lean back and take a visual journey across the night sky then step outside and repeat your voyage through space on foot – at Ireland's leading astronomical education centre, you can do both and learn a great deal about our solar system in the process.

The traditional domed ceiling of the planetarium is illuminated by a state-of-the-art digital projection system and plays host to a changing programme of family-friendly shows (prebooking advised), from close-up tours of the Red Planet to learning how to identify those constellations visible with the naked eye. Aside from the planetarium itself, there is an engrossing exhibition area featuring, among other displays, a recently acquired 4.5-billion-year-old meteorite. Both the planetarium and the nearby Armagh Observatory are located in the fourteen-acre Astropark, whose rolling green landscape reveals all sorts of educational models that complement the starry scenes you'll have seen inside. Wandering round the impressive scale model of the universe, for example, gives you an immediate grasp of the relative sizes of the nine planets, the distances between them and the supremacy of the sun.

The planetarium complex is straightforward to navigate, with ramped walkways approaching the main entrance and all areas of the ground floor, and two Blue Badge spaces nearby. A lift provides access to the first floor and there are designated viewing areas for wheelchair users in the theatre itself. There's a unisex wheelchair accessible toilet on each floor. Signage in the main areas and the lift are given in Braille and assistance dogs are welcome – bear in mind, though, that the special effects used in the theatre could be unsettling for dogs, and the revolving images overhead can take a little getting used to for human visitors too! Both the reception and theatre have an induction loop. Lastly, paved walkways weave around the Astropark and there are plenty of places to sit down en route.

Food & drink ▶▶ The café on site serves a good range of hot and cold drinks and snacks. In Armagh city, there are a lot of cafés to choose from, but both the snack bar and restaurant in the *Market Place Theatre* (Ⓦwww.marketplacearmagh.com) are recommended.

175 Quoile Countryside Centre and Castle, County Down

Address: 5 Quay Road, Downpatrick BT30 7JB **Website:** www.ni-environment.gov.uk/quoile **Telephone:** 028 4461 5520 **Hours:** park daily Easter–Sep 10am–6pm; Oct–Easter Sun only noon–4pm; Castle Island bird hide usually 10am–4pm **Dates:** closed 25–26 Dec **Entry:** free

This pleasant and relaxing countryside area has accessible riverside walks and an abundance of wildfowl and other birds. Quoile is a National Nature Reserve, with a countryside centre and castle tower at its heart, and a fantastic bird hide on its eastern fringe.

The riverbanks have been transformed from tidal inlet to freshwater grass and woodland since a tidal barrage was constructed in 1957, to prevent flooding of the area. A 1.5-mile path with a hard surface runs through woodland along the riverbank, from the floodgates at the Downpatrick end of the reserve to steps climbing to Steamboat Quay, once a busy port with a paddleboat steamer to Liverpool. The reserve is a haven for wildfowl and you'll see large numbers of ducks, swans and geese. The countryside centre has displays on the wildlife and history of the area, an attractive, small garden with raised organic beds, and a picnic area beside the stream. They also offer introductory birdwatching courses – call them for dates. Also worth a visit for views of the seashore and Strangford Lough is the 2.5-mile drive to the Castle Island Road, where the large and attractively constructed Castle Island bird hide overlooks the reserve from the south and offers ornithologists wonderful viewing opportunities.

Quoile Countryside Centre is just north of Downpatrick, on the road to Strangford (signposting is poor so keep your eyes peeled), and effectively situated on both sides of the Quoile River. The paths and buildings within the nature reserve are all ramped and suitable for wheelchair access, though it's best to park at the countryside centre to avoid steeper ramps up to the other two car parks further along the river. Steps lead up to the castle tower, and to Steamboat Quay. Castle Island bird hide has ramped access.

Food & drink ▶▶ In the nearby town of Downpatrick the *Oakley Fayre Café* (☎028 4461 2500) on Market Street and the *Cathedral Garden Café* in the St Patrick's Centre (Ⓦwww.saintpatrickcentre.com) both offer tasty hot and cold snacks and pastries.

USEFUL CONTACTS

This **Useful Contacts** chapter features the Rough Guide pick of the specialist organisations and independent companies that provide advice, assistance and services to help disabled people with holidays and day-trips in Britain. **Getting Around** has the lowdown on practical services for your day-to-day travel needs. **Travel Advice** flags up the disability charities and organisations that, in addition to their everyday work, provide travel and leisure advice and aid. Here we also champion the specialist providers of UK accessible travel and holiday information. And finally, **British Tourism** highlights the regional and national tourist boards and keepers of national heritage whose access information and advice stands out from the rest.

GETTING AROUND

BBNav – Blue Badge enhanced GPS navigation www.bbnav.co.uk Sat-Nav system with all the usual functionality as well as coverage of Blue Badge on-street parking bays, car park access and local council parking rules for over 150 major UK cities and towns.

Blue Badge Parking Map www.blue badge.direct.gov.uk Online interactive map with locations of Blue Badge parking, car park access, accessible toilets and railway stations in many UK areas. Click on points of interest to get further details, such as detailed access information for railway stations.

Bus pass scheme, England Free off-peak travel on the whole English local bus network is now available for over 60s and disabled people. Passes are usually available from the local council. Some councils offer additional benefits such as peak-time travel. Further information is available at www.direct.gov.uk or www.dft.gov.uk.

Bus pass schemes, Wales, Scotland and Northern Ireland Wales, Scotland and Northern Ireland operate independent bus pass schemes. In Wales, contact your local council for a pass you can use on buses at any time of day. A simliar scheme is run by Transport Scotland www.transportscotland.gov.uk and requires a National Entitlement card. In Northern Ireland, you can apply to Translink www.translink.co.uk for a half-fare SmartPass that can be used on bus and rail services.

Changing Places www.changing-places.org **England, Wales and Northern Ireland:** 020 7696 6019 changingplaces@mencap.org.uk **Scotland:** 01382 385154 pamischangingplaces@dundee.ac.uk This consortium campaigns for public toilets for people who require non-standard access features, including hoists and height adjustable changing benches. The website has a map of current and planned Changing Places toilet locations with opening hours.

Disabled Persons Railcard www.disabledpersons-railcard.co.uk 0845 605 0525 textphone 0845 601 0132 disability@atoc.org Concessionary railcard that costs £18 annually, but allows 1/3 off most standard and first class rail fares for those with a disability (plus an adult companion), if train travel presents difficulties. The website also has useful links to contacts for booking assistance with individual rail operators.

Door to Door www.dptac.gov.uk/door-to-door Website run by the Disabled Persons Transport Advisory Committee (DPTAC) providing transport and travel advice for disabled people. A great starting point for basic information on all forms of transport, with good detail on London travel, if you can get beyond the sometimes obvious advice.

Mobilise (incorporating Disabled Drivers Association) www.mobilise.info 01508 489449 enquiries@mobilise.info A charity campaigning for improvements in access for disabled motorists, passengers and Blue Badge holders. Members receive a monthly magazine and can access information officers who advise on individual transportation issues. Check the website for updates on disability schemes and legislation. Annual membership costs £16.

Motability www.motability.co.uk 0800 923 0000 minicom 0845 675 0009) Car, powered wheelchair and scooter scheme for disabled people (for more information see p.6).

National Express www.nationalexpress.com/coach/ourservice/disabled.cfm Disabled Persons Travel Helpline 08717 818179 textphone 0121 455 0086 Aiming to run a 100 percent accessible coach network by 2012, new vehicles are being steadily rolled-out. To check serviced routes see the website or call the travel helpline. Adapted coaches have a wide entrance, lift access, level flooring and a large toilet.

Reduced fares for disabled passengers of up to half price are available on some services.

National Federation of Shopmobility UK ⓦwww.shopmobilityuk.org ⓣ08456 442446 ⓔinfo@shopmobilityuk .org Most towns and shopping centres have a Shopmobility scheme that lends manual wheelchairs, powered wheelchairs and scooters. Schemes operate differently from place-to-place with some charging and others free. The website has a searchable database of affiliated schemes.

Need a Loo? ⓦwww.needaloo.org Online directory of publicly accessible disabled toilets. Whilst not totally comprehensive, there are a lot of loos listed. Locations displayed via Streetmap and Google Maps.

RADAR ⓦwww.radar.org.uk ⓣ020 7250 3222 ⓔradar@radar.org.uk Campaigning network of organisations and disabled people who operate the National Key Scheme for accessible toilets. They also publish a guide to the key scheme that lists details of the 7000 UK toilets.

Stations Made Easy ⓦwww.nationalrail .co.uk Search for any station via the "stations and destinations" page on the National Rail website, and you'll be provided with a handy station floor plan and invaluable images of facilities including ticket desks and platforms, to help with route planning.

Transport for London (TFL) ⓦwww.tfl .gov.uk The TFL website provides transport accessibility information and a journey planner that allows you to find a route that suits your mobility requirements. TFL also produce a range of accessibility guides including audio, large print and step-free tube maps and information on assisted transport services.

TRAVEL ADVICE

Ableize ⓦwww.ableize.com Online directory of links to further information and services, including those involved with travel, recreation, arts, sports,

holidays and accommodation. Not a very easy website to navigate, but if you can forgive the clumsy presentation, it is worth spending time trawling through the extensive listings here.

Contact A Family ⓦwww.cafamily.org .uk ⓣ0808 808 3555 textphone 0808 808 3556 Publishes a guide to Holidays, Play and Leisure **containing advice on available facilities for** children with disabilities and details of holiday providers along with possible sources of funding. The guide can be downloaded for free from the website –search under "leisure".

Direct Enquiries ⓦwww.directenquiries .com ⓣ01344 360101 ⓔcustomer services@directenquiries.com Online directory with a great London Underground accessible route planner that has platform-to-platform and platform-to-street-level information for every station. Access reviews for many services (hotels, shops etc) are available, but solely for companies that have registered. Don't miss the detailed guides of accessible nature reserve trails, complete with photographs.

Directgov ⓦwww.direct.gov.uk/en/dis abledpeople Government website for public services with an area dedicated to people with disabilities. Contains background on the National Accessible Scheme for accommodation in England, the Blue Badge parking scheme and advice on places of interest, leisure and accessing the arts.

Disabled Go ⓦwww.disabledgo .info ⓣ0845 270 4627 ⓔquestions@ disabledgo.info Heavily detailed access information for restaurants, hotels, cinemas, tourist attractions, pubs and train stations etc. All attractions and sites are researched in person with invaluable minutiae detail on points such as the best transfer side in an adapted toilet. An incredibly useful website – the only downside is that they haven't yet covered the whole country.

Disabled Holiday Info ⓦwww .disabledholidayinfo.org.uk ⓔinfo@ disabledholidayinfo.org.uk A very useful website with advice on accessible attractions, transport and activities in selected regions of the UK – most comprehensively Shropshire and Cheshire. Factsheets are available on subjects including accommodation with wheel-in showers and accessible accommodation with fishing. See box on p.171 for details of their handy accommodation database.

Disabled Information from the Disabled ⓦ www.disabledinfo.co.uk A website where disabled people can share their experiences and expertise with others by submitting "articles" on various subjects – the result of which is a diverse mix of informative pieces and some obvious promotion. Features some useful advice for drivers.

Disability Now ⓦ www.disabilitynow .org.uk Magazine published by Scope with some travel articles. The website has a listings section for accessible hotels, cottages and B&Bs.

Good Access Guide ⓦ www.good accessguide.co.uk ☎ 01502 566005 Essentially an online directory of services, businesses and venues that advertise themselves as accessible and disabled-friendly. Far from a comprehensive list but definitely a good starting point.

National Autistic Society ⓦ www.nas .org.uk Features some advice on planning holidays and days out when you have a child with autism, plus lists of holiday providers and accommodation suitable for adults with autism. Also features the extensive Autism Services Directory which lists organisations providing play and leisure services.

National Blind Children's Society ⓦ www .nbcs.org.uk Organises days out for children with visual impairments at many attractions in the UK. An activity planner is downloadable from the website.

Open Britain ⓦ www.openbritain.net Two former RADAR publications and Tourism for All's Easy Access Britain Guide have been amalgmated to create the Open Britain Guide. Particularly useful for find-ing places to stay, it can be ordered from the website. An Open London Guide is planned for 2010.

Ouch! ⓦ www.bbc.co.uk/ouch BBC website concerning disability issues with news, blogs and an active forum. There isn't a specific message board for travel but posting a question on the general board is likely to gain a good response.

RNIB ⓦ www.rnib.org.uk Advice on leisure activities and holidays for those with visual impairments, including a list of accessible museum and gallery events. There are also links and ideas for shopping, cinemas, theatre trips and spectator sports. They also provide advice on finding holiday accommodation.

RNID ⓦ www.rnid.org.uk Check the "entertainment" section for details of signed theatre, subtitled and audio-described cinema, and BSL-interpreted gallery and museum tours.

Special Needs Kids ⓦ www.special -needs-kids.co.uk The "fun & leisure" section on this website has some useful suggestions for days out for families with children who have special needs. Also has details of disabled sporting organisations and children's activity clubs.

Tourism For All ⓦ www.tourismforall .org.uk ☎ 0845 124 9971 Holiday Care, the Tourism for All Consortium and IndividuALL merged several years ago to form Tourism For All, a national charity dedicated to making tourism welcoming for all. The website has lots of ideas for places to visit.

Youreable.com ⓦ www.youreable.com Online community site with a travel section offering advice on planning a trip. Also has links to providers of holidays and accommodation suitable for the disabled.

The Wheel Life Guide ⓦ www.thewh ellifeguide.com A helpful directory specialising in leisure and lifestyle, in association with thewheellife. com (a social networking site). Useful organisations, accommodation, activity holidays and tour operators are listed and there is a particularly good section on disabled sporting associations.

BRITISH TOURISM

Accessible South West ⓦ www.accessiblesouthwest.co.uk A website produced by South West Tourism with a directory of accessible services and places. The accommodation directory is useful but places to eat are harder to find as they are listed under "businesses and services" with contacts including laundrettes.

English Heritage ⓦ www.english-heritage.org.uk ⓣ 0870 333 1181 textphone 0800 015 0516 ⓔ customers@english-heritage.org.uk Owners of over 400 historic properties, English Heritage operates an Access for All policy. They publish an Access Guide that features properties with good provisions for visitors with limited mobility and sensory needs. However as heritage sites, even those that are more accessible inevitably have inaccessible parts. Access information for individual properties is listed on the website, though unfortunately you can't search by accessibility in the "search for a property" function.

Enjoy England ⓦ www.enjoyengland.com The accommodation search function on the Enjoy England website allows you to search by type of disability (physical, visual or hearing). However information for disabled visitors on the rest of the website is limited to one page – for the whole of England they seem only able to recommend a handful of accessible places to visit.

National Trust ⓦ www.nationaltrust.org.uk ⓣ 01793 817634 ⓔ accessforall@nationaltrust.org.uk The National Trust welcomes visitors with disabilities. The dedicated Access for All office runs a policy that includes an Admit One card scheme allowing free entry for an essential companion. The website has further info on policies as well as access details for individual properties. An annually published Access Guide has details for every property. The guide does regularly highlight steps and uneven surfaces, which can make parts of it depressing reading, but bear in mind the publication

exists to warn you of problems, rather than state what is possible. Predictably with heritage sites, there are some largely inaccessible areas of certain properties – but the assessments in the Access Guide have been written by disabled people so you can feel confident of accurate, considered information.

Visit Birmingham ⓦ www.visitbirmingham.com/information/access_for_all ⓣ 0121 202 5115 Undoubtedly the most useful regional tourist board website. It's not perfect, but the Access for All section has tips on getting around Birmingham, including a link-up with Direct Enquiries to provide photo journeys of routes to tourist destinations from the nearest public transport. Birmingham City Centre Partnership run two great schemes – Meet and Greet to help people get around ⓣ 0121 616 2259 and Wayfinder Talking Signs ⓦ www.birmingham.gov.uk/wayfinder for blind and visually impaired people.

Visit Britain ⓦ www.visitbritain.co.uk Britain's national tourism agency also run the National Accessible Scheme – a nationally recognised rating for accessible accommodation (more information about the scheme is available from the website). Disappointingly on the site you can't use the scheme's symbols as search criteria on the accommodation database. There is however a satisfactory section for "people with physical and sensory needs".

Visit Lancashire ⓦ www.visitlancashire.com ⓣ 01257 226600 ⓔ info@visitlancashire.com This website has an online list of accessible accommodation and some access information for attractions but unfortunately the fairly comprehensive "food and drink" listings section doesn't include access details.

Visit Scotland ⓦ www.visitscotland.com ⓣ 0845 225 5121 ⓔ info@visitscotland.com Tourism Scotland runs its own quality assurance scheme for disabled access. Accommodation and attractions are searchable on the website using accessibility criteria, making this by far the most useful of the national tourism websites. A printed guide is also available.

CREDITS

Reviewers: Emma Bowler, Chris Cammiss, Karen Darke, Richard Farrant, John Hargreaves, Andrew Healey, Joy & Nic Jansen, Dot Kirby, Carol Lawley, David Livermore, Alice Masters, Lara Masters, Andy Macleod, Glenys Mashford, Frank & Sue Napper, James Rawlings, Lucy Robinson, Richard Shakespeare, Helen Smith, Rob Smith, Paul Talbot, Jeanette Travis, Viv Watton **Additional contributions:** Douglas Campbell, Dom Hyams, Sue Kelley, Phil Lee, Jane MacNamee, Eva McCracken, Gary McGladdery **Editing & typesetting**: Emma Traynor **Design**: Diana Jarvis **Cartography**: Maxine Repath **Proofreader**: Susannah Wight **Picture research**: Mark Thomas **Production**: Rebecca Short, Liz Cherry **Project manager:** Emma Traynor (Rough Guides), Delia Ray (Motability) **Account manager**: Dunstan Bentley (Rough Guides)

This third edition published March 2010 by
Rough Guides Ltd, 80 Strand, London WC2R 0RL
in association with
Motability Operations, City Gate House,
22 Southwark Bridge Road, London SE1 9HB

© Rough Guides, 2010

ISBN 9781848366589

Printed in Italy by LegoPrint S.p.A

All photography © Rough Guides except for the following:

Colour introduction:

Gondola on the Nevis Range © Andy Gray/Nevis Range; Wicken Fen © Diana Jarvis; Cairngorm funicular © Lucienne Sencier; Lara Masters © Jan Gamble; Eden Project © Mark Thomas; Brunel's ss Great Britain © Mandy Reynolds; Pedalabikeaway Monmouth © Sue Napper; Charlecote Park © Rob Smith; Culloden Battlefield © Doug Houghton/Alamy; Brunel's ss Great Britain © Mandy Reynolds; Churchill Museum © Imperial War Museum; Interior of Tate Britain © Mark Thomas; Culloden Battlefield © Epicscotland/Alamy; Steam trains © Locomotion National Railway Museum; Gallery interior © Horniman Museum and Gardens; Interior of the National Gallery © The National Gallery; National Waterfront Museum © Diana Jarvis; The Fountain at The Alnwick Garden © The Alnwick Garden; Owls © Krys Bailey/Alamy; Legoland Windsor © Viv Watton; Cairngorm funicular © StockShot/Alamy; Manchester Velodrome © Anthony Collins Cycling/Alamy; Wicken Fen © Diana Jarvis; Sled-dogs © Cairngorm Sled-dog centre; Family with bikes © Pedalabikeaway

Black and white images:

Spitalfields © Stefano Paterna/Alamy; The National Gallery © Mark Thomas; Kensington Gardens © Art Kowalsky/Alamy; View of the O2 © The O2; Man boarding plane © British Disabled Flying Association; The Pavillion Gardens © World Pictures/Alamy; Samphire Hoe © Manor Photography/Alamy; Dungeness © Tony Lilley/Alamy; RHS Wisley © RHS Wisley; Beth Chatto Gardens © Rodger Tamblyn/Alamy; Henley-on-Thames © Oxford Picture Library/Alamy; Legoland © Viv Watton; National Space Centre © Robin Weaver/Alamy; Ferrari racing cars © Silverstone; Southwold Pier © Terry Matthews/Alamy; View towards Chatsworth © Chatsworth House; Warwick Castle © Colin Underhill/Alamy; West Midland Safari Park © Glyn Thomas/Alamy; National Arboretum © James Osmond/Alamy; Stourhead © Emma Traynor; Buckfast Abbey © Terry Harris/Alamy; View of the Scilly Isles © Hemis/Alamy; Ravenglass & Eskdale Railway © Imagebroker/Alamy; RSPB Ribble © Conrad Elias/Alamy; Manchester Velodrome © Anthony Collins Cycling/Alamy; The Albert Dock, Liverpool © Topix/Alamy; Quarry Bank Hill © National Trust/Alamy; View of the fountain © The Alnwick Garden; BALTIC centre © Mark Thomas; Fountains Abbey © National Trust; The Yorkshire Sculpture Park © Eric Murphy; Llangollen Wharf © Mike Haywood/Alamy; Llanberis Railway © Jack Sullivan/Alamy; Boys on CAT attraction © CAT; Red Kite © Andrew Walmsley/Alamy; View of the glasshouse © National Botanical Gardens Wales; Sailing on Loch Insh © Mike Rex; Gondola on the Nevis Range © Nevis Range; Glider © Walking on Air; Interior of House for an Art Lover © House for An Art Lover; The Grand Opera House © Scenicireland/Alamy; Interior of the Ulster Museum © The Ulster Museum; The Museum of Free Derry © Joe Fox/Alamy; Visitors centre © Belleek Pottery

We've gone to a lot of effort to ensure that the third edition of The Rough Guide to Accessible Britain is accurate and up to date. However, things change – opening hours and entry fees change seasonally, attractions improve their facilities, restaurants raise prices and close down. If you feel like we've got it wrong, or there is something new that we ought to know about, we'd really like to hear from you. Please send your comments to accessibleguide@motabilityoperations.co.uk.

Many thanks to Mobilise, Disabled Holiday Info, Attitude is Everything and Direct Enquiries for their assistance with the production of this guide.

USEFUL CONTACTS